Accounting: Novel Concepts and Applications

Accounting: Novel Concepts and Applications

Edited by Hollie Montgomery

Clanrye International
www.clanryeinternational.com

Clanrye International,
750 Third Avenue, 9th Floor,
New York, NY 10017, USA

ISBN: 978-1-64726-071-2

Cataloging-in-Publication Data

Accounting : novel concepts and applications / edited by Hollie Montgomery.
p. cm.
Includes bibliographical references and index.
ISBN 978-1-64726-071-2
1. Accounting. 2. Bookkeeping. I. Montgomery, Hollie.
HF5636 .A23 2021
657--dc23

For information on all Clanrye International publications visit our website at www.clanryeinternational.com

CLANRYE INTERNATIONAL

Contents

Preface

The measurement, communication and processing of financial or non-financial information regarding economic entities is known as accounting. It measures the results of a firm's economic activities. Accounting also conveys this information to various users like investors, creditors, regulators and management. Accounting can be divided into various branches including financial accounting, management accounting, external auditing, tax accounting and cost accounting. Financial accounting deals with reporting of an organization's financial information. Management accounting is involved in measuring, reporting and analyzing the information in order to be used by the management. This book traces the progress of this field and highlights some of its key concepts and applications. It picks up individual branches and explains their need and contribution in the context of a growing economy. Through this book, we attempt to further enlighten the readers about the new concepts in this field.

The researches compiled throughout the book are authentic and of high quality, combining several disciplines and from very diverse regions from around the world. Drawing on the contributions of many researchers from diverse countries, the book's objective is to provide the readers with the latest achievements in the area of research. This book will surely be a source of knowledge to all interested and researching the field.

In the end, I would like to express my deep sense of gratitude to all the authors for meeting the set deadlines in completing and submitting their research chapters. I would also like to thank the publisher for the support offered to us throughout the course of the book. Finally, I extend my sincere thanks to my family for being a constant source of inspiration and encouragement.

Editor

1

Strategic cost management, contingent factors and performance in services

Odysseas Pavlatos [a,1]

[a] *Athens University of Economics and Business, Greece*

Abstract: The purpose of this paper is to investigate the relationship between contextual factors identified from contingency-based research, the extent of the use of strategic cost management (SCM) techniques and business performance in services. An empirical survey was conducted on a sample of 88 services in Greece. The analysis of the survey data indicates that the use of strategic cost management techniques in services can be considered quite satisfactory. By drawing on the grounds of contingency theory, five factors were identified as potentially exhibiting an emergent relationship with strategic cost management. The five factors are; (1) Perceived environmental uncertainty, (2) Structure, (3) Organizational life cycle stage, (4) Strategy and (5) Size. The survey revealed that SCM usage is positively affected by these five contingent factors, while SCM usage, in turn, positively affects performance. A significant mediating effect of SCM usage on performance is evident.

Keywords: strategic cost management, contingent factors, performance, services, Greece

[1] *Corresponding authors*: Department of Business Administration, Athens University of Economics and Business, Aminiou Str. 3, 1163 Athens; email addresses: opaulatos@gmail.com

1. Introduction

In the recent literature has presented many innovative management accounting tools, such as strategic cost management tools (Abdel-Kader & Luther, 2008; Zawawi & Hoque, 2010).

As a matter of fact, the last few years have seen a growing interest in Strategic Cost Management (SCM) despite the considerable discourse on strategic cost management that has prevailed since the early 1980s (Bromwich, 1990; Roslender & Hart, 2003). Nevertheless, very little has been achieved in terms of empirical enquiry designed to further our appreciation of the nature and the context of SCM application (Cadez & Guilding, 2008). However, there ought to be further research that is geared towards developing the test hypotheses on factors that relate to SCM adoption and usage.

Chenhall (2003) reports that there is a need for more research into service organizations on management accounting system design and contextual variables since these entities become increasingly important within most economies. More recently, Chenhall and Moers (2015) report little management accounting system design work considering innovative tools, in services. The role of management accounting system related to service areas offer many opportunities to research (Chenhall & Moers, 2015).

Existing research in service organizations tends to focus on organizations in one industry (e.g. health care industry, communication industry, banking industry, hospitality industry) or in a single organization, or focusses on not- for profit organizations (Auzair, 2015). As services range across retail, health care, education, hospitality and professional services, limited generalizations can be drawn from such a narrow focus (Auzair, 2015).

Performance management literature suggests that there is a relationship between performance management system design and previous performance in services (Naranjo-Gil *et al.*, 2009). The historical performance of an organization is another factor that might influence the need to adopt innovative management accounting tools (Naranjo-Gil *et al.*, 2009). Firms which have performed relatively badly over the previous period will experience a relatively high, and perhaps urgent, need to change their systems, as has been widely recognized in the general management literature (e.g. Pavlatos, 2015). Previous research has explored the impact of historical performance and firm characteristics (direct and interaction effects) on strategic cost management usage (e.g. Pavlatos, 2015).

Instead, this research explores how contingencies affect business performance through strategic cost management adoption and usage (indirect effects). This study examines the effect of contingent factors on strategic cost management and, in turn, the mediating effect of SCM on company performance. This paper explores the effect of using strategic cost management tools on business performance, which has not been explored, as far as we know, in the service sector (Chenhall & Moers, 2015).

The present study contributes to the literature on organizational configurations in particular by examining the systematic nature of effective service organizations when adapting to their contextual settings. The findings provide support for contingency theory's central proposition that organizational performance depends on the fit between organizational context and structure in a service context. This research concludes that the application of SCM systems are not necessarily related to superior performance, but that superior performance is a product of an appropriate match between contingent factors and SCM application.

The remainder of the paper is structured as follows. The next section provides a synthesis of the most pertinent literature. Hypotheses are then developed concerning factors that might impact upon the usage rates SCM. This is followed by an analysis of the research methodology and thereafter the survey results. Conclusions, limitations and implications for future research are presented in the final section.

2. Theory and hypothesis development

"The increasing research on strategic cost management or strategic management accounting is as a result of its increasing importance to managers of information from all boundaries of the firm" (Simmonds, 1981, p.360). It was in fact pointed out that the external focus of SCM and further research has been consistent with their premise (Cinquini & Tenucci, 2010).

To help in the progress, Guilding *et al.* (2000) provided an original distillation of SCM techniques as well as criteria for viewing a particular accounting technique as "strategic". They further drew 12 SCM techniques from the literature. Furthermore, Cravens and Guilding (2001) added another three techniques and finally, 16 SCM techniques have been identified by Cadez and Guilding, (2008). There are an evident number of surveys of SCM practice that have been carried out (Carr *et al.*, 1991; Carr & Tomkins, 1996, 1998; Guilding *et al.*, 2000; Cravens & Guilding, 2001; Guilding & McManus, 2002; Cinquini & Tenucci, 2010). These surveys have found out that competitor focused accounting and strategic pricing are the most widely used techniques. However, some also suggest that the term SCM is not widely used in companies, and its meaning is not always clear to managers (Tillmann & Goddard, 2008). The above surveys have been conducted only in manufacturing industries.

The literature search reveals no overdue enquiry on the validity of viewing SCM as a coherent empirical construct in a service environment. Moreover, no prior empirical work concerned with the application of SCM techniques in a service context has been yet reported.

The contingency theory approach to studying SCM practice is one of the techniques that have been used by most researchers (Simons, 1987; Chenhall & Langfield-Smith, 1998; Guilding, 1999; Anderson & Lanen, 1999; Abernethy and Brownell, 1999; Cinquini & Tenucci, 2010). Otley (2016) reviews the literature on the contingency theory of management accounting since the 1980. He suggests that the narrow view of contingency that relies on responses to generally applicable questionnaires needs to be replaced by a more tailored approach that takes into account the context of specific firms.

In line with the above, Cadez and Guilding (2008) examined the effect of strategic choices, market orientation, and company size on two distinct dimensions of SCM and the mediating effect of SCM on company performance in a comprehensive contingent model.

This research was based on the framework of Cadez and Guilding (2008), and was expanded on the following: Firstly, this study examined the impact of those contingencies that have not yet been studied. Such contingent factors include; "Perceived environmental uncertainty", "Structure", "and "Organizational life cycle stage" on strategic cost management practices which have not been previously studied. It is for that reason that they have been included in this study.

Furthermore, this research was restricted to including only service organizations. Messner (2016) explained how industry matters of management accounting practice and how this type of context can be accounted for in empirical studies. Prior research regarding the investigation of the factors that influence the use of SCM has been mainly related to large manufacturing companies. In the service sector, Pavlatos (2015) examined the impact of contingent factors on Strategic Management Accounting in the Greek hospitality industry. He found that firms characteristics and specific industry factors affect the use of strategic management accounting tools in a service context.

Moreover Auzair (2015) used a configuration approach to examine the relationships between multiple contingent variables (e.g. strategy, process type, size, organizational lifecycle stage) and management control systems (MCS) in service organizations from various industries. She found that strategic orientation plays an important role in high-performing firms and the ability to incorporate various contingent situations determines the effectiveness of an organization.

2.1 Perceived environmental uncertainty (PEU)

The external environment is a powerful contextual variable that is at the foundation of contingency- based research. Perceived environmental uncertainty (PEU) is defined as a situation where managers perceive elements of the environment to be uncertain, with uncertainty distinguished from risk "as uncertainty defines situations in which probabilities are not attached" (Chenhall, 2003, p. 137). Perceived environmental uncertainty is seen to be an important contextual factor in the design of MCS because increased PEU makes managerial planning and control more difficult (Lawrence & Lorsch, 1967).

Chenhall and Morris (1986) and Gordon and Narayanan (1984) report that as decision makers perceive greater environmental uncertainty, they tend to seek external, non-financial and ex ante information in addition to other types of information. Gul and Chia (1994) found that when PEU is low, management is able to make relatively accurate predictions about the market, while when PEU is high management may require additional information to cope with complexities of the environment. According to Abdel-Kader and Luther (2008) there is positive association between management accounting sophistication and PEU. Guliding and McManus (2002) found that there is a weak association between customer focused accounting and competition intensity.

Based on these arguments and findings, the perceived environment is likely to play a positive role in affecting the extent to which strategic management accounting practices is used by firms. Firms perceiving a higher degree of environmental uncertainty may use more strategic cost management than firms that perceived lower environmental uncertainty. The intensity of price competition, the economic environment, the legal and political constraints, the market activities of the competitors and the preferences of the customers may affect the extent of the use of SCM.

In the service industries, firms facing relatively high environmental uncertainty may place greater emphasis on SCM to help them to reduce uncertainty and improve managerial decision-making, managerial planning and control. Furthermore, it is suggested that managers perceive their environment to be highly uncertain may require more strategic cost management information to manage the uncertainty. Based on the above discussion, the following hypothesis will be tested in the research:
H1: *There is a positive association between PEU and Strategic cost management usage.*

2.2 Structure

According Chenhall (2003) organizational structure is about the formal specification of different roles for organizational members, or tasks for groups, to ensure that the activities of the organization are carried out. For this research, structure has been conceptualised in terms of the centralisation/ decentralisation dimension (Chenhall & Morris, 1986; Merchant, 1981). A decentralised structure distributes authority for decision making to a large number of lower level managers; whereas, a centralised structure focuses decision making authority at the headquarters level with few managers involved.

In the service context, organizational structure is likely to play a positive role in affecting the extent to which strategic cost management tools are used. It is suggested in this study, that firms which are more decentralised are likely to require a greater volume of information at lower levels of management to assist in decision making relative to centralised firms. Therefore, decentralised firms would have a greater need for SCM tools, as these provide additional information to help lower level managers in their decision-making processes. Therefore, it is hypothesised that:

H2: *There is a positive association between organizational structure and strategic cost management usage*

2.3 Organizational life cycle stage

According to Miller and Friesen, (1984) a firm's life cycle stage is a contingency to which organizational responses have to be matched. This implies that the use of management accounting systems differs across the stages of organizational life cycle as different systems are needed in different stages (Kallunki & Silvola, 2008). Additional research by Miller and Friesen (1984) show that firms in the maturity phase put significantly more emphasis on formal cost controls than firms in the growth stage. On the contrary, Auzair and Langfield-Smith (2005) used a self-categorization measure based on the firm's own assessment of its life cycle stage and reported that organizational life cycle, among other contingent variables, has a significant effect on the design of a firm's management accounting systems. Furthermore, Kallunki and Silvola (2008) found out that the organizational life cycle stage affects the use of innovative management accounting techniques, such as ABC.

Further findings by Chenhall and Langfield-Smith (1998) indicated that greater organizational size leads to greater complexity of tasks, which requires more division of labour. According to Chenhall and Langfield-Smith, (1998) more sophisticated integrative mechanisms such as information systems are then developed to coordinate the activities of subunits. "Management accounting innovations are examples of such information systems" (Kallunki & Silvola, 2008). In addition, firms in the maturity stage as result of greater organizational size have greater resources to experiment with administrative innovations such as innovative management accounting tools (Kallunki & Silvola, 2008). Kallunki and Silvola, (2008) report that greater organizational size and greater resources is expected to lead to more widespread use of strategic management accounting techniques among firms in the maturity stage as opposed to firms in the growth stage.

The above literature therefore indicates that there is a correlation between the organizational life cycle stage and the use of strategic cost management techniques. In the service context, the mature firms may have a more analysis of the competitor positions within the industries. This is because they use more cost data based on strategic and marketing information to develop and identify superior strategies so that may produce a sustainable competitive advantage. This is in order to analyse to a great extent of strategic factors in the pricing decision process in comparison with growth firms. In this case, the following hypothesis is tested:
H3: *There is a positive association between organizational life cycle stage and strategic cost management usage.*

2.4 Extent of the use of SCM and performance

The relationship between management accounting usage and performance has been subjected to extensive empirical investigation (Chenhall & Moers, 2007). According to 'contingency-based' research, a state of equilibrium in the relationship between the contingency factors and the type of MCS is best described by "fit" (Chenhall, 2003).

According to Cadez and Guilding (2008) "while most studies provide some support for the view that greater management accounting usage is positively associated with performance in many of these studies the relationship is inconclusive and context dependent" (see Cadez & Guilding, 2008 for a review). While respecting these studies' mixed outcomes, Cadez and Guilding (2008) found that there is a positive association between SCM usage and performance.

This study proposes service firms that use more strategic cost management tools may enhance their performance relative to their competitors that use less strategic cost management practices. Thus, the following hypothesis is tested:
H4: *Greater SCM usage is positively associated with firm performance.*

3. Research methodology

3.1 Sample characteristics and data collection

In order to test the hypothesized relations among strategic management accounting techniques, contingent factors and performance, empirical data was collected from the Greek services industry. Greece economy is based on service sector (85%) and industry (12%), while the agricultural sector consists only 3% of the national economic output. The most important economic industries in Greece are tourism and merchant shipping. In fact, about 15 million international tourists visit Greece every year, which makes it the 7th most visited country in the EU and the 16th in the world. As for merchant shipping, Greece has the largest merchant marine in the world as it covers 16% of the world's total capacity.

We focused on sizable companies that would be likely to have an established management accounting function. The survey instrument was sent by email to 500 large Greek firms which are included in the ICAP database (Gallup's subsidiary in Greece). The selection criteria used for sampling purposes were the sales revenues and the number of employees for year 2016. The collection of data lasted for four months, from February to May 2017. The questionnaire, accompanied by a cover letter where a brief reference to the scope of the study was made, was addressed to the Chief Financial Officers (CFO) of each firm. It should be noted that the questionnaire was accompanied also by one glossary that explained the terminology of the strategic cost management tools adopted by Cadez and Guilding (2008).

Before starting the dissemination of the survey instrument, the questionnaire was pilot tested. Interviews were conducted with the Chief Financial Officers of 10 large firms. The pilot test did not reveal any shortcomings regarding either the content or the phrasing of the questions. Several procedures from Dillman (2000) were taken to optimize the response rate, such as the promise of strict anonymity, the use of high-quality printing with handwritten signatures, the use of pre-stamped envelopes and separate cards to request the study's results. A total of 88 firms fully completed and returned the questionnaire, yielding a 18% response rate. Companies that did not express interest in the research replied that the main reasons for not taking part in the survey were the lack of time and the fact that answering questionnaires was not one of their top priorities. The questionnaires were answered by Chief financial officers who have firm knowledge of the management accounting practices used within their companies and have the primary responsibility for product costing, planning and control decisions.

Tests for non-response bias were performed to determine (a) whether the distribution of the 500 organizations in the response (n = 88) or non-response (n = 232) categories was independent of available demographic characteristics and (b) whether early and late respondents provided significantly different responses. Chi-square tests indicated no significant differences in the demographic characteristics. Hotelling's T^2 statistic also indicated no significant differences in the multivariate means of early versus late respondents.

3.2 Variable measurement

The variable "Extent of use of strategic cost management techniques" was measured drawing on the scale by Cadez and Guilding (2008). It was slightly adapted to be understandable in services based on information from the interviews with six managers who specialize in management accounting. It comprises of a ten-item seven-point Likert-scaled instrument anchored by (1) 'to no extent' to (7) 'to a great extent', in which respondents were asked to indicate the extent of the use of strategic cost management techniques.

The measurement of "Organizational life cycle stage" was based on the Kazanjian and Drazin (1990) self-categorization measure, with modifications as the original instrument was designed for technology-based ventures; this instrument was used by Auzair and Langfield-Smith (2005). The description offered at each stage of the life cycle by Kazanjian and Drazin was compared with Quinn and Cameron's (1983) summary of nine life cycle models. Consequently, three stages of organizational life cycle were measured: formation, growth and mature stages (Auzair and Langfield-Smith, 2005). Respondents were asked to select one box only that described their stage of development: formation (stage1), growth (stage 2) and maturity (stage 3). As only a few firms self-classified as stage 1 (2 firms), responses for stage 1 and stage 2 were combined into a single category, namely growth. Thus, only two stages were analysed – growth (35 firms) and maturity (53 firms) stages– which now resembles the dichotomous distinction used by Dodge *et al.* (1994) and by Auzair and Langfield-Smith (2005).

"Structure" was measured by the Gordon and Narayanan (1984), six-item, seven point, Likert-scaled, fully-anchored instrument. Respondents were asked to strongly disagree (ranging 1) or strongly agree (ranging 7) with five statements regarding that the authority has been completely delegated to appropriate managers or employees to make decisions and one more statement which was: "The most operating decisions are made at lower managerial level".

"Perceived environmental uncertainty" was measured by the Gordon and Narayanan (1984), point, Likert-scaled, fully-anchored instrument. It was slightly adapted to be understandable in the hotel context. Respondents were asked to strongly disagree or strongly agree with six statements regarding the perceived environmental uncertainty. These statements were (1) "The price competition in the industry is extremely intense", (2) "The economic external environment facing your firm changing rapidly", (3) "During the past 5 years many new services have been marked by industry", (4) "The market activities of your competitors during the past 5 years becoming less predictable", (5) "During the past 5 years, the tastes and preferences of your customers have become much harder to predict" and (6) "During the past 5 years, the legal, political and economic constraints surrounding your firm have proliferated greatly". Next to each statement, a seven-point scale was provided, ranging from "1" (strongly disagree) to "7" (strongly agree).

"Performance" was measured using a slightly modified version by Cadez and Guilding (2008). It was slightly adapted to be understandable in a service context based on information from the interviews with six managers who specialize in management accounting. For each of these 6 dimensions, respondents were asked to indicate their firm's performance relative to their competitors on a scale ranging from "1" (below average) to "7" (above average). We included a number of control variables (strategy, size, age of the organization). Table 1 reports the descriptive statistics of variables in the study.

Table 1. Descriptive statistics of the variables in the study

Variable	N	Mean	Std. Deviation	Theoretical Minimum	Theoretical Maximum	Actual Minimum	Actual Maximum
Strategic cost management usage	88	4.24	0.58	1	7	1	7
Organizational life cycle stage[a]	88	0.58	0.51	0	1	0	1
Perceived environmental uncertainty	88	4.44	0.68	1	7	1	7
Structure	88	4.05	0.54	1	7	1	7
Performance	88	4.09	0.48	1	7	2	7
Control variables							
Strategy	88	4.91	0.89	1	7	1	7
Size (No of employees)	88	285.11	24.81	-	-	85	625
Age of the organization	88	34.12	16.14	-	-	1	51
Industry classification	N	%					
Health care	16	18					
Travel and leisure	17	19					
Telecommunications	8	9					
Banks	4	5					
Insurance	8	9					
Real estate	6	7					
Financial services	4	5					
Technology	15	17					
Financial services	7	8					
Other	3	3					
Total	88	100					

[a] Organization life cycle is a categorical variable. It was translated as a dummy variable that reflected whether a sampled organization belongs to the maturity stage.

"Organizational strategy" is based on Porter's classification scheme (Porter, 1980) and measured by the response to a single question drawn from Govindarajan (1988). This question asks the respondents to indicate their belief as to the best description of the business's strategic emphasis, ranging from cost leadership (ranging 1) to product differentiation (ranging 7).

"Size" was measured using the number of employees. The variable "Age of the organization" was measured by Kallunki and Silvola (2008). Respondents were asked to indicate the age of the firm in years since it was founded.

4. Data analysis and results

We test the research model using Partial Least Squares (PLS), a multivariate analysis technique for testing structural models (Chin, 1998). PLS is a general method for the estimation of path models involving latent constructs indirectly measured by multiple indicators (Chin & Newsted, 1999). The measurement model in PLS is assessed in terms of individual item reliability, construct reliability and discriminant validity. Table 2 shows that the correlations between variables are generally low. The low correlations also suggest no problems exist with regard to multicollinearity (no correlation exceeds 0.30 in absolute value). Also, all VIF scores are below 2.5. The correlation between organizational life cycle stage and size is marginally significant, indicating that the organizational size of the firms is greater in maturity phase than it is in the growth phase which is consistent with prior research (Kallunki & Silvola, 2008; Auzair & Langfield-Smith, 2005). Table 3 shows the reliability and validity statistics of multi-item constructs.

Table 2. Correlations from PLS model (n=88)

Variable	1	2	3	4	5	6	7	8
1. Strategic Cost Management usage	1							
2. Perceived environmental uncertainty	0.214*	1						
3. Structure	0.154*	0.082	1					
4. Organizational life cycle stage	0.208*	0.124	0.122	1				
5. Strategy	0.192*	0.078	0.133	0.024	1			
6. Size	0.125*	0.104	0.132	0.101*	0.205	1		
7.Age of the organization	0.114	0.019	0.152	0.132	0.134	0.182	1	
8. Performance	0.285*	0.134	0.125	0.194	0.154	0.104	0.140	1

NOTE: * indicates Correlations is significant at the .05level (2 tailed)
****indicates Correlations is significant at the .01 level (2 tailed)**

Table 3. Reliability and validity analysis of multi-item constructs (n= 88)

Variable	ICR[a]	Alpha[b]	AVE[c]	Item	Loading
Strategic Cost Management Usage	0.855	0.824	0.644	Benchmarking	0.822
				Competitor cost assessment	0.824
				Competitive position motoring	0.788
				Competitor performance appraisal	0.781
				Customer profitability analysis	0.792
				Integrated performance measurement	0.801
				Life cycle costing	0.789
				Strategic pricing	0.812
				Valuation of customers as assets	0.762
				Value chain costing	0.731
Perceived environmental uncertainty	0.815	0.809	0.687	Price competition	0.831
				Economic (external) environment	0.815
				New services by industry	0.764
				Market activities of competitors	0.779
				Tastes and preferences of customers	0.722
				Legal, political and economic constraints surrounding firm	0.789
Structure	0.824	0.809	0.652	Initiating ideas for new services	0.806
				Hiring and firing managerial personnel	0.815
				Budgeting allocations	0.836
				Pricing decisions	0.787
				Selecting large investments	0.797
				Operating decisions are made at manager level	0.807
Performance	0.841	0.814	0.681	Return on investment (ROI)	0.811
				Margin of sales	0.801
				Customer satisfaction	0.872
				Market share	0.776
				Service quality	0.783
				Development of new services	0.824

[a] **Internal composite reliability**

[b] **Cronbach's alpha**

[c] **Average variance extracted**

Table 4. Extent of the use of strategic cost management techniques (n=88)

Technique	Actual Percentages (%)						
	1	2	3	4	5	6	7
Benchmarking	1	2	8	28	34	24	3
Competitor cost assessment	6	10	22	25	21	15	1
Competitive position motoring	2	6	18	30	24	16	4
Competitor performance appraisal	3	9	20	26	20	19	3
Customer profitability analysis	3	5	12	28	30	18	4
Integrated performance measurement	4	9	17	24	23	17	6
Life cycle costing	6	10	23	24	20	14	3
Strategic pricing	4	5	16	33	23	16	3
Valuation of customers as assets	5	10	20	23	20	17	5
Value chain costing	5	9	17	25	19	18	7

NOTE: 7-point rating scale: 1: No extend; 7: great extent

Table 4 shows the frequencies use of strategic cost management techniques. The figures in this table confirm that at the moment of the survey the majority of the firms in our sample use strategic cost management tools. The extents of the use of benchmarking and customer profitability analysis were somewhat more widespread that the other strategic cost management practices.

According to Hulland (1999), one consequence of the comparison between covariance structure analysis modelling approaches and PLS is that no proper overall goodness-of-fit measures exist for models using the latter. The structural model is evaluated examining the R^2 values and the size of the structural path coefficients. Consistent with Chin (1998), bootstrapping based on 500 runs is used to generate standard errors and t-statistics. This allows us to assess the statistical significance of the path coefficients.

Table 5 reports the path coefficients, t-values observed with the level of significance achieved and the proportion of explained variance of the endogenous variable (R^2) for the whole sample (n=88).

Table 5. Results from PLS analysis (n= 88)

Path to:	SCM usage	Performance
Path from:	Path coefficient	Path coefficient
Perceived environmental uncertainty	0.244* (2.403)	
Structure	0.188* (2.132)	
Organizational life cycle stage	0.189* (2.012)	
SCM usage		0.324* (2.599)
Control variables		
Strategy	0.233* (2.235)	0.162 (0.234)
Size	0.192* (2.019)	0.175 (0.184)
Age of the organization	0.154 (0.148)	0.164 (0.178)
	R^2=0.214	R^2=0.234

NOTE: * indicates Correlations is significant at the .05level (2 tailed)

Regarding perceived environmental uncertainty, there is strong support for H1, as expected. The results show that perceived environmental uncertainty (β= 0.244 p< 0.05) has a significantly positive effect on the use of strategic cost management techniques. The results support H2, since the path coefficient from structure to SCM use is positive and significant (β= 0.188, p<0.05). Moreover, the results support H3, since the path from organizational life stage on the use of strategic cost management tools is positive and significant (β= 0.189, p<0.05). The data analysis shows that the use of strategic cost management is greater among firms in maturity phase than among firms in a growth phase. Consistent with expectations, strategy (β= 0.233, p<0.05) and size (β= 0.192, p<0.05), which I add as control variables, are positively and significantly associated with SCM usage. On this note, firms following a differentiation strategy use more SCM than firms following a cost leadership strategy.

With respect to the relationship between SCM and performance, SCM use exhibits a statistically significant positive relationship (β= 0.324, p<0.05), so there is a strong support of H4. The results of the structural model show that contingent factors, such as PEU, structure, organizational life cycle stage, strategy and size do not directly related to performance.

5. Conclusion and discussion

This study focuses on the organizational framework of strategic cost management (Cadez & Guilding, 2008). The analysis of the survey data obtained from 88 Greek service firms indicates that the use of strategic cost management techniques can be considered quite satisfactory. According to the survey, the use of benchmarking and customer profitability analysis is much more widespread than other strategic cost management practices including life cycle costing, strategic pricing, competitive position motoring, competitor cost assessment, competitor performance appraisal, integrated performance measurement, valuation of customers as assets and value chain costing.

The findings provide support for contingency theory's central proposition that firm performance depends on the fit between organizational context and structure. The survey revealed that SCM usage is positively affected by these five contingent factors (PEU, Structure, organizational life cycle stage, strategy size). while SCM usage, in turn, positively affects performance. A significant mediating effect of SMA usage on performance is evident. The findings emanating from the PLS model provide support for all the hypothesized relationships. The survey results provide support for the application of contingency theory in management control system design in services. The extent of the use of SCM is not necessarily related to superior firm performance, but that superior firm performance is a product of an appropriate match between contingent factors and SCM usage. Thus, the results support the argument that performance is related to its choice of strategic cost management practices. The extent of the use of SCM tools, in turn, also positively affects performance Given that in a PLS model fit is depicted as a statistically significant (Gerdin & Greve, 2004); these results provide support to contingency theory.

However, the findings presented in this paper are subject to a number of limitations. Some of these limitations are inherent to the survey method used such as the use of perceptual measures and the potential of common-method bias. By closely following the guidelines of Dillman (2000) however, we have tried to limit these limitations as much as possible. We have also used more objective data where possible.

The study has helped in adding to the knowledge in management accounting practices in services. The results provide the first empirical evidence of the relation between the use of strategic cost management techniques, organizational factors and performance in service organizations.

This study extends prior research in several ways. Firstly, it has provided additional insights into areas relating to factors influencing the use of SCM. More specifically, the constructs perceived environmental uncertainty, structure and organizational life cycle stage are introduced as factors that influence the use of strategic cost management practices. Secondly, this paper adds to the limited body of knowledge of the design of MAS in a service context (service management accounting system design). While most of the previous research has focused on SMA in manufacturing firms, this study focuses on a service context and contributes to the meager knowledge that we have about contextual variables that influence the design of SMA systems in service industries.

The study can also be seen as constituting an enquiry into the validity of viewing strategic cost management as an empirical construct in a service environment. Finally, the results provide insights potentially useful for accounting practitioners, academics, and owners of service firms to design strategic cost management systems that "fit" with their contextual factors in order to enhance performance.

Future research should consider incorporating other important variables that have been omitted from other studies and are likely to influence the use of SCM. The most notable omitted variables are organizational variables, such as technology, TQM and organizational culture (Chenhall, 2003; Abernety & Bouwens, 2005). Moreover, the SCM systems of service firms could be studied in depth in order to examine the perceived benefits and usefulness that arise from their implementation. Finally, should be investigated whether the heterogeneity of the sample (different sub - industries) affects the results.

References

Abdel-Kader, M. & Luther, R. (2008) "The impact of firm characteristics on management accounting practices: A UK-based empirical analysis", *The British Accounting Review*, vol. 40: 2-27.

Abernethy, M. A. & Bouwens, J. (2005) "Determinants of accounting innovation implementation", *Abacus*, vol. 41: 217-240.

Abernethy, M.A. & Brownell, P. (1999) "The role of budgets in organizations facing strategic change: an exploratory study", *Accounting Organization and Society*, vol. 24: 189–204.

Anderson, S.W. & Lanen,W.N. (1999) "Economic transition, strategy and the evolution of management accounting practices: the case of India", *Accounting Organization and Society*, vol. 24: 379-412.

Auzair, S. (2015) "A configuration approach to management control systems design in service organizations", *Journal of Accounting & Organizational Change*, vol. 11: 47-72.

Auzer, S. & Langfield-Smith, K. (2005) "The effect of service process type, business strategy and life cycle stage on bureaucratic MCS in service organizations", *Management Accounting Research*, ol. 2: 227-248.

Bromwich, M. (1990) "The case for strategic management accounting: The role of accounting information for strategy in competitive market", *Accounting, Organizations and Society*, vol. 15: 27-46.

Cadez, S. & Guliding, C. (2008) "An exploratory investigation of an integrated contingency model of strategic management accounting", *Accounting Organization Society*, vol. 33: 836-863.

Carr, C. & Tomkins, C. (1996),"Strategic investment decisions: the importance of SCM. A comparative analysis of 51 case studies in U.K., U.S. and German companies", *Management Accounting Research*, vol. 7: 199-217.

Carr, C. & Tomkins, C. (1998), "Context, culture and the role of the finance function in strategic decisions. A comparative analysis of Britain, Germany, the U.S.A. and Japan", *Management Accounting Research*, vol. 9: 213-239.

Carr, C., Tomkins, C. & Bayliss, B. (1991) "Strategic controllership – a case study approach", *Management Accounting Research*, vol. 2: 89-107.

Chenhall, R. (2003) "Management controls systems design within its organizational context: Findings from contingency-based research and directions for the future", *Accounting, Organizations and Society*, vol. 28: 127-168.

Chenhall, R.H. & Langfield-Smith, K., (1998) "The relationship between strategic priorities, management techniques and management accounting: an empirical investigation using a systems approach", *Accounting Organization Society*, vol. 23Q 243-264.

Chenhall, R. & Morris, D. (1986) "The impact of structure, environment, and inter-dependence on the perceived usefulness of management accounting systems", *The Accounting Review*, LXI: 16-35.

Chenhall, R. H., & Moers, F. (2007) "The issue of endogeneity within theory-based, quantitative management accounting research", *European Accounting Review*, vol.16: 173-195.

Chenhall, R., & Moers, F., (2015) "The role of innovation in the evolution of management accounting and its integration into management control" *Accounting, Organization and Society*, vol. 47:1-13

Chin, W. W. & Newsted, P. R. (1999). *Structural equation modeling analysis with small samples using Partial Least Squares*, in: R. Hoyle (Ed.) Statistical Strategies for Small Sample Research, pp. 307-341, Thousand Oaks, CA: Sage.

Chin, W. (1998) "*Issues and opinion on structural equation modelling*", *MIS Quarterly,* March: vii-xvi.

Cinquini, L. & Andrea Tenucci. A. (2010) "Strategic management accounting and business strategy: a loose coupling', *Journal of Accounting & Organizational Change*, vol. 6: 228-259.

Cravens, K. S. & Guilding, C. (2001) "An empirical study of the application of strategic management accounting techniques" *Advances in Management Accounting,* vol. 10: 95-124.

Dillman, D. (2000). *Mail and Internet surveys: The Tailored Design Method*, New York: Wiley.

Gerdin, J. & Greve, J. (2004) "Forms of contingency fit in management accounting research – A critical review", *Accounting, Organizations and Society*, vol. 29: 303-326.

Gordon, L. & Narayanan, V. (1984) "Management accounting systems, perceived environmental uncertainty and organization structure: an empirical investigation", *Accounting, Organization and Society*, vol. 9: 33-47.

Govindarajan, V. (1988), "A contingency approach to strategy implementation at the business level: integrating administrative mechanisms with strategy", *Academy of Management Journal,* vol.31: 828-853.

Guilding, C., and McManus, L. (2002) "The incidence, perceived merit and antecedents of customer accounting: an exploratory note", *Accounting, Organizations and Society,* vol. 27: 45-59.

Guilding, C. Cravens, K. S. & Tayles, M. (2000) "An international comparison of strategic management accounting practices" *Management Accounting Research,* vol. 1: 113-135.

Gul, F. & Chia, Y. (1994) "The effect of management accounting systems, perceived environmental uncertainty and decentralization on managerial performance: a test of three-way interaction, *Accounting, Organization and Society*, vol. 19: 413-426.

Hulland, J. (1999) "Use of Partial Least Squares (PLS) in strategic management research: a review of four recent studies", *Strategic Management Journal*, vol. 20: 195-204.

Kallunki, J. & Silvola, A. (2008),"The effect of organizational life cycle stage on the use of activity-based costing", *Management Accounting Research*, vol. 19: 62-79.

Kazanjian, R.K. & Drazin, R. (1990) "A stage-contingent model of design and growth for technology-based new ventures", *J. Business Venturing*, vol. 5: 137-150.

Lawrence, P. & Lorsch, J. (1967). *Organization and Environment*. Irwin, Homewood, IL.

Merchant, K.A. (1981) "The design of corporate budgeting system: influences on managerial behaviour and performance", *Accounting Review*, vol. 56: 813-829.

Messner, M. (2016) "Does industry matter? How industry context shapes management accounting practice", *Management Accounting Research,* vol. 31: 103-111.

Miller, D. & Friesen, P.H. (1984) "A longitudinal study of the corporate life cycle", *Management Science*, vol. 30: 1161-1183.

Naranjo-Gil, D., Maas, V. & Hartmann, F. (2009) "How CFOs determine management accounting innovation: an examination of direct and indirect effects", *European Accounting Review*, 1 vol. 8: 667-695.

Otley, D. (2016) "The contingency theory of management accounting and control: 1980–2014", *Management Accounting Research,* vol. 31:45-62.

Porter, M. (1980). *Competitive Strategy*. The Free Press, New York.

Quinn, R. & Cameron, K., 1983 "Organizational life cycles and shifting criteria of effectiveness: some preliminary evidence", *Management Science*, vol. 29: 33-51.

Pavlatos, O. (2015) "An empirical investigation of strategic management accounting in hotels", *International Journal of Contemporary Hospitality Management*, vol. 27: 756-767.

Roslender, R. & Hart, S. (2003) "In search of strategic management accounting: Theoretical and field study perspectives", *Management Accounting Research,* vol. 1: 255-279.

Simmonds, (1981). *The Fundamentals of Strategic Management Accounting*. CIMA.

Simons, R. (1987) "Accounting control systems and business strategy" *Accounting, Organizations and Society*, vol. 12: 357-374.

Tillmann, K. & Goddard, A. (2008) "Strategic management accounting and sense-making in a multinational company", *Management Accounting Research*, vol. 19: 80-102.

Zawawi, N. & Hoque, Z. (2010) "Research in management accounting innovations: An overview of its recent development", *Qualitative Research in Accounting & Management*, vol. 7:505-568.

2

Offshoring Accounting Services: New opportunities for developing countries

Jadranka Mrsik[a,1] and Ninko Kostovski[a]

[a]*University American College, Skopje, Macedonia*

Abstract: The aim of this paper is to explore the viability of off-shoring of accounting services to foreign companies by providers of such services located in Republic of Macedonia. We have assessed the potentials of accountants in Republic of Macedonian to offer off-shored accounting services by using the criteria for assessment of outsourcing destinations in general as established by the McKinsey Institute. We have founded that there is considerable potentials for off-shoring of accounting and related services. Exploitation of these potentials would result in significant contribution to the accounting profession development and the employment of young graduates in accounting. In these terms, we offer some practical recommendations to the profession and to the policy-makers for further promotion of this business opportunity

Keywords: Accounting Services, Outsourcing, Off-shoring, Accountants

1. Introduction

Companies today operate simultaneously in many countries worldwide and consequently need to employ accountants with international accounting knowledge. In addition, the off-shoring and near-shoring of selected accounting activities is becoming increasingly attractive option for many of them pursuing

[1] Corresponding author: Jadranka Mrsik, University American College, 1000 Skopje, Macedonia, Email: jadranka.mrsik@uacs.edu.mk

greater competitiveness. Therefore, the accounting profession worldwide is developing towards much broader interdisciplinary knowledge and towards variety of skills. The accounting information systems development, the globalization of the accounting services and the international standardization of the financial reporting are the primary factors of changes of the accounting profession that need to be adequately tackled by the formal education and by the lifelong training of the accountants.
The market for off-shore-based Financial and Accounting (F&A) services is improving despite a very challenging economic environment according to Sahni *et al.* (2012) expecting the worldwide F&A services market to grow from US$27 billion in 2010 to $38.45 billion in 2015.

Stark *et al.* (2011) recognized the offshore services industry as opportunity for developing countries by offering increased employment in service jobs, facilitating the entry of these countries into the knowledge economy, and providing access to new markets. Everest Group (2014) considers Central and Eastern Europe (CEE) as one of the leading delivery in Finance and Accounting because of availability of multi-lingual and highly qualified finance talent, close cultural ties with Western Europe and North America, proximity to western markets, and favourable business environment.

In the latest A.T. Kearney Global Services Location Index, nine countries from the CEE region are among the 40 top destinations for global offshoring (Appendix One). The index is made up from three categories: Financial attractiveness, Skills' availability and Respective business environment.

The McKinsey Global Institute (2012) new growth model for CEE countries identifies the outsourcing (off shoring) as one of the three major opportunities for CEE-nations to raise both the volume and the value of their export. The Report underlines the need of targeted investments in education and development to capture more high-value-added O&O work will require, as well as, engaging in international marketing efforts and sharing best practices in the industry. Outsourcing is expected to grow regionally, aided by the financial crisis in Western Europe, which is pushing companies to shift some expensive functions to the east of the continent (Cienski, 2013). The developing countries should consider this off-shoring service opportunity in their strategies for growth.

In Europe, countries such Poland, Czech Republic, Slovakia, Hungary, Romania and Bulgaria are also well-known destinations for offshoring various business services, holding app. 8% share of the global off-shoring market. In Poland, these services expansion outpaced the rest of Central Europe and grew three times faster than in India (McKinsey Institute, 2015). Aided by the financial crisis in Western Europe, outsourcing is expected to grow even further, pushing companies to shift expensive functions to the east of the continent, claims Cienski (2013). Forbs indicated on Romania as the next most convenient destination for procurement of outsourced accounting services (Păvăloaia, 2011).

This trends provide an opportunity for developing countries like Macedonia that possess or can develop considerable competitive advantage on the global market of off-shoring accounting and related services. Macedonia, due to its economy small size, is not on the offshoring landscape and in the focus of the consultant companies` assessment of the countries where the companies may decide to locate offshore operation. Therefore, in this paper we have examined the potential of Macedonia to offer offshore services by employing the criteria established by McKinsey Institute. Cattaneo and Walkenhorst (2012) have recognized international relationships, language ability, and professional expertise, and access to a quality communications infrastructure being important factors of the level of outsourcing opportunities for accounting firms and we agree with. They have stressed the significance of the knowledge of international accounting standards and consequently the need of certification through the International Organization for Standardization, as well.

In this paper we have analysed the capacity of Macedonian accountants to provide services to clients outside the country. We apprise off-shoring of selected accounting activities as attractive option for developing countries like Macedonia. Therefore, we analyse the position of the accounting profession and it qualification to develop considerable competitive advantage on the global market of off-shoring accounting and related services and we implement our findings in a SWOT diagram. Consequently, we have offered several propositions to the profession and the policy-makers in the same line.

2. Literature review

The off-shoring is not new activity but it has become increasingly sophisticated over the last few decades, according to Kwacz *et al.* (2013). In their study they describe the evolution of off-shoring over time which has started by sending operational processes abroad, predominantly manufacturing tasks. The second wave from 1990s related primarily to contact centres and information technology support, initiating the services off-shoring stage. And the third one relies more heavily on high-value and complex tasks, such as research, product and design development, and programming. Ives (2013) have recognized even six generation of business process outsourcing evolution: starting from financial, accounting and HR services through back and middle office to everything as a service.

Gal (2014) indicates two aspects of service exports as a new channel to growth – specialization within service exports, and the sophistication of service exports. His analysis suggests that increasing sophistication of services is positively related to growth. Blinder (2007) analyses the impact of outsourcing on a wide spectrum of jobs and predicts that it will become a major phenomenon in the oncoming decades, and even postulates that it could be on the same level as a "new industrial revolution."

Based on the transaction cost economics, Ellram *et al.* (2007) findings confirm that low transactions volumes for offshore outsourcing of services are unattractive because of the high upfront fixed cost of the administrative and set-up costs. However, it partly supports the premise that organizations are less likely to offshore outsource services with high asset specificity and that firms are less likely to offshore outsource items when they are unsure of the requirements or when they cannot determine whether the supplier actually performed as agreed to in the contract.

Farrell *et al.* (2005) indicated on the further liberalization and on the improvements in the information technology as contributors to the decrease in the perceived risk of operating abroad and on the shortage of labour in developed countries as main factors for outsourcing to the low-wage locations, offshore. Mishra *et al.* (2012) found positive relationship between the quality of the business services in a given country and its growth performance. They stress that the increases in the sophistication of the business services provide valuable foundation for sustained economic growth. Moreover, the offshore services are recognized as potential vehicle for low and middle-income countries to participate in the global knowledge economy. These services offer attractive compensation and career development opportunities for graduate professionals in these countries. Hence, these services are important, not only for employment, but for the creation of additional demand for education, business formation and higher level of consumer services in these countries, too (Stark et al, 2011). These countries additionally benefit by adopting policies that increase the value-added of these services, improve productivity, eliminate obstacles to sophistication in many related service activities and promote service export performance (Mishra *et al.*, 2012).

There is consensus among the researchers and the organizations that the developing countries, in general, should consider the introduction of offshoring accounting in their search for viable strategies for growth. The availability of appropriate human capital and adequate knowledge and skills are the key prerequisites for that, according to UNKTAD Global Services Forum (2013). However, Kwacz *et al.* (2013) added some additional factors, when ranking emerging economies as providers of offshoring services, such as their overall business acumen and the type of the leadership.

Stark *et al.* (2011) expect the established trend in offshoring to continue, explaining it by the persistence and further intensification of the labour shortages in the developed economies, while the wage differences between the countries are likely to persist. Admittedly, the emerging economies will likely remain the most desirable sites for offshoring, because of their large, young talent pools and their lower wage costs. Greater investment in education, coupled with shortages of qualified talent in developed countries, will continue to constitute critical advantage for the emerging countries, they claim.

While studying the outsourcing in the accounting industry, Daley (2008) stated that the firms have positive experience with the new service offering due the variety of the available services and the decreased prices. Furthermore, the online "portals" which enable the outsourcing of accounting become much more secure and the workflow software has grown increasingly user-friendly, efficient, and cost effective, claims Daley (2008). Professional service firms, according to Sako (2014), are outsourcing providers and also users of outsourced services and they may to acquire a larger or a smaller segment of the market depending on the successfulness of their playing of the intermediary role.

According to Daley (2008), the phenomenon of outsourcing has engulfed the entire accounting industry and now offers wide range of services, starting from bookkeeping, accounts payable, debt collection, billing and invoicing, ending with complex tax returns preparation. Cienski (2013) considers countries of central Europe as most attractive providers, since they are in the EU and thus share common legal code, have well-educated population, fluent in many languages, while the labour costs are still less than in the case of the other countries of Europe. He argues that, while the labour rates remain significantly lower in India, China and Philippines, the European offshore destinations by sharing same culture and the time zone with the major European business centres, are still the best candidates for the higher-valued "near shoring" arrangements and investments. This is in line with Bunyaratavej *et al.* (2007) finding that differences in wages might not be the only factor that firms use to consider offshoring of their services and that the education and the cultural distance are important factors determining the location of offshore services activities.

A study of the European Union apparel sector concludes "labour costs, along with geographical and cultural proximity are the most important reasons for the original choice of a given country as a processing partner" (Baldone *et al.*, 2001). In line with this approach, distance, promptness in delivery and flexibility in organisation of production are important variables in choosing the off-shoring location (Evans and Harrigan, 2003). Sass and Fifekova (2011) consider availability of skilled labour with strong language skills, low costs, favourable business and stable political environment, well-developed infrastructure and geographical and cultural proximity to Western Europe as favourable factors for the Central and Eastern European (CEE) region to become a business service offshoring and outsourcing destination.

Despite the belief that the service industry is promising opportunity for the CEE economies, Gal (2010) states few threats concerning the region's future prospects as major offshoring centre. According to him, the size of the talent pool is still limited to the CEE region, (2) the population is limited and fragmented, (3) the providers are more attached to the local market instead of seeking out the global market and (4) the bureaucratic environment.

Stark *et al.* (2011) suggest that the policy makers in the case of the countries providers, while evaluating their workforce development policies should consider the rapid evolution and the high competitive nature of the outsourcing industry, calling for much more in-depth understanding of the workforce profiles needed for these higher-level services. Moreover, the skills and the qualification of the workforce effectively determine the point of entry and the market potential for growth of these the host nations, claim Stark at al. (2011). They also suggest combined institutional approach and collaboration between the business, public authorities and education sector in narrowing the gaps between the demand and the supply of labour able to meet the global standards of these services.

According to the McKinsey's Global Institute Report (2012) the offshore talent pool exceeds that of the high-wage countries by a factor of two. Only Russia has almost 10 times more finance and accounting professionals than Germany, for example. However, only 13% of this talent supply from the low-wage nations is suitable to work for multinational companies. The lack of appropriate language skills, the inability of the educational system to convey the needed practical skills and the lack of cultural fit and readiness for high workload and flexible working hours are the main reasons for that situation. Even so many researches indicate that the university graduates from the Eastern European countries are well suited to work for multinational companies the mentioned skills will remain to be the essential prerequisites for offshoring of the advanced business services. Even in the case of the countries in which education provides modern skills, according to Stark *et al.* (2011) the majority of the workers still need extensive on the job training to meet the high-quality standards required for serving the global market.

3. Methodology

The methodology used is based on a desk research of the documents from government agencies, independent institutions and financial agencies, universities and other educational institutions and relevant journals. We also use database of the State Statistical Agency of Macedonia for the number of the registered accountants and the amount of their salaries or declared income.

To assess the potential of the Macedonian accountants to offer offshore services we have used the criteria for evaluation of outsourcing destinations as established by the McKinsey Institute: (i) the cost savings, (ii) talent pool, quality of providers, (iii) language skills and (iv) cultural and market proximity. We have examined the cost savings by comparing the salaries in Macedonia with those in other CEE countries. We have assessed the talent pool by reviewing the accounting educational programs and the language skills and assess the cultural "proximity" of the country. We have used the Eurostat data of Foreign language learning statistics to evaluate language skill of Macedonians. Results of the survey are presented in suitable S.W.O.T country analysis.

4. Evaluation criteria for accounting services off shoring

The institutional framework

Republic of Macedonia has accepted the International Accounting Standards for large and medium-sized companies in 2005. Since 2012, even the micro companies and the sole proprietors have to keep their accounting in accordance with the related International Standards. The institutional framework for the accounting, auditing and the reporting system in Macedonia was established when the Institute of Chartered Auditors in 2006 and the Institute for Chartered Accountants in 2012 were inaugurated. These two institutions are now authorized for certification of the auditors and accountants and for continuing training of the certified providers of these services. Other accounting professional associations that were established meanwhile are the Association of the accountants of the Republic of Macedonia and the Chamber of the Accountants.

The cost of the accounting services

In 2014, in the sector of Administrative and support service activities, there were 1,067 registered entities, with 17,769 employees, who turned app. 220-million-euro revenue. The payroll cost was 70 million euro, or each worker cost app. 4,000 euro (State Statistical Office, 2016). Comparison with the other countries shows that Republic of Macedonia would be cost competitive destination for offshoring. As it can be seen from the Table 1 in the Appendices, accountants are less paid only in Philippines and China.

The quality of providers

The Law for the Accounting Profession, adopted in 2012, imposed the basis of the development of the accounting services by regulating their licensing, examination and continuous professional training. Certification is undertaken in the interim by the Ministry of Finance, which has issued certificates to some 12,000 accountants and certified accountants, of which 9,000 are temporary certificates (World Bank, 2014). The 2012 Law on Accounting Services improves regulation and the knowledge and skills level of accountants in Macedonia. The Law on Accounting Services defines the roles of the institutions, the licensing framework (the knowledge and skills and the examination) and the two categories of certified professionals, Accountant and Certified accountant. The Table 1 lists the Law requirements for accountant and for certified accountant professional.

Table 1. Requirements for accounting practice in Republic of Macedonia

Requirement	Accountant	Certified Accountant
Education	Four Years High School	Baccalaureate in business or economics
Exam	Required	Required
Training	90 hours in last three years, minimum 20 hours in last year	120 hours in last three years, minimum 30 hours in last year
Prior work experience	No	at least three years in accounting
Entitlement for endorsement	Sole proprietorships, civil associations and foundations	All types of business entities
Legal form of operations	Sole Proprietorship	Company
Minimum headcount	One Accountant	One Accountant and One Certified Accountant
Professional insurance	2,000 to 5,000 euro	20,000 euro

(Source: The authors own work based on the Law on Accounting Services)

Talent availability

Republic of Macedonia has a relatively well-established system of education. With the transition from the previous socialist system into free trade economy, Republic of Macedonia constantly upgrades the system introducing various business and entrepreneurial courses in the curricula at all levels of education and all types of schools. The high school education is compulsory. The number of enrolled high school students in 2014/15 was 83,522. The number of the university students in 2013 reached 56,094, and 9,166 graduated that year (MAKSTAT, 2016). Both private and public schools are allowed. There are several foreign high schools and universities and many students from Republic of Macedonia study abroad. The institutions of higher education (there are twenty accredited) provide various courses in accounting at undergraduate and graduate level. The universities in the country offer basic accounting course as part of economics and business administration degrees and advanced courses dedicated for accounting and auditing majors. The number of students in the business school in 2013 was 8,473, out of which 1,344 or app. 16% enrolled in accounting and auditing programs (State Statistical Office, 2014). Accounting subjects offered cover foundation, intermediate and advanced accounting, financial reporting, international accounting, managerial accounting and auditing. The syllabi incorporate key aspects of international accounting and financial reporting standards and ethics. However, the quality of the delivery varies in a very broad range with the reputation of the school and the skill and experience of the teachers. Although, there is a new generation of educators who slowly change the paradigm, somehow the state universities still put forward and value memorizing before critical thinking. On the other hand, private universities foster new standards of teaching and emphasize skills of the students, but they are doing that by downplaying the formal knowledge of the profession.

We surveyed the publicly declared programs of the six best ranked universities in Republic of Macedonia, as merited by the Ministry of Education. We used the ratio between the accounting courses and the total load with undergraduate subjects as a proxy for the perceived "importance" of the programs in accounting. In five of the universities that load was 2/30 or 6.67% and in one 3.37%. Five of the surveyed institutions offer accounting and auditing undergraduate degree, with 30% of the total load in case of one university, 13% in case of two, and only 10% load in the other three. Information Systems for Accounting or any kind of training in computerized accounting (Quick Books or similar) are not offered by any of the surveyed institutions. However, the institution that currently does not offer such undergraduate specialization plans to offer it from the next academic year. They will collaborate and align with the requirements of the Association of Chartered Certified Accountants (ACCA) as widely recognized and reputable professional organization. We conducted several interviews with professors involved in delivery of accounting subjects. They stress that due to the so-called Bologna Process their students practically lack one full undergraduate year of schooling, which means that the Introduction in business is omitted, putting extra pressure to the professors who teach Principles of accounting. Moreover, since the intermediate accounting is also omitted students while still struggling with the basic concepts have to wrestle with the complicated issues of financial accounting. As a consequence, they tend to develop hesitation to the accounting and auditing programs and generations of business graduates in the Country are almost entirely focused on marketing, human relations and other soft skills and the pool of potential candidates for accounting and auditing graduate degrees is very limited.

However, due to the low population growth and the high emigration, Republic of Macedonia also shows depopulation and shortage of workforce. The low wages are not attracting young graduates to stay at home. Open borders drive them towards the regions of Europe that pay much more for educated workers. The emigration rate among young graduates is app. 22% or every fifth young graduate leaves the country. This issue might turn critical for the aspirations of Republic of Macedonia to offer a suitable destination for offshoring of accounting and the related services. The other critical issue is the quality of the potential providers and the common perception of their establishment and integrity as accounting professionals.

Cultural and language issues

Some of the common disadvantages of the workforce of the so-called ex-communist countries, like the lack of the proper attitude to the work and lack of internal drive, loose discipline and commitment are present in the case of the workforce in Republic of Macedonia, too. However, the lack of proficiency in foreign languages, at least in the case of English, with the young generations is practically eliminated. According to Eurostat (2016) all pupils in primary education in Macedonia learn English languages and near 55% of Macedonian students learn two or more languages in upper secondary education.

5. Presentation of the findings in S.W.O.T. Matrix

We present our findings from the evaluation of the criteria of the potential of Republic of Macedonia in offering offshored accounting services in the Table 4 in form of S.W.O.T. Matrix.

Table 3. SWOT- Analysis of the Republic of Macedonia as Outsourcing Destination

STRENGTHS	WEAKNESSES
Relatively educated workforce Good proficiency in English International standards implemented Very competitive salary ran Advanced ICT infrastructure	Weak work culture Weak professionalization Lack of widely recognized certifications
OPPORTUNITIES	**THREATS**
Good location (time-zone) Conducive Government Policy Large diaspora worldwide	The economic crisis in EU Political instability in the region Potential shortage of work force

6. Conclusions and recommendations

Accounting and the related services, like payroll were not traditional domain of offshoring. Only the second wave of outsourcing added advanced services based on high-value and complex tasks such as accounting. Offshoring and nearshoring today offer wide range of services from simple bookkeeping, accounts payable, debt collection, billing and invoicing, up to tax return preparation. Countries of Central Europe are attractive nearshoring destinations, since they share the common legal environment with the rest of the European Union; people are fluent in English or German, while the wages are still considerably lower. Offshoring of business services are increasingly recognized as potential vehicles for many other low and middle-income countries interested to participate in the global knowledge economy. These services offer attractive compensation and career development opportunities for graduate professionals in these countries.

Research shows that the sophistication of the business services, including the accounting, provide valuable foundation for sustained growth. These emerging economies will likely remain desirable sites for offshoring, due to their large, young talent pools and the lower cost of the labour. Greater investment in education in the emerging countries coupled with the shortage of qualified talent in the developed countries will continue to constitute the critical advantage of the emerging countries. Consequently, the policy makers in these countries should foster creation of new generations of workforce able to cope with the challenges of these new outsourcing. The availability of the workforce will determine the ability of a given country to tap the market of outsourcing of advanced services like accounting. However, the talent pool is limited since just 13% of it in low-wage nations has appropriate language skills. The educational systems fail to convey practical skills to students and there is lack of cultural fit and readiness for high workload and flexible working hours. Having all of this in mind, Republic of Macedonia should also consider higher involvement in this growing world marketplace. The Country has accepted the International Financial Reporting Standards for all accounting entities starting from the micro companies and sole proprietors up to the companies listed at the Stock exchange.

Analysing the strengths, weaknesses, opportunities and threats we can conclude that Republic of Macedonia is relatively well located (same time zone) and has large diaspora that can serve as Agent Bridge between the providers and customers. Policy makers should comprehend the full potentials of the offshoring of accounting services. Republic of Macedonia should learn from countries like Poland that is a leader among all CEE countries in taking advantages of this trend. The country just recently started to recognize the full potential of the services in general for the employment of its higher educated workforce. The contribution of the services in the GDP reached 9.8% in 2014 (State Statistical Office, 2016). Due to the higher prices of the services relative to manufacturing, this drives up the productivity in the country. In addition, these services require much lower capital investments, do not pollute or harm the environment as the traditional industries were doing for decades. Regarding the education, only 16% of business students are enrolled in some accounting and auditing program. Only one university tries to align its program in accounting and auditing to the requirements and standards of ACCA as reputable professional organization.

Recognizing this, the recommendation to the policy makers and to the professional associations would be to include better coverage of accounting in the business schools, combined with stricter professional education and licensing, additional foreign languages, better communication and improved ICT skills and knowledge.

The accounting associations should consider introduction of some widely recognized professional designations and certifications in parallel with their national certificates. The move will add value to the national certificates and will make Republic of Macedonia recognizable destination for offshoring of accounting and other related services.

References

Association of Business Service Leaders (ABSL) (2014) "Business services sector in Poland", Retrieved from: emerging-europe.com/files/22221/file/ Business_Services_Sector_in_Poland_2014.pdf

AT Kearney (2016) "On the Eve of Disruption". Available at: https://www.atkearney.com/documents/10192/7094247/On+the+Eve+of+Disruption.pdf/49fa89fa-7677-4ab8-8854-5003af40fc8e

Blinder, A. S. (2006) "Offshoring: the next industrial revolution", *Foreign Affairs*, vol. 85, No. 2: 113-128, Available at http://www.foreignaffairs.com /articles/61514/alan-s-blinder/offshoring-the-next-industrial-revolution

Bunyaratavej, K., Hahn, E. D. & Doh, J. P. (2007) "International offshoring of services: A parity study", *Journal of International Management*, vol. 13: 7-21

Cattaneo O. & Walkenhorst, P. (2012) "Accounting services: ensuring good governance, financial stability, and economic growth through trade", World Bank

Cienski, J. (2013) "Outsourcing: Businesses go east to offshore costly services", Available at: http://www.ft.com/intl/cms/s/0/66e94cbe-8667-11e2-ad73-00144feabdc0.html#axzz3CYQtAYCW

Daley, R. P. (2008) "The accounting industry in the age of globalization and offshore outsourcing", Senior Capstone Project. Retrieved from: http://digitalcommons.bryant.edu/cgi/viewcontent.cgi?article=1001&context =honors_economics

Ellram, L. M., Tate, W.L. & Billington, C. (2007) "Offshore outsourcing of professional services: A transaction cost economics perspective", *Journal of Operations Management*, vol. 26: 148-163

Eurostat (2016) "Foreign language learning statistics", Retrieved from: http://ec.europa.eu/eurostat/statistics-explained/index.php/Foreign_language_learning_statistics#Further_Eurostat_information (on-line access: September 17th 2016)

Evans, C.L. & Harrigan, J. (2003) "Distance, time and specialization", NBER Working Paper, 9729, May. Retrieved from http://www.nber.org /papers/w9729.pdf

Everest Group (2014) "Central & Eastern European (CEE) Locations for Finance & Accounting Services Delivery – Delivery Options Bloom in Western Europe's Backyard", Available at: https://research.everestgrp.com /Product/EGR-2014-2-R-1300/Central-Eastern-European-CEE-Locations-for-Finance-Accounting-(on-line access: May 12th 2016)

Farrell, D, Laboissière, M., Rosenfeld, J., Stürze, S. & Umezawa, F. (2005) "The Emerging Global Labor Market: Part II—The Supply of Offshore Talent in Services", The McKinsey Global Institute.

Gal Z. (2010) "Future Bangalores? The increasing role of Central and Eastern Europe in the global services offshoring market: evidence from trade statistics", MPRA Paper No. 28360,

Gal, Z. (2014) "Relocation of business services into Central and Eastern Europe (Evidence from trade and local statistics)", *Romanian Review Of Regional Studies*, vol. X: 67-78

Ives, R. (2014) "Outsourcing becoming a necessity more than a need: Evolving with the generations", Global Services Forum, May 28, Beijing

Kwacz Y., Ruiz, M. & Scasso, J. I. (2013) "Services offshoring ranking: A comparative analysis of emerging economies", Tower Watson. Available at: http://www10.iadb.org/intal/intalcdi/PE/CM%202014/14410.pdf

McKinsey Global Institute (2012) "A new dawn: Reigniting growth in Central and Eastern Europe". Available at: www.mckinsey.com/insights/economic_studies/a_new_dawn_reigniting_growth_in_central_and_eastern_europe (on-line access: June 25th 2016)

McKinsey Global Institute (2015) "Poland 2025: Europe's new growth engine." Retrieved from: http://www.mckinsey.com/~/media/mckinsey/business%20functions/economic%20studies%20temp/our%20insights/how%20poland%20can%20become%20a%20european%20growth%20engine/poland%202025_full_report.ashx. (on-line access: June 25th 2016)

Mishra, S., Lundstrom, G.S. & Anand, R. (2012) "Service export sophistication and economic growth", World Bank. Retrieved from: https://openknowledge.worldbank.org/bitstream/handle/10986/3372/WPS5606.pdf?sequence=1

Păvăloaia, V. (2011) "Aspects of accounting and financial analysis service outsourcing: A Romanian approach", *Acta Universitatis Danubius. Economica.* vol. 7(3): 21-33

Sahni, M., Wong, C.-C. & Bangah, S. (2012) "Offshore outsourcing service trends - A Malaysian perspective", Special Study for MDeC

Sako, M. (2014) "Outsourcing and offshoring of professional services", The Oxford Handbook of Professional Service Firms

Sass, M. & Fifekova, M. (2011) "Offshoring and outsourcing business services to Central and Eastern Europe: some empirical and conceptual considerations", *European Planning Studies*, vol. 19: 1593-1609

Stark, K. F., Bamber, P. & Gereffi, G. (2011) "The offshore services global value chain: economic upgrading and workforce development", Center on Globalization, Governance & Competitiveness. Available at: http://www.cggc.duke.edu/pdfs/2011-11-11_CGGC_Offshore-Services-Global-Value-Chain.pd

State statistical Office of Republic of Macedonia (2014) “Labor cost survey, 2012”, Retrieved from: http://www.stat.gov.mk/Publikacii/2.4.14.08.pdf (on-line access: June 27th 2016)

UNCTAD (2013) “The Global Services Forum - Services: A new frontier for sustainable development”, Available at” http://unctadxiii.org/en/Pages/DisplaySession.aspx?sessionid=4Web pages

World Bank (2014) “Report on the Observance of Standards and Codes on Accounting and Auditing”, Report No: ACS12571

Appendices

1. Top countries in Outsourcing in 2015

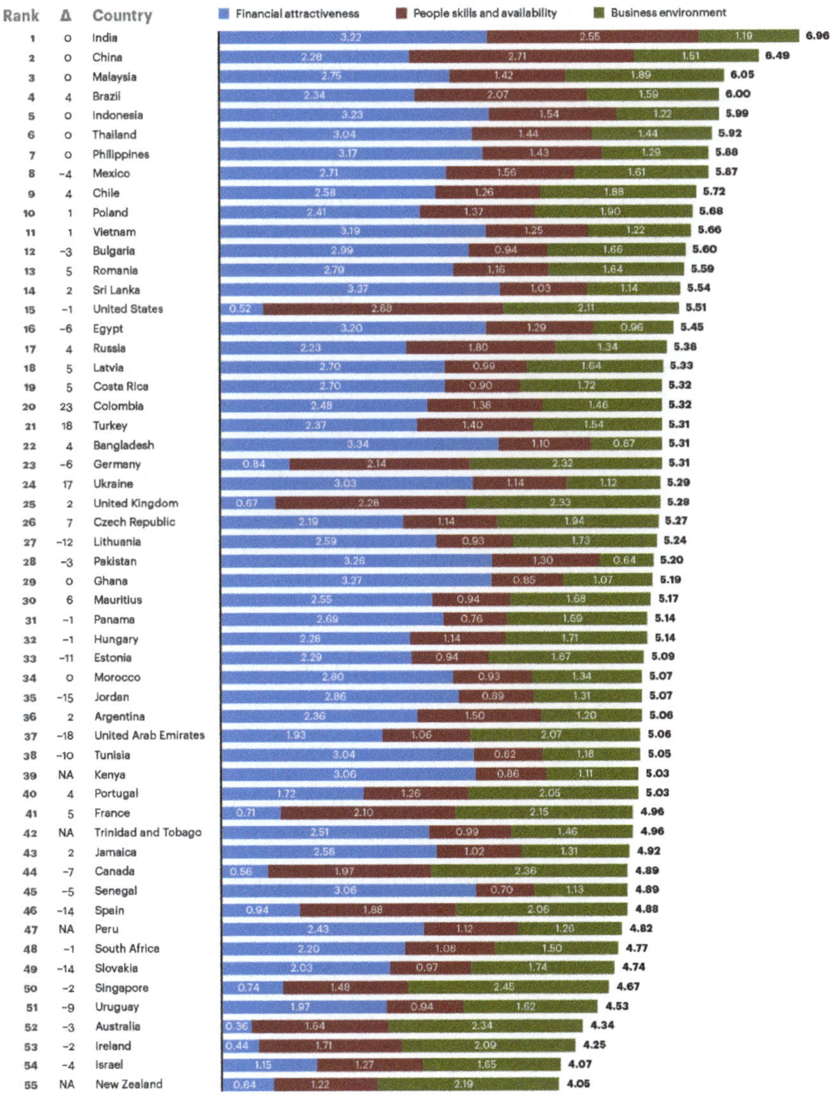

(Source: Kearney - The 2016 Global Services Location Index)

2. Average Gross and Net Salaries (Income) of Accountants

Country	Gross	Compulsory Deductions	Net
U.S.	3,370	22%	2,629
Finland	3,308	38%	2,051
Germany	2,977	34%	1,965
Korea	2,789	14%	2,399
Italy	2,785	37%	1,755
Kuwait	2,697	0%	2,697
Australia	2,578	20%	2,062
Canada	2,352	32%	1,599
Austria	2,179	36%	1,395
Singapore	1,682	22%	1,312
Portugal	1,553	23%	1,196
Brazil	1,351	20%	1,081
Hungary	1,136	45%	625
Taiwan	1,111	10%	1,000
Czech Republic	928	29%	659
Mexico	831	15%	706
Latvia	709	29%	503
Slovakia	646	22%	504
Thailand	621	6%	584
Poland	617	35%	401
Romania	597	33%	400
Lithuania	493	31%	340
Macedonia	377	25%	283
Philippines	278	16%	234
China	165	8%	152

(Source: www.worldsalaries.org/accountant.shtml and makstat.gov.mk)

3

Accountants and the cloud – Involving the professionals

Dragoş Mangiuc[a,1]

[a] *Bucharest University of Economic Studies, Romania*

Abstract: As the cloud-based technologies gain more customers each day, the need for understanding the "economics of cloud" arises, together with the need for strategic measurement of different cloud or non-cloud-based infrastructure options. In such context, the option for the cloud technologies cannot be the duty of the IT department only, as the economic drivers are at least as important as the technological ones. Economic measurement of the future cloud computing implementations is required for at least two reasons. First, all types of implementations are investment projects and, by consequence, need to be fully justified before being chosen or rejected. Second, once a cloud strategy is adopted and an infrastructure is implemented, the implementation must be continually monitored, so the organization can be sure that it continues to deliver an optimal return on investment. Gaining maximal return on the implementation of a cloud computing strategy is predicated on the ability to understand the economic metrics. Therefore, the accounting professional can no longer be a simple observer in the process of cloud migration and cloud adoption, but a central piece and a "voice of reason" standing between the typical enthusiasm of the IT department and the typical skepticism of the management.

Keywords: Cloud computing economics, accounting profession, CAPEX, OPEX, ROI, TCO

---

[1] *Corresponding author*: Department of Management Information Systems, Bucharest University of Economic Studies; 6, Romană Square, 010371, Bucharest
email address: dragos.mangiuc@cig.ase.ro

1. Introduction

Contemporary organizations are the target of a continuous "data bombardment", therefore they quickly reach the need for an efficient way to convert the received data into correctly structured information, able to provide decision support or competitive advantages. Any decision taken at the organizational level, may it be the construction of a new building, or the migration of a business service towards the cloud, requires pertinent and usable information. The accounting professionals working in IT organizations, or in any kind of organization which takes into account the adoption of cloud-based services, often considered that the final decision for or against the adoption of such services exceeds their competence, being the exclusive prerogative of the IT department (Mahlindayu *et al.*, 2014). The current paper is an attempt to demonstrate the way an accounting or audit professional may be implied in the final decision regarding a migration towards the cloud, and also the way such professional may use her own knowledge and experience in order to positively influence the final decision, by providing solid points and properly performed efficiency calculations

This paper aims to create an image as objective and accurate as possible of the cloud migration process, in an environment usually dominated by massive bias and diametrically opposed views. Between the "tech" group in an organization, having advanced technical knowledge that tending to see only the advantages of cloud-based solutions, and the group lacking technical knowledge, which tends to see the migration to the cloud as an unnecessary expense, the accounting professional may be able to exercise a mediation position, by making strong and valid economic points. To this end, the accounting professional may use a number of generally accepted indicators for evaluating investment decisions, whose understanding does not require deep economic and financial knowledge. The paper starts from the premise that the organization's management was confronted in the past with investment decisions and as a result, is familiar with the contents and significance of the proposed indicators.

After describing the research methodology, the paper identifies a number of financial indicators applicable in assessing a cloud based solution and makes a series of proposals on the specific treatment required for the design of these indicators when assessing information technologies. Further, the paper attempted to identify a set of costs-concerning specific issues, to be taken into account in the design of the performance indicators, and a number of specific elements that enable an accounting professional to perform estimates of the cost as close as possible, with a minimum of technical knowledge.

The next section of the paper is a comparative case study that illustrates the manner that the previously proposed indicators can be used in order to support investment decision in a cloud-based solution. To this end, two different technical solutions were presented: a "traditional" one, incorporating massive capital expenses based on the in-house management of necessary hardware components and on the in-house development of the required software applications; the second one completely based on cloud technologies, incorporating major operational expenses and completely relieving the beneficiary of IT management tasks. As the author believes that a comparison between the two is not relevant in the short term, the paper has opted for a realistic comparison on a timespan of five years for both solutions, the TCO (Total Cost of Ownership) indicator being used for this purpose. The analysis results are synthesized in a tabular format that facilitates comparison, a number of observations on the best manner to correlate the investment decision with the actual situation of the organization (start-up, development, maturity) being made.

In order to deepen the analysis performed by the of the accounting professional, and also, in order to ensure the comparability of potential investment alternatives, the next section proposes a way of calculating the ROI (Return On Investment) indicator, providing alternative computation formulas, and also a number of the author's views on how to interpret the results. In this section, the comparative case study is revisited for exemplification purposes, the ROI indicator being calculated and interpreted for each of the two solutions.

The conclusions section summarizes the author's findings, while cautioning about the limits of the evaluation model and reiterating the original assertion, that the accountant may have a relevant role in the final decision for the adoption or rejection of cloud-based solutions.

2. Research methodology

The paper addressed the issue of the accounting professional's status in relation to the final decision for the adoption or the rejection of cloud-based services, in the context of a less and less forgiving economic environment. Its main objective is to provide insight regarding the tools that an accounting or auditing professional can use to select between different solutions, without the need for complex IT knowledge, only by applying the standard treatment of any new investment opportunity.

The information is provided in the form of a case study. Two different scenarios are analyzed, each of them considering an option for the investment in a new IT infrastructure. The purpose of the case study is to reveal the actual manner an accountant should approach and form an opinion, when the organization has to choose between an in-house solution and a cloud-based one. The analysis is based on a set of key performance indicators, like the total cost of ownership, the return on investment or the ratio of the capital and operational expenses, which are traditionally used in the financial analysis of investment options.

The value added by the current analysis consists in approaching the investment options for IT solutions in a manner which considers all the IT implications of each investment opportunity, form the perspective of an IT specialist, but can be used by an accounting or auditing professional when asked to select an option. The advantages and disadvantages of each financial analysis tool for the investment opportunities are also discussed, from both IT and financial perspectives.

3. Financial estimation for a migration to the *cloud*

The final decision on a migration to the *cloud*, usually followed by the development and implementation of a coherent *cloud* strategy, involves the evaluation and consideration of large amounts of information, much of which is not technical, but economic in nature (Sujeet *et al.*, 2016). In these circumstances, the accounting professional's role in formulating the final decision is not just a formal or complacent one, but becomes an important role as the accountant or the auditor has a range of knowledge that makes her to be in the best position to review, organize and synthesize a variety of data and information that cannot be eliminated from the decision-making process. In this context, the accounting professional will be able to start from the information at her disposal in order to compute a number of indicators with high informational content, so as to decide based on the aforesaid indicators whether a *cloud*-based infrastructure is the right choice. Out of these indicators, the leading importance for the final decision belongs to:

- **Total Cost of Ownership (TCO)** – is a financial estimate of all direct and indirect costs associated with ownership of an asset, as, for example, a *cloud*-based infrastructure (Visani *et al.*, 2016). The proper understanding of the costs which are part of the TCO of the existing IT infrastructure helps to understand how the organization and its business processes are able to benefit from such infrastructure. Also, the computation of this indicator is extremely useful when comparing different alternative options for financing a possible migration. When evaluating a *cloud*-based solution, it is necessary to estimate the total cost of ownership both in the traditional way and in the light of the new meaning of TCO: total operating cost.
- **Capital expenditure (CAPEX) and operational expenditure (OPEX)** – CAPEX term refers to the way large purchases having an expected life of more than one year will be managed from an accounting perspective. The ultimate goal is to reconcile the manner an acquisition is used and the income generated by the acquisition (Almeida *et al.*, 2011). OPEX usually

refers to those purchases of an organization which are consumed during the current year.

- **Return on Investment (ROI)** – is an indicator that can quickly and effectively show how financially inspired an investment was. It may also have an important decisional component, when comparing multiple investment options, each with its own estimated value for ROI.

In relation to the manner the indicators described above will be used, the *cloud computing strategy* of an organization can be defined as the medium and long term plan of an organization to adopt and use technologies whose defining characteristics fall within the *cloud* area. The existence and implementation of such a strategy changes the role of the IT department in an organization, which migrates from the design and implementation of solutions, to the delivery of services. It is generally accepted (Al-Ayyoub *et al.*, 2015) that the existence of such strategy inside an organization promotes the innovation process, because migration to the *cloud* can have major effects on the cost and implementation duration of a solution. This is especially noticeable when the organization uses the services of some external providers instead of the in-house development of a solution.

As noted above, TCO involves identifying all the costs driven by the ownership of an asset. The costs taken into account depend on the nature and specifics of the assessed project, and their structure differs from one project to another. The concept of "total cost of operation" extends the basic model for the computation of the cost of ownership, so that it also takes into account the operating costs. According to some authors, TCO can be defined as the total cost incurred by the ownership of an asset and by its operation (Helms, 2016).

In the case of a project for the adoption of *cloud* technologies, the TCO indicator must be a financial estimate which includes all direct and indirect costs involved in the purchase of such a solution, as well as the costs involved by the current use of that solution. For example:

- **Direct costs** – when acquiring information and communications technology, direct costs include purchase cost, installation costs and maintenance costs. Depending on the nature of implementation, direct costs may also include the cost of testing the purchased solution, the cost of the location where equipment was deployed (for data centers, these costs can be considerable), environmental costs, costs to ensure the optimal operation conditions - the fine tuning of air temperature and electricity parameters.
- **Indirect costs** – although not directly associated with the acquisition of *cloud*-based solutions, these costs are real and unavoidable for the implementation to be successful. Costs of this kind should be included in any financial review of an acquisition of technology (Sohn *et al.*, 2015). Indirect costs can include qualification and specialization of personnel,

losses due to planned or accidental unavailability of service, different types of security breaches (physical or virus-related in nature), the ability to deal with a disaster and to resume work after a disaster, other development related costs, or even the expenses with the decommissioning of the investment.

- **Operating costs** – are costs associated with operating a *cloud*-based infrastructure. They have as their main component the purchase cost of services from the corresponding suppliers. If the *cloud*-based solutions require the employment of additional staff, the cost of the additional staff will also be included in the operating costs.

The following table (Table 1) summarizes the main components that require to be taken into consideration when estimating the TCO indicator of a *cloud* based solution. In such cases, the assessment of direct costs and operational costs is easily achieved, but determining the indirect costs may prove to be much more difficult (Plaza, 2015). However, it is essential that any necessary and probable indirect cost to be included in all financial estimates.

Table 1. Total cost of ownership structure

Direct costs	*Indirect costs*	*Operating costs*
Purchase price	Training	Additional staff needed to support
Maintenance	Outage	*cloud*
Installation	Breach	implementation
Upgrades	Disaster preparedness	Cost of services from *cloud*
	Disaster recovery	service and data providers
	Floor space	
	Testing	
	Development	
	Decommissioning	

An in-depth analysis of the migration process to a *cloud*-based solution reveals a number of aspects which are specific to this situation. The following list is not considered to be exhaustive, but still could be a valid starting point for analyzing the phenomenon of migration to the *cloud*:

- *Cloud*-based infrastructure should lead to a high level of innovation – an increase in the level of innovation may require a high growth of the computing infrastructure and, as a result, an overall increase in cost levels. Such increases can lead to additional costs for the personnel involved to operate facilities, or other cost categories covering the need for the additional infrastructure.
- *Cloud*-based infrastructure should provide better conditions for working remotely – a *cloud*-based implementation has as an important consequence the fact that any employee can work anywhere there is a reasonable Internet connection and a suitable device available (laptop, tablet,

smartphone, etc.). This can lead to additional costs for the Internet connection, the required devices, and also, it may require major changes in the organizational culture.

- The cost of the software licenses, the hardware and the facilities needed in order to properly host the hardware change significantly in the case of a *cloud*-based infrastructure. Although migration to the *cloud* has the ability to reduce these costs in the initial phase, the total cost of operation may be higher over time, when compared with the total operating cost of an in-house solution. The decision to migrate to the *cloud* should take into account all benefits of such a solution, but also all the involved expenses, so that the ROI indicator can be calculated correctly, or, at least, to a reasonable level (Misra & Mondal, 2011).

The total cost of operation has different values in different scenarios, especially when the development of an in-house applicative solution and the purchase of the necessary services from the *cloud* service providers are compared in terms of effectiveness. When the hardware infrastructure and the corresponding software are built in-house, there are significant costs for development, and, most of all, significant time-related costs, because the development effort is time-consuming, there is a need of a coherent testing system for the internally built applications etc. When the needed services are purchased, many of the costs described above are significantly reduced or even disappear, but instead, the organization may face important costs for the integration of the new external services purchased with the existing internal business processes and the existing internal infrastructure. In many cases, the decision to build or purchase may be finally determined by the value of the length of time that the organization has to wait in order for the in-house solution to be designed, developed and implemented, in contrast with the ability to immediately benefit from those services through their purchase from a *cloud* service provider. Although the differences in the cost structure, in the case of a "build or buy" decision, are more numerous than those described herein, the provided examples allow to form an overall idea on the differences between the two approaches.

The total cost of operation may be an extremely useful and important indicator in comparing multiple options, because some variants cost significantly more compared to others, when evaluation is performed for their entire useful life, and not limited to the time of purchase, or the first few years following the acquisition. Evaluating several options, each one requiring different costs of ownership and costs of operation, can lead to very different values of the overall TCO, calculated for the lifetime of the solution. While TCO is not the only financial indicator that should be considered, is one of the most important. Along with TCO, the professional accountant in the position to decide the optimal solution should consider the ROI, the value of the time factor expressed as money, the cost of the investment capital sources, the effects of the investment on the financial statements of the organization, the tax implications of the investment, and the net present value of the investment (Liu *et al.*, 2016). It is of utmost importance that every financial indicator taken into account in order to estimate an investment alternative, or to compare multiple investment variants, to be calculated (where possible) for the lifetime of the investment, not only for the initial access thereto (or start-up costs). Proper use of the TCO indicator has the ability to provide quite a clear image on how the investment in infrastructure, may it be traditional or *cloud*-oriented, will affect the financial position of the organization over time (Alkhanak, 2016). In no case analysis should be limited to the costs of start-up or the first year, but has to be performed for the whole lifetime of the investment.

The main proposal of this article is that the accounting professional becomes a mediating factor between any existing contrary opinions, for and against the adoption of cloud-based solutions. However, some recent studies (Gullhav & Nygreen, 2016) reveal that many practitioners in the field of accounting and law are seriously reluctant to achieve a transition to the cloud-based technologies, particularly due to the perceived losses in the field of security and data protection, and also due to the complexity of the overall IT system. This perspective is, in the author's opinion, a subjective one, while cloud-based technologies, like any product of human intelligence, have their own set of strengths and weaknesses.

The contemporary accounting professional is often put under pressure by the management of the organization to increase its work efficiency and become competitive. In these circumstances automating the accounting activity as much as possible is the obvious answer, but not all technologies are created equal.

The migration of an organization's accounting function to the cloud can enable the accounting department to pay only for what they use, eliminating the need for purchase and installation of software licenses (Koutsandria *et al.*, 2016). The business model where the amounts paid for the use of software applications increase or decrease depending on the volume of activity allows a very good alignment of costs to the added value created by applications and to the benefits obtained. In an unstable accounting environment, heavily burdened by taxation (as is the case of Romania), the costs of making quick updates at short intervals, largely due to changes in the regulatory and legislative environment, are no longer relevant to the client organization, building and implementing updates being the exclusive contractual duty of the cloud service provider. On the other hand, professional accountants should consider not only the cost savings involved in migration to the cloud, but also the cost increases. For example, if a management or accounting information system has already outsourced some of its components to the cloud, the interconnection of each subsystem with the main cloud-based system, may prove to be much more expensive than it appears on a first examination. The interfaces between cloud systems can be much more complicated than the simple transfer of text or database files (He *et al.*, 2016).

Cloud-based technologies enable access to information and the ability to process it at any time and from any location. Receiving information in real time allows the accountant to work faster and to be better informed, but also increases the level of pressure that the accounting professional must bear in order to sync own activities with the "speed of the organization". The scalability feature of cloud-based accounting information systems allows flexible adaptation to the increases or decreases in the volume of activity, the payment being made based on the monthly number of transactions registered, processed or stored. In terms of flexibility and scalability, not all IT solutions are equivalent. For increased flexibility, certain functionality may be enabled or disabled on request (Shuja *et al.*, 2016), and some solutions provide a modular approach, allowing the organization to choose and pay for only those components it needs and actually use. According to the author, it is recommended to avoid organizational "lock-in" by purchasing a very long term subscription for a very consistent application package.

In the case of a very large accounting department, or if accounting information supports validation on multiple levels (from the control department, internal audit department, external auditors, etc.), the ability to define multiple users and grant them individual rights can prove to be a major advantage, facilitating collaboration between participants to the process, regardless of each one's location. The implementation of customized user roles and the integration of audit trails attached to each transaction, can facilitate detection and in-depth analysis of any fraudulent transactions before they manifest their effect on the financial statements.

According to some authors (Carniani *et al.*, 2016), a key issue that must be considered when opting for a cloud based accounting solution is its ability for horizontal integration. The authors state that a vital importance criterion is the ability of the cloud-based accounting applications to integrate in the cloud with other managerial applications from the organizational ecosystem (human resources management, production management, financial management, budgeting), thereby increasing not only the overall versatility of the organization's business processes, but also the general level of control exercised.

Traditionally, a number of accounting professionals avoid the cloud-based accounting solutions for reasons related to the loss of security (Lins *et al.*, 2016). Their perception may be inaccurate, in the sense that the cloud-based solution may benefit more rapidly and efficiently from updates, patches and other security enhancements when compared to an in-house solution, where the skill level and the experience of the organization's own IT department is the maximum limit up to which they can get in terms of security. However, in the author's opinion there are also some potential drawbacks, which are not too large to completely compromise the cloud migrated accounting solutions, but should be taken into account when the option for or against the cloud is made, and the accounting professionals should consider minimizing their negative effects, either through contractual terms or through equivalent methods:

- For a start-up or a small business, a package of cloud-based accounting software will always involve higher costs, when compared to a package of desktop accounting applications, and the extra cost will be completely unjustified if the included online backup service of the cloud-based solution not wanted or used.
- Storing accounting information in the cloud involves a loss of control which the accounting professional and the organization as a whole suffers for its own data and the place where it is stored. The most important manner the organization might be affected by this fact is a potential legal issue, where data may be under the law of the country or area where it is stored, instead of the law of the country or area where the organization exists. Sometimes, private or governmental external entities may require the cloud service provider access to the organization's accounting data for audit or control purposes, and the service provider would have to allow access under the law of the area where data is stored.
- Regardless of the chosen cloud accounting package, there will always be limitations on the available applications, operating systems and infrastructure options, in other words, there will be things that the cloud-based accounting application will not make. In these conditions, some cloud-based applications may be more rigid and more difficult to set up compared to their desktop counterparts.
- Although almost all cloud-based accounting applications are offering online storage as part of the package, very few of them offer real tools for local backup, in other words, the possibility that the accounting professional to download accounting data from the cloud to his own server and, if applicable, export the data to a different provider, or use it to build custom statements and reports that the cloud-based application does not offer. Switching to another service provider or keeping existing data for a long time without paying the subscription fee can raise serious issues, if not dealt with explicitly in the service level agreement contracts.

Considering the advantages and disadvantages of a cloud-based solution, it can be concluded that the recourse to such an accounting solution allows the accounting professional to better focus on the core business of the organization without wasting time with the repetitive tasks of updating applications and assuring compliance with the accounting and fiscal normative environment.

4. Financial measurements for a migration to the *cloud*

Starting from the perspective of the analysis based on the TCO type indicators presented above, two indicators of a financial of financial may be considered whose value estimate is essential for any initiative to migrate to the *cloud*:

- The ratio of operating expenses (OPEX) and capital expenditures (CAPEX);
- The value of return of an investment (ROI).

It is considered that the use of a perspective based on the total cost of ownership and the total operating cost, together with the CAPEX/OPEX ratio and ROI provide sufficient data for the organization to make informed choices on the opportunity of the migration to the *cloud*, even in the absence of knowledge of a technical nature. In the following, the paper will present two scenarios by means of which it will be explained how a professional in accounting or auditing can understand the impact of the migration to the *cloud* on the organization, even without advanced technical knowledge in the field.

- **Option 1**. An organization acquires information and communications technology in the amount of €150,000 (including hardware infrastructure and software applications), with an estimated useful life of five years. If the investment is depreciated using the straight-line method, the estimated expenditures will be in the amount of €30,000 per year, which means that the organization's income will be reduced by the same amount annually. These expenses should be compared against any revenue generated during the period. It is assumed there is also a needed additional amount of €65,000 as start-up costs, an annual maintenance expenditure of €59.500, and also €160,000 are needed annually in order to maintain the level of employees' qualification and the adequate working conditions for the equipment (these expenditures are estimated to increase by 5% per year).
- **Option 2**. The organization decides to move its IT services to an external *cloud* services provider. In this case, the development of the necessary applications will involve an initial cost of technology of €15,000, annual associated costs of installation and configuration of €15,000, personnel costs of €75,000, maintenance costs of €5,400, and total costs of the *cloud* service of €210,000 (personnel costs, maintenance and *cloud* services are estimated to increase by 5% per year).

A major element to be considered when evaluating a migration of the IT infrastructure to the *cloud* is represented by the major trade-offs which occur between capital expenditures (CAPEX) and operational expenditures (OPEX). In the case of a private *cloud* solution, which can even be operated by the beneficiary, the trade-offs from CAPEX to OPEX can be significantly reduced, or even non-existent (Altmann & Kashef, 2014). The CAPEX/OPEX ratio depends on context, to a large extent, and it should be assessed separately for each considered scenario.

If organizations make major IT infrastructure investments, these are traditionally treated as CAPEX, which means that are recorded as assets on the organization's balance sheet and depreciated over time. On the other hand, when the organization makes operational expenses in the normal course of business, these expenses are normally settled in the same year in which they were realized. Accordingly, the purchase of infrastructure the organization needs in order to operate its own IT solution is CAPEX, while the purchase of services from a *cloud* services provider is OPEX. When the organization's applications are migrated to an external *cloud* services provider, there is a trade-off of expenditures from CAPEX to OPEX, these two options being regarded as two fundamental models of financing the implementation of an IT solution, each having its own set of effects on the organization's balance sheet and income statement:

- In the CAPEX-based financing model, the organization requires cash, which can be obtained from its own funds, or borrowed, in order to purchase an asset. Therefore, the organization assumes a series of long-term liabilities in relation to the acquired asset, which it owns. Moreover, if the organization no longer needs the asset (may it be depreciated or not), it must decide how to dispose of the asset. During the useful life of the asset, the organization's staff is responsible for that asset's management. This creates some requirements of a financial nature, which may also be regarded as disadvantages:
    - The costs associated with the purchase, maintenance and disposal of the asset;
    - The personnel cost required to operate the asset;
    - A proactive effort to keep the asset in a condition to generate value, since the organization has invested in it.
- In the OPEX-based funding model there are no long-term liabilities of the organization and the initial cash requirements will be significantly reduced as compared to the previous option. The organization will pay a subscription (usually on a monthly basis) to use the IT assets of an external *cloud* services provider, who has ownership of the assets. The subscription value is usually calculated based on the leased computing power or on the filled storage space (although other charging models are available). The asset's ability to generate value throughout its useful life is the exclusive concern of the provider. When the organization does no longer want to use those assets, it simply waives the subscription without assuming any liabilities associated with the assets, in terms of disposal or realization thereof. Also, the OPEX model involves a trade-off in terms of responsibility and the involved personnel. The organization's staff is responsible only for managing applications, while the *cloud* services provider has the responsibility to manage the IT assets which provide these applications. It can be concluded that this type of relationship creates the following trade-offs in the IT solution funding model:

- The IT assets are owned by a third party, and the organization only pays for what they use (e.g., computing power, storage space, live memory etc.), instead of assuming long-term liabilities regarding the assets they use;
- The organization does not require personnel to maintain the infrastructure in operation, it only requires the necessary staff for the operation of the applications received as a service from the provider;
- The initial capital needed for the investment will be significantly reduced, as compared to the previous option, but the total operating costs for the project's useful life will be higher. These issues must be considered and analyzed for each project, so that it can be determined which option provides optimal results. It should be considered the fact that a significant decrease of the project's initial costs may constitute a solid foundation for entrepreneurship and innovation initiatives across the organization.

The fact that the organization no longer needs to assume long-term financial liabilities for an asset is important, but this solution can generate significantly higher costs than the ownership of that asset. When an organization leases an application from an external *cloud* services provider, a trade-off occurs between CAPEX and OPEX. However, it rarely happens that the implementation of an IT solution requires only one type of the two expenditures. Even an organization that relies heavily on external *cloud* services providers will still hold an internal infrastructure (although much more reduced), which will have to be managed. Even in these conditions, a migration of costs will happen, having effects on organizational strategy and on its financial position. Generally, a CAPEX and OPEX analysis is necessary when a decision must be made in terms of an organization's specific IT solutions. The services of an external *cloud* provider can be recorded as expenditures during the current accounting year, while the purchased infrastructure (as in option 1 above) is recorded as capital expenditure and depreciated over time. From a financial perspective, analyzing IT costs, in order to determine whether it is advisable to develop a proprietary solution or to use a *cloud* services provider entails the analysis of how the effects of these decisions are reflected in the balance sheet of the organization, its income statement, as well as the level of taxation. Under GAAP, when the company makes a capital expenditure, the amount will be allocated over the entire period in which associated economic benefits flow toward the company. To exemplify, the costs for the first option are described in Table 2, the costs of the second option are described in Table 3, and a comparative analysis of the two options is described in Table 4.

Table 2. Total costs of an in-house solution (in Euro)

VARIANT 1 – ACQUISITION OF AN IN-HOUSE SOLUTION						
		Year				
	Start-up costs	One	Two	Three	Four	Five
CAPITAL EXPENSES						
Initial in-house ICT	150.000	30.000	30.000	30.000	30.000	30.000
In-house setup	65.000	13.000	13.000	13.000	13.000	13.000
Annual CAPEX		**53.000**	**53.000**	**53.000**	**53.000**	**53.000**
Total 5-year CAPEX						**215.000**
OPERATING EXPENSES						
In-house personnel		160.000	168.000	176.400	185.220	194.481
In-house ICT maintenance		59.500	62.475	65.599	68.879	72.323
Annual OPEX		**219.500**	**230.475**	**241.999**	**254.099**	**266.804**
Total 5-year OPEX						**1.212.876**
EXPENSES TO THE PROFIT AND LOSS STATEMENT						
Annual expenses		**262.500**	**273.475**	**284.999**	**297.099**	**309.804**
Total 5-year expenses						**1.427.876**

Table 3. Total costs of a cloud-based solution (in Euro)

VARIANT 2 – ACQUISITION OF AN EXTERNAL CLOUD SOLUTION						
	Start-up costs	Year One	Two	Three	Four	Five
CAPITAL EXPENSES						
In-house setup	15.000	3.000	3.000	3.000	3.000	3.000
Annual maintenance		15.000	15.000	15.000	15.000	15.000
Annual CAPEX		**18.000**	**18.000**	**18.000**	**18.000**	**18.000**
Total 5-year CAPEX						**90.000**
OPERATING EXPENSES						
In-house Personnel		75.000	78.750	82.688	86.822	91.163
In-house IT maintenance		5.400	5.670	5.954	6.251	6.564
Cloud computing service		210.000	220.500	231.525	243.101	255.256
Annual OPEX		**290.400**	**304.920**	**320.166**	**336.174**	**352.983**
Total 5-year OPEX						**1.604.643**
EXPENSES TO THE PROFIT AND LOSS STATEMENT						
Annual expenses		**308.400**	**322.920**	**338.166**	**354.174**	**370.983**
Total 5-year expenses						**1.694.643**

Table 4. Costs comparison for the two solutions (in Euro)

SUMMARY	*VARIANT 1*	*VARIANT 2*
Total 5-year CAPEX	215.000	90.000
Total 5-year OPEX	1.025.005	1.604.643
Total 5-year expenses to Profit & Loss Account	1.240.005	1.694.643
Year 1 Cash Needs	400.500	380.400
5-year Expenses	1.240.005	1.694.643

Analyzing the three tables presented, there can be noticed the CAPEX to OPEX migration in the case of the *cloud*-based solution, as well as how this migration affects profit or loss. By analyzing the comparative data in Table 4, there can be noticed the following consequences of the migration from an in-house IT solution to a *cloud* services provider:

- CAPEX and OPEX values are very different in the two scenarios, with important consequences for the organization's balance sheet and its income statement;
- The required initial cash investment, as well as its evolution over the useful life of the investment is very different for the two options. *Cloud*-based infrastructure will require lower costs at the beginning (during the first year), but the total cost, over the useful life, will be higher.

Such differences may cause the *cloud*-based services to become a very attractive option, financially. In addition, as the emphasis moves from CAPEX to OPEX, there is a decrease of the accumulation of assets in the balance sheet of the organization. In the second option (the *cloud*-based one), the total expenditures will change, the majority of purchases will be recorded as expenses, and the value of assets in the balance sheet will decrease massively as compared to the first option. This can be viewed as a positive or a negative effect, depending on the organization's overall financial strategy.

The life cycle of a business, presented in Figure 1, summarizes the position of an organization, as it progresses from the start-up phase to the maturity and then to the maintenance phase. The evolution stage of an organization in relation to its lifecycle should be considered when discussing the implementation of a *cloud*-based infrastructure. In the early stages of the lifecycle, many organizations are limited in terms of available cash and, therefore, a *cloud*-based solution may seem like a good idea, with its reduced cash requirements for the first year and with the strong emphasis on operating expenses. This approach may also be desirable for investors (especially those who operate in the capital brokerage business). Investors may be concerned that, in the case of business failure, they will be burdened by expensive infrastructure, which will have to be sold for less than the cost of purchase. As the business progresses and develops, entering the stages of growth, maturity and maintenance, the value of available cash may be significantly higher and, from an accounting perspective, an OPEX-based model may not be attractive enough. A business having reached maturity will prefer to develop their own assets, focusing on CAPEX. This does not mean that a *cloud* infrastructure is excluded. It only means that a private *cloud*-based solution or a hybrid solution may be preferred, involving significant capital expenditures. Whichever the selected model, the CAPEX and OPEX balance should be considered, based on the financial needs of the organization.

5. Return on investment (ROI)

Value returned by an investment (*Return on Investment – ROI*) is an accounting valuation method. The comparison between ROI values for the various investment options, including those in information technology, is an extremely useful indicator. In its simplest form, the ROI can be calculated as ratio between net income generated by an investment and the book value of assets associated with that investment. In accounting practice, ROI is also determined using other formulas such as, for example:

ROI = (Net income + Interest) / Book value of assets

The formula can be modified to take into consideration a number of factors that influence the cost and outcome of the investment. For example, the ROI associated with the implementation of a project can be calculated using the formula:

ROI = (Gain from investment - Cost of investment) / Cost of investment

The way in which ROI is calculated should include those values which are the best indicators for the organization. As a result, a professional in the marketing department can determine ROI as the ratio between the revenues from each product and the associated costs, an IT manager can include in the formula the parameters in which he is the most interested. Table 5 includes a number of estimates of income for each of the two types of investment decisions described above:

Table 5. ROI comparison for the two variants (in Euro)

EXPECTED REVENUE FROM THE NEW SOLUTION						
			Year			**TOTAL**
	One	**Two**	**Three**	**Four**	**Five**	
Revenue	260.000	286.000	314.600	346.060	380.666	**1.587.326**
VARIANT 1 – ACQUISITION OF AN *IN-HOUSE* SOLUTION						
Annual CAPEX	43.000	43.000	43.000	43.000	43.000	**215.000**
Annual OPEX	234.500	246.225	258.536	271.463	285.036	**1.295.761**
Total Annual Expenses	277.500	289.225	301.536	314.463	328.036	**1.510.761**
Return on Investment	**-6.31%**	**-1.12%**	**4.33%**	**10.05%**	**16.04%**	**5.07%**
VARIANT 2 – ACQUISITION OF AN EXTERNAL *CLOUD* SOLUTION						
Annual CAPEX	18.000	18.000	18.000	18.000	18.000	**90.000**
Annual OPEX	290.400	304.920	320.166	336.174	352.983	**1.604.643**
Total Annual Expenses	308.400	322.920	338.166	354.174	370.983	**1.694.643**
Return on Investment	**-15.69%**	**-11.43%**	**-6.97%**	**-2.29%**	**2.61%**	**-6.33%**

In Table 5, the indicator ROI was calculated using the formula:

ROI = (Gain from investment - Cost of investment) / Cost of investment

As a result, in this example ROI considers the cost associated with each investment option, as well as the predicted earnings for each option. It was assumed that income has the same value in both scenarios. However, if there are additional information available in this regard, different amounts of income may be considered for each option. Once the accounting professional makes an adequate quantification of TCO and expected revenues, ROI can become a very useful tool for selecting the option with the highest investment results. The interpretation of ROI values (for the previous formula) are as follows:

- If ROI is a negative amount, the investment cost is higher than its outcome. In these circumstances the organization should not make the investment, unless it is mandatory to comply with legal requirements, in which case it will select the option with the lowest negative impact on ROI;
- If ROI is used to compare investment alternatives, the option with the highest value of ROI will be selected.

Calculation of ROI enables the organization's management to determine whether the level of investment results is acceptable, before initiating an investment project. Assuming, for example, that an organization intends to evaluate its potential investment in an infrastructure upgrade; the accounting or auditing professionals can determine the costs of upgrading infrastructure, estimating also the additional earnings obtained from the investment. However, it should be noted that the accounting valuation method based on ROI has some limitations and overestimates the value of the indicator for the following reasons:

- Projects whose implementation requires massive time resources will have an overestimated ROI value. The longer the implementation, the stronger the overstatement of ROI.
- The time lapse between the beginning of the investment and the moment it generates earnings can alter the accuracy of estimates, which do not account for the time lapse between expenditures and revenues, considering them simultaneous.
- Organizations that operate in markets where market share, revenues or expenses increase rapidly will have lower ROI values, as compared to companies in stagnating or slowly growing markets.

It can be considered that, despite the aforementioned limitations, the ROI indicator provides a sufficient primary estimate, being a useful tool for assisting in the understanding of financial effects of different investment options.

6. Discussion and conclusions

This paper is an effort towards strengthening the role of the professional accountant or auditor in deciding on an investment in *cloud*-based technology services, where, on first examination, only members of the IT department would have the knowledge to select the correct option. To this end, there were presented three important tools (ROI, TCO and the CAPEX/OPEX ratio) that a professional accountant can use to assess the true costs and effects of an IT investment option, or to compare options, when it is prompted to choose between an in-house option and one based on the services of an external *cloud* supplier.

In calculating the CAPEX/OPEX ratio, the value of ROI or any other indicators considered to be useful in the analysis, it is recommended to use the "TCO approach", i.e. estimating these indicators throughout the life of the investment, not only for the first year or for part of its useful life. The analysis of the CAPEX/OPEX ratio is important because it highlights different expenditure types needed to implement an in-house solution or to migrate to the *cloud* and it allows the selection of an option that aligns with the organization's overall financial policy. The ROI indicator is important because it summarizes the potential income from a specific investment option.

Analyzed concurrently, TCO, CAPEX/OPEX and ROI form the foundation for the analysis of IT investment options and for determining the quality of the desired IT infrastructure, regardless of its type: the organization's own infrastructure or infrastructure "leased" through the *cloud*. The use of these indicators can be generalized as follows:

- TCO is a mixture of ownership costs and operating costs when using *cloud*-based services from an external supplier. This means that the analysis process requires a sufficient level of detail, so that all costs and all categories of expenses are taken into account.
- From the perspective of the CAPEX/OPEX ratio, an internal infrastructure implies that the amount is capitalized for a number of years – the CAPEX model. Using an external provider of *cloud*-based services means that the organization can benefit from lower initial costs, but will incur higher total costs over the lifetime of the investment, which requires further analysis.
- ROI allows to estimate the investment outcomes and can be used to choose one of the available options, when the costs are known and the revenues can be estimated for each of the options considered. In addition, ROI can also be used retrospectively, with certain values of financial data.

All presented indicators and all implementation options proposed should be used to make an organization to increase its agility. Business agility is the ability of an enterprise to grasp and react quickly and accurately to changes in its economic environment. Such changes may be, for example, the fact that a competitor exits the market or introduces a new product, the gain or loss of significant customers, significant legislative changes etc. An organization's ability to seize and respond to the changes in the economic environment depends on how all its employees addresses the relationship with the organization; accounting professionals are included in this group. Many signals from the economic environment are not accessible to members of the IT department, requiring advanced economic knowledge. In these circumstances, accounting and auditing professionals should consider *cloud*-based technologies as a way to respond rapidly and effectively to the challenges of the economic environment. Recourse to the *cloud* enables an organization to reduce the overall duration of business cycles, to increase the level of innovation, to react faster as a general trend, increasing its chances of success on the market.

Acknowledgements

A previous version of this paper was presented at the AMIS 2016 international conference, in order to receive further feed-back from the academic community before the final version is published.
Part of this paper is the result of a research stage performed at ESSEC in Paris during December 2016, financed by the "*Development of accounting research and accounting education internationalization*" research project.

References

Al-Ayyoub, M., Wardat, M., Jararweh, Y. & Khreishah, A. A. (2015) "Optimizing expansion strategies for ultrascale cloud computing data centers", *Simulation Modelling Practice and Theory*, vol. 58, no. 1: 15-29

Alkhanak, E.N., Lee, S.P., Rezaei, R. & Parizi, R. M. (2016) "Cost optimization approaches for scientific workflow scheduling in cloud and grid computing: A review, classifications, and open issues", *Journal of Systems and Software*, vol. 113, no. 3: 1-26

Almeida, H., Campello, M. & Weisbach, M. S. (2011) "Corporate financial and investment policies when future financing is not frictionless", *Journal of Corporate Finance*, vol. 17, no. 3: 675-693

Altmann, J. & Kashef, M. (2014) "Cost model based service placement in federated hybrid clouds", *Future Generation Computer Systems*, vol. 41, no. 12: 79-90

Carniani, E., D'Arenzo, D., Lazouski, A., Martinelli, F. & Mori, P. (2016) "Usage control on cloud systems", *Future Generation Computer Systems-The International Journal of Escience*, vol. 63, no. 1: 37-55

Gullhav, A.N. & Nygreen, B. (2016) "A branch and price approach for deployment of multi-tier software services in clouds", *Computers & Operations Research*, vol.75, no.1: 12-27

He, L., Huang, F., Zhang, J., Liu, B., Chen, C., Zhang, Z., Yang, Y. & Lu, W. (2016) "Dynamic secure interconnection for security enhancement in cloud computing", *International Journal of Computers Communications & Control*, vol. 11, no. 3: 348-357

Helms, T. (2016) "Asset transformation and the challenges to servitize a utility business model", *Energy Policy*, vol. 91, no. 4: 98-112

Koutsandria, G., Skevakis, E., Sayegh, A. A. & Koutsakis, P. (2016) "Can everybody be happy in the cloud? Delay, profit and energy-efficient scheduling for cloud services", *Journal of Parallel and Distributed Computing*, vol. 96, no.1: 202-217

Lins, F., Damasceno, J., Medeiros, R., Sousa, E. & Rosa, N. (2016) "Automation of service-based security-aware business processes in the Cloud", *Computing*, vol. 98, no. 9: 847-870

Liu, S., Chan, F.T.S. & Ran, W. (2016) "Decision making for the selection of cloud vendor: An improved approach under group decision-making with integrated weights and objective/subjective attributes", *Expert Systems with Applications*, vol. 55, no. 8: 37-47

Mahlindayu, T., Siti, Z., Abdul, R., Bakhtiar, A. & Rusli, A. R. (2014) "Cloud computing awareness and adoption among accounting practitioners in Malaysia", *Procedia - Social and Behavioral Sciences*, vol. 164, no. 12: 569-574

Misra, S. C. & Mondal, A. (2011) "Identification of a company's suitability for the adoption of cloud computing and modelling its corresponding Return on Investment", *Mathematical and Computer Modelling*, vol. 53, no. 3–4: 504-521

Plaza, M. (2015) "Balancing the costs of human resources on an ERP project", *Omega*, vol. 59, no. 3: 171-183

Shuja, J., Gani, A., Shamshirband, S., Ahmad, R.W. & Bilal, K. (2016) "Sustainable cloud data centers: A survey of enabling techniques and technologies", *Renewable & Sustainable Energy Reviews*, vol. 62, no. 1: 195-214

Sohn, S. Y., Jeon, J. & Han, E. J. (2015) "A new cost of ownership model for the acquisition of technology complying with environmental regulations", *Journal of Cleaner Production*, vol. 100, no.8: 269-277

Sujeet, K. S., Ali H. A.B, Srikrishna, M.G. & Al-Kharusi, M. (2016) "Predicting motivators of cloud computing adoption: A developing country perspective", *Computers in Human Behavior*, vol 62, no. 09: 61-69

Visani, F., Barbieri, P., Di Lascio, Marta L. F, Raffoni, A. & Vigo, D. (2016) "Supplier's total cost of ownership evaluation: a data envelopment analysis approach", *Omega*, vol. 61, no. 6: 141-154

4

The relation between the CSR and the accounting information system data in Central and Eastern European (CEE) countries – the evidence of the Polish financial institutions

Justyna Fijałkowska [a], Beata Zyznarska-Dworczak [b1] and Przemysław Garsztka [b]

[a]*University of Social Sciences,*
[b]*Poznan University of Economics and Business*

Abstract: Financial institutions play a fundamental role in determining the sustainability of economies, both in developed and developing countries. However, the worldwide financial crises made many financial institutions lost their credibility and CSR engagement has been perceived as a remedy. The aim of this paper is to analyze the interrelation between being socially responsible and tangible financial outcome of financial institutions in one of the CEE countries - Poland. Financial and market data of all the public companies from the financial sector in Poland – 116 financial institutions. The analyzed period is 2012-2015 that gives 257 observations. The empirical results reveal that in case of financial institutions in Poland the slack resources are strongly related to CSR involvement, however being socially responsible is not reflected in the bottom line. Polish market and the public are reluctant in considering the CSR importance and the CSR engagement is not rewarded. This undermines the role of CSR commitment in financial institutions in CEECs. It may be assumed that CSR efforts in Poland are not focused properly, or they are not communicated effectively. On the basis of comparative analysis is

[1] *Corresponding authors*: Department of Accounting, Poznan University of Economics and Business; Al. Niepodległości 10, 61-875 Poznań; email adresses: jfijalkowska@spoleczna.pl; b.zyznarska-dworczak@ue.poznan.pl; przemyslaw.garsztka@ue.poznan.pl;

presented there is a significant difference between CEE countries and other transitional countries in CSR implementation and communication. The findings are important in better understanding of the link between CSR engagement and its tangible outcomes in CEE countries. The conclusions may lead to the improved decision-making processes concerning CSR activities and their communication.

Keywords: CSR, financial performance, financial institutions, banks, Central and Eastern Europe, CEE, CEE countries.

1. Introduction

Financial institutions play a fundamental role in determining the stability of financial markets, sustainability of modern economies and economic fortunes of nations. However, after the financial crises of 2008 many financial sector institutions have lost their credibility in the eyes of the consumers and investors. The economic crises originated from the financial markets and led to the lower trust in financial institutions, inferior investments and the recession (Fijałkowska & Zyznarska, 2017). Social responsibility has been found to be a way for banks and other financial institutions to earn back their credibility (Cornett *et al.*, 2014). Accounting information system is responsible for the collection, storage and processing of financial and accounting data that is used for internal management decision making, including nonfinancial transactions that directly affect the processing of financial transactions (Belfo & Trigo, 2013: 537).

Reporting is probably the most important feature of accounting information system. As Huang and Watson (2015: 3) underline "there is a natural link between CSR and accounting because the accounting profession has a general responsibility for the measurement, disclosure, and assurance of information, including CSR-related information". Rogošić and Čaljkušić (2015) indicate that "sustainability accounting is considered as a complement to the traditional financial accounting with a purpose to evaluate the environmental, social and governance performance of a company and to provide the report on this matter". Accounting information system should be therefore adjusted to the requirements of the public that becomes highly aware and sensitive regarding the accountability and disclosure of financial institutions.

The accountability and responsibility accounts may play an important role in the legitimizing of the financial institutions' activities and may be crucial in the reconstruction of the public trust. This issue becomes even more important nowadays, in the face of the new directive concerning the non-financial information disclosure by the biggest companies in the European Union (Directive 2014/95/EU), that is applicable also to the biggest financial institutions. As Yilmaz (2016: 96) underlines “The concepts of responsibility, accountability, transparency, equality and protection of interests, which represent the main components of corporate management, are impactful and important concepts not only in terms of social responsibility of accounting, but the whole information system of the business and specifically the accounting information system”.

CSR value has attained extensive interest among practitioners and academics. Moreover, the substantial investments in the CRS makes the question concerning the link between CSR and Corporate Financial Performance continuously noteworthy. The interest of investors in company’s non-financial performance has grown significantly over the past few years (Ernst & Young, 2009). It is assumed that 67 % of investors, while taking economic decisions, consider the non-financial information disclosed by companies, 89% of investors threats them as the most important source of information influencing their decision (ACCA, 2013: 50). Moreover, it is expected that CSR activities may have an influence on the companies’ overall performance and financial results.

Although CSR is often regarded as a universal concept, it should be highlighted that its actual meaning changes over time and differs between regions due to varying socio-political and cultural circumstances (Moon, 2007). This is due to the fact that the economic conditions, cultural inheritance, political grounds and government decisions influence the expectations of the users in general and the stakeholders’ ones in particular, regarding the extent and the domains of the CSR. “While CSR has a particularly strong resonance in parts of Western Europe, it took root slowly in Central and Eastern Europe” (Feltham, 2016: 1).

According to the research conducted by Centrum CSR (2009:66) the recognition and level of implementation of principles of corporate social responsibility was “most likely still low among corporations in CEE region (there may be a case of non-communicated CSR)”. However, as it is underlined in the research mentioned “there is great potential for cooperation between business, civil society groups, trade unions and the authorities, as well as academics, in the field of social policy, including outward foreign investment (both incoming and outgoing) in every country in Central and Eastern Europe”. Although CSR policies would be crucial to gaining comparative advantage for this region, there are many different obstacles of CSR implementation and communication, like: negative image of business, dysfunctional legal background, corruption, weakness of the III sector, difficult economic situation of many companies, the lack of an ethics and ethical standards, and difficult situation on the job market (Lewicka-Strzalecka, 2006: 440).

Furthermore, some studies prove also that less developed and more turbulent business regulatory and legal systems in CEE countries lead to the situation that financial considerations take higher precedence over social and environmental responsibility activities of organizations (Filatotchev *et al.* 2000, Vynoslavska *et al.* 2005). The research of Inglehart and Welzel (2005) indicates that in richer and more stable countries such as those in Western Europe, individuals are more likely to have adapted to their current material level with the result that they focus more on such issues as social welfare and environmental sustainability. Moreover Steurer and Martinuzzi (2012), prove that Western European countries, particularly Anglo-Saxon and Scandinavian, governments are significantly more active in promoting CSR than governments in CEE countries and they conclude that public policies on CSR reinforce rather than offset the European "CSR gap".

Market participants in Western European countries have significantly different perspectives on the importance of corporate responsibilities than those in Central and East European countries". Furrer *et al.* (2010) investigate corporate responsibilities practices across different societies and different generations within those societies and they indicate that in Central and East Europe, there is less tangible evidence that CSR has been high on the business agenda. The accession of ten Central and East Europe countries to the EU in 2004 and two more in 2007 has raised significant concerns regarding corporate responsibility priorities in these transitional economies (Vaughan-Whitehead, 2003). Csafor (2008:115) notices "Corporate Social Responsibility (CSR) has only a short past in the former socialist countries of Eastern Europe, but growing demand for CSR can be felt in these states as well". CSR research in accounting is definitely more visible within the international academic community than 40 years ago, but it still seems to be a research niche in countries that do not have a long CSR tradition and practice, such as the CEE countries (Albu *et al.* 2016: 202). While the international CSR research grew significantly over the last decade, there is a shortage of research investigating the nature and extent of CSR in CEE[i] countries, as compared to more developed countries (Albu *et al.*, 2016: 203).

The primary objective of this paper is to empirically analyze if there is an impact of being socially responsible on the tangible financial consequences of financial institutions in one of the CEE countries, namely in Poland. The empirical analysis aims also in analysis if the financial resources make companies get involved in CSR. The paper is structured as follows: the next section concerns the social responsibility and sustainability in financial institutions, the third sections focuses on the relation between CSR and corporate financial performance. This part is based on the CSR / CFP relation analysis based on assumptions concerning the social impact hypothesis, available funding hypothesis (slack resources hypothesis), positive synergy hypothesis, negative synergy hypothesis, trade-off hypothesis and managerial opportunism hypothesis. The fourth section contains the results of empirical analysis and is followed by concluding remarks and comparison with the results of other studies concerning different CEE countries. The findings of this study are important for the financial institution sector in order to better understand the link between their CSR investment and tangible outcomes that may lead to the improved decision-taking processes. In the paper the normative approach to accounting and management is adopted.

2. Corporate social responsibility and financial institutions

The financial services sector is viewed as a central pillar of modern capitalist economies (Merton,1995; Levine, 1997; 2005). Financial institutions have an impact not only on financial and economic system, but on a wider community as well. Their socially responsible practices in particular may have important social implications, hat is even more emphasized within bank-centric financial systems, typical of CEE countries (Hernaus & Storjanovic, 2015). The services executed by banks and other financial institutions are characterized by information asymmetry and uncertainty which makes trust a necessary condition for doing business (Beck, 2006; Schanz, 2006). Trust is a central strategic issue for financial services firms (Llewellyn, 2005; Olsen, 2008) and is strictly related to the reputation, that is a multi-faceted concept embracing many components. Rossier (2003) highlights a number of reasons why bankers, in particular, have to consider issues of reputation. The bankers and other participants of financial sector trade money which represents other people's security and well-being. They are also involved in a profession that has been held in contempt, since medieval times because of usury (Fijałkowska, 2012: 141).

Today the credibility, accountability and reputation of financial sector is in its foundations and determines the stability of financial markets (Gaultier-Galliard & Louisot, 2006). Decker and Sale (2009: 137) notice that "reputation is built on the trust that is established with all stakeholders and as an intangible asset it directly affects the value of financial services firms and is crucial to their sustainability and to the economic sustainability of society". As Stansfield (2006: 470) states reputation in financial institutions concerns "financial performance and strength, client trust and confidence, client service, corporate social responsibility, corporate governance practices, corporate ethics, corporate disclosure practices, as well as relations with regulatory authorities and compliance in a broad sense". Decker and Sale (2009: 137) add that "key CSR principles such as accountability and transparency are at the heart of regulatory efforts to ensure banks and bankers operate with trust". They continue underlining that "reputation is built on the trust that is established with all stakeholders and as an intangible asset it directly affects the value of financial services firms and is crucial to their sustainability and to the economic sustainability of society".

UNEP (2004) indicates "The financial sector can play a critical role in the transformation to a more sustainable environment. As financial intermediaries in an economy, financial institutions can contribute to mitigating environmental problems, while at the same time taking advantage of the opportunities that sustainability offers to the finance sector". Bossone (2000) and Olson (2006) argue that trust and confidence in banking will continue to be important and vital to society's financial well-being. The concept of Corporate Social Responsibility (CSR) is closely related to trust and reputation and therefore it is an increasingly important issue in the international banking industry (Scholtens, 2009) and in the financial sector as a whole. According to Minor (2009), when managers are asked why they engage in CSR, they claim it is to secure a better brand and reputation. However, as Fombrun (1996: 53), suggest "the activities that generate CSR do not directly impact the company's financial performance, but instead affect the bottom line via its stock of 'reputation capital' –the financial value of its intangible assets".

Financial institutions face various pressure to shift to a new business framework that requires social responsibility approach to their activates. Corporate social responsibility has been a subject of great interest for more than 30 years among scholars from multiple management perspectives (Wang *et al.*, 2016: 1084). CSR can be defined as "the process of communicating the social and environmental effects of organizations' economic actions to particular interest groups within society and to society at large" (Gray *et al.*, 1987: ix). The concept of CSR is related with sustainability. The relation between CSR an sustainability is underlined in the definition published by International Organization for Standardization's, stating that "Social responsibility is the responsibility of an organisation for the impacts of its decisions and activities on society and the environment, through transparent and ethical behaviour that contributes to sustainable development (..)" (ISO 26000).

CSR is widely understood as an obligation of entrepreneurs to contribute to the sustainable socio-economic development (IBLF 2003). Sustainable business models "follow a comprehensive sustainability logic that integrates economic, ecological, and social considerations with regards to present and future generations" (Schneider, 2015: 525) - while disclosing information concerning CSR and sustainability financial institutions often use those two related concepts interchangeably. As Jurek (2016: 68) underlines "CSR in financial institutions should not be seen only in terms of interactions between different stakeholders (Shareholders, investors, depositors, borrowers, regulators) and financial institutions" in the fields of economic, legal, ethical and philanthropic responsibility, but "also in the context of their distinctive function of financial intermediaries" The figure below presents the main internal and external groups of financial institutions' stakeholders (as the most important players in the whole financial institutions' sector) towards which they should be responsible.

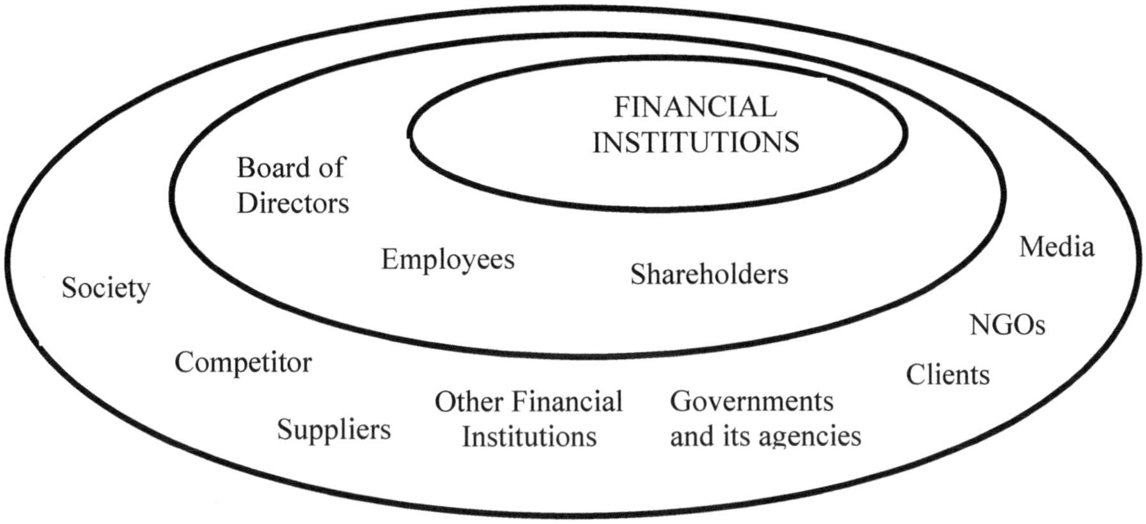

Figure 1. Internal and External stakeholders of financial institutions

As it was underlined during the World Economic Forum in 2012 "finance plays a critical role for society at large, serving individuals, families, businesses, governments and civic institutions. The financial sector performs indispensable functions such as enabling saving and investment, providing protection from risks and supporting the creation of new jobs and enterprises. It is critical that the sector operates to provide these functions for society in a stable, sustainable way". The dimensions of CSR in financial institutions, based on the Carrols' (1991) framework are presented in the Table 1.

Table 1. Dimensions of CSR in financial institutions

Dimension of responsibility	Description
Economic	Financial institutions should improve the wealth of the owners, create new opportunities for risk management and offer the efficient transfer of funds
Legal	Legal responsibility is largely determined by legal regulations concerning for example the requirement of maintaining confidence, the limitations of risk taking, arbitrate relationship between the financial sector and society. Regulations constitute a pillar of financial institutions' responsibility and are supposed to rebuild trust and prevent from similar to 2007 and 2008 crises.
Ethical	Ethical codes should be implemented in financial institutions. Honesty and good faith, professional integrity, transparency and accountability are ethical values crucial financial institutions, to achieve by: • Integrity –to generate trust that is vital for a financial system

Dimension of responsibility	Description
	to flourish; • Responsibility – the responsibility to act fairly, i.e. they have the responsibility not to exclude certain groups.
Philanthropy	Philanthropy is concerned with altruistic acts not required by law that create social reputation and represent a social distribution of some proportion of profits. Philanthropy may be expressed also by the volunteering actions and charitable donations of the employees.

Financial sector due to the crisis in 2007 and 2008 suffers the loss of trust and credibility. The study of Barjaktarović *et al.* (2013) proved negative effects of the economic crisis on the banking sectors of the selected CEE countries. The financial and economic crisis strongly influenced the entire world, however, Central and Eastern Europe (CEE) was particularly severely affected. Živković and Aktan (2009) stress that the emerging countries are faced with lower liquidity level, more frequent internal and external shocks, as well as a higher degree of insider trading causes. These countries are more vulnerable to the factors that generally lead to banking turbulences and that amplify their impact such as banks and private agents exposure to currency and maturity mismatch, disruption in international capital markets, banks panic (Furceri & Zdzienicka, 2010). However, it is worth mentioning that in 2009, immediately after the crisis, while most of the EU was wallowing in a recession, the GDP of Poland actually grew by 1.7%. (Eurostat) This is compared to its European neighbours (the EU27) whose aggregate loss of GDP fell to 4.2% (Eurostat). Before the crises banks were generally not extensively involved in CSR and in its disclosure (Novokmet & Rogosic, 2016: 115). Vigano and Nicolai (2006) indicate that European bankers have been slow in considering issues of sustainability.

Moreover, the financial sector was traditionally viewed as not having much negative environmental impact, relatively non-polluting. The main impact on the society was always concerned mainly with its significant size. After the financial crisis however, the situation changed; financial sector reputation suffered from the consumers' perceptions of the sectors' crucial role in the crisis. Therefore, since then CSR activeness and CSR reporting in financial institutions have become one of the main tools of rebuilding trust (Novokmet & Rogosić, 2016: 115). It was always more important for financial institutions to focus on the "sustainable finance" that is defined by Strandberg (2005) as the provision of financial capital and risk management products and services in ways that promote or do not harm economic prosperity, ecological and community wellbeing. The imperative for the financial sector became also the proper communication on the responsible attitude to the business running. Nowadays, one of the most important ways to express the social responsibility of financial institutions is the publication of CSR / sustainable reports and website disclosure. The question arises if the involvement and communication on CSR brings the concrete tangible results that can be expressed by improved financial results. The empirical analysis is the subject of the research that is included in part 4 of this article.

3. Relation between corporate social responsibility (CSR) and corporate financial performance (CFP) – literature review

There are three major theories which suggest that companies should be sustainable and should incorporate corporate sustainability in their core strategic goals, namely legitimacy theory, stakeholder theory and agency theory (Zyznarska-Dworczak, 2016: 308). In the literature these theories are often contrasted with Friedman's (1970) well-known criticism of a firm's corporate social responsibility initiatives. These theories primarily suggest positive relationship between corporate sustainability and company performance (Aggarwal, 2013: 63). Together with slack resources theory they give foundations to our analysis.

The relationship between CSR and corporate financial performance (CFP) has been a subject of numerous scientific studies since 50 years (Friedman, 1970; Preston & O'Bannon, 1997; Waddock & Graves, 1997; McWilliams & Siegel, 2001; Smith, 2002; Orlitzky *et al.*, 2003; Allouche & Laroche, 2005; Margolis *et al.*, 2007; Aggarwal, 2013; Kleine *et al.*, 2013; Wang *et al.*, 2016). The results do not lead to uniform conclusions, moreover they are inconclusive and conflicting. Some of these contradictory results stem from conceptual, operationalization, and methodical differences in the definitions and application of both social and financial performance (Griffin & Mahon, 1997: 7).

There is a group of researchers that empirically confirm that the relation between CSR and CFP is stronger for firms from advanced economies than for firms from developing economies. This relationship is also significantly different between industries, sectors and institutions (Wang *et al.*, 2016; Ioannou & Serafeim 2010). Furthermore, the researchers affirm that the heterogeneity of the CSR and CFP relationship may result from the measurement strategies of the two key constructs of CSR and CFP (Wang *et al.*, 2016: 24). There is no common way of the CSR measurement. One approach to judge a company as a socially responsibility is its inclusion into one of the CSR indexes, e.g. Indexes of Corporate Governance (CG), Indexes of Corporate Social Responsibility (CSR), index of Corporate Social Performance (CSP), GRI-based Disclosure Index Scores, Respect Index. Another way to define that a company is socially responsible is the publication of

CSR/sustainability reports. These approaches of CSR measurement are combined to the various types of CFP indicators that may be generally divided into two groups:

1. Accounting-based measures – like ROE (Return of Equity), ROA (Return of Assets), ROS (Return of Sales), Debt/Equity, Current Ratio, Debt/Assets, EBIT/Interest Expense, Quick Ratio, Total Assets, EPS, and
2. Market-based measures – like Alpha, Beta, Price/Earnings, CAR (Capital Adequacy Ratio), Total Return, Mean Abnormal Returns, Risk Adjusted Return, Stock Price, Market to Book Value.

Combination of these different approaches to CSR and SFP results in multitude of diverse applications and results of empirical analysis. Additionally, the interrelation between CSR and CFP may be analyzed twofold :

1. the direction of the CSR-CFP relation,
2. the causality of the CSR-CFP relation:
   (a) prior CSR related to subsequent CFP;
   (b) prior CFP related to subsequent CSR;
   (c) concurrent and across relationship between CSR vs CFP.

The direction of the relationship may indicate positive, negative, mixed or neutral linkages between CSR and financial performance. Separately, it is possible that changes in CSR influence financial performance, or the opposite, that change in financial performance influence CSR (Waddock & Graves 1997: 305), or there is a synergistic relationship between the two, either positive or negative. By combining these two dimensions of variation Preston and O'Bannon (1997) yield the six possible causal and directional hypotheses (Preston & Bannon, 1997: 419-424):

1. with positive direction: social impact hypothesis, available funding hypothesis (slack resources hypothesis) and positive synergy hypothesis;
2. with negative direction: negative synergy hypothesis, trade-off hypothesis and managerial opportunism hypothesis.

Positive impact of social performance on financial performance explains social impact hypothesis, which is a "social impact" version of the stakeholder theory. This hypothesis assumes that CSR enhances the satisfaction of various stakeholders – and consequently the firm's external reputation – leading to better financial performance, in particular by increasing the efficiency of their organization's adaptation to external demands "by addressing and balancing the claims of multiple stakeholders" (Orlitsky *et al.*, 2003: 405).

Social impact hypothesis assumes that CSR increases managerial competencies, contributes to organizational knowledge about an entity's market, social, political, technological, and other environments, and thus enhances organizational efficiency (Orlitsky *et al.*, 2003:407. All these "good" effects of CSR are labeled by Waddock and Graves (1997) under "good management theory". Other scholars (McGuire *et al.*, 1988; Waddock & Graves, 1997; Orlitzky *et al.*, 2003; Seifert *et al.*, 2004; Daniel *et al.*, 2004, Margolis *et al.*, 2007; Albertini, 2012) suggest that CSR and CFP are positively associated, "but that the causal relationship is from financial to social performance" (Preston & O'Bannon, 1997: 423). This slack resources hypothesis means that better financial results potentially effect the availability of slack (financial and other) resources that support companies in investing in social performance activities, such as employee and community relations, or environmental protection (Waddock & Graves 1997: 312). In this theory CSR is treated as an outcome of better financial performance and not a cause of it. The positive synergy hypothesis supposes that higher levels of CSR lead to an improvement of CFP, which offers the possibility of reinvestment in socially responsible actions (Allouche & Laroche, 2005). There is a kind of "virtuous circle" formed by a simultaneous and interactive positive relation between CSR and CFP (Waddock & Graves, 1997: 306).

However, there is also a negative synergy hypothesis that indicates a "vicious circle"; higher levels of CSR may lead to decreased CFP. Therefore, synergy hypothesis assumes that social and financial performance are synergetic, but whether positive or negative it should be detected based on the available statistical data (Preston & Bannon, 1997: 424).

Negative social-financial performance relationships can be predicted by other 2 hypothesis: trade-off hypothesis and the managerial opportunism hypothesis. The trade-off hypothesis indicates, in accordance with Friedman`s attitude (1970) and other neoclassical economists' arguments, that "a firm's higher levels of social performance may lower its financial performance as compared to competitors" (Preston and O'Bannon, 1997: 421). "Because social action will have a price for the firm it also entails a competitive disadvantage" (Smith, 2002: 232) to other firms that are less socially active. The trade-off hypothesis claims that social accomplishments involve higher costs for an entity, for example capital expenditures on special equipment, machinery and real estate devoted to CSR, cost materials and services by purchase of inputs from suppliers who are socially responsible, higher wages and benefits as well as additional workers to enhance policies social performance (McWilliams & Siegel 2001: 123). The costs, according to this argument, fall directly to the bottom line, reducing profits and thus shareholder wealth (Waddock & Graves 1997: 310).

The managerial opportunism hypothesis indicates negative social-financial performance relationships stating: higher levels of financial performance lead to lower levels of social performance and in the opposite direction. While gaining better financial performance, the management may attempt to cash in by reducing social expenditure in order to increase their own short-term private gains. Inversely, with worse financial performance managers may attempt to offset and justify their disappointing results by engaging in conspicuous social programs (Preston & O'Bannon, 1997: 423).

Some theorists (Griffin & Mahon, 1997; McWilliams & Siegel 2001) have a generally negative attitude to the CSR and CFP analysis; they ponder that the link between CSR and CFP disappears when more accurate variables are introduced into econometric models, such as research and development intensity (Allouche & Laroche, 2005). They argue also that there are so many intervening variables between CSR and CFP that there should be no reason to expect any relationship at all. Additionally, the measurement problems are still so wide that it alone can mask any real linkage that could exist (Waddock & Graves, 1997: 310).

These theoretical assumptions concerning CSR and CFP relationship are summarized, through the literature review covering the period of 1963-2013 in the Table 2. They focus in two perspectives regarding CSR / CFP relation: its direction and its causality. The analysis of literature review presented in Table 2 indicates that the most popular causality regards social impact hypothesis. Most of analyzed results (Margolis & Walsh, 2001; Peloza, 2009; Aggarwal, 2013; Clark *et al.*, 2015; Kochalski, 2016) indicate the positive impact of CSR on corporate financial performance (CSR as dependent variable). The strength of this relation varies from 44% to 85%. Furthermore, some of the researchers (Margolis & Walsh, 2001; Orlitzky *et al.*, 2003; Margolis *et al.*, 2007; Albertini, 2012) indicate an inverse existing positive impact, in which the financial results determine the results of the CSR activities. This finding, in turn, confirms the assumption of slack resources hypothesis. Margolis and Walsh (2001) indicate that 53% of the empirical research reviewed confirms a positive impact of good financial performance on CSR activities, while 24% shows no relation, 19% mixed and 5% negative relation. This kind of causality of CSP and CFP researched is often the subject of integrative, quantitative meta-analyses with a methodologically more rigorous review in many substantive areas of the bidirectional relationship between CSR and CFP (Orlitzky *et al.*, 2003; Daniel *et al.*, 2004; Allouche & Laroche, 2005; Margolis *et al.*, 2007; Wang *et al.*, 2016). Meta-analysis however concentrates on the strength but not on the direction of the relation.

Table 2. The results of studies of the empirical relationship between CSP and CSR presented in the literature

Positions of literature	The causality of CSP		The time interval	The number of empirical research reviewed	The direction of the CSP-CFP relationship			
	CSP as dependent variable: CSP=> FP	CSP as independent variable CFP=>CSP			Positive	No relation*	Mixed	Negative
Mikołajewicz, Nowicki 2016	X		1970-2013	85	85.0%	6.0%	13.0%	1,0%
Clark *et al.* 2015	X		1970-2014	110	85.5%	5.1%	0.9%	8.5%
Kleine *et al.* 2013	X		1963-2011	182	30.8%	31.9%	7.7%	29.7%
Albertini 2012	X	X	1975-2011	52	meta-analysis			
Aggarwal 2013	X		2005-2012	11	45.5%	36.4%	9.1%	9.1%
Peloza 2009	X		1972-2008	159	63.0%	22.0%	15.0%	0%
Margolis et al 2007	X		1972-2007	192	meta-analysis			
Margolis *et al.* 2007		X	1972-2007	66	meta-analysis			
Orlitzky *et al.* 2003	X		1970-2002	52	meta-analysis			
Orlitzky *et al.* 2003		X	1970-2002	52	meta-analysis			
Margolis, Walsh 2001		X	1972-2002	95	53.0%	24.0%	19.0%	5,0%
Margolis, Walsh 2001	X		1972-2002	95	68.0%	16.0%	16.0%	0,0%
Griffin, Mahon 1997	X		1990s	10	70.0%	-	-	30.0%
			1980s	32	43.8%	9.4%	-	46.9%
			1970s	17	70.6%	23.5%	-	5.9%

* also insignificant/inconclusive

The negative relation, confirming the trade-off hypothesis, was observed only in one direction: negative impact of CSR on the CFP. According to the analyze presented in Table 2 most of the tested research indicates the ratio of CSR-CFP influence below 10%. The exception - with the much strongest influence - was a research conducted by Griffin and Mahon (1997). The researchers stated that in the 1980s almost 47% of tested literature position was a study that indicated the negative impact of CSR on the CFP and in the 1990s - 30%. One more study (Kleine *et al.*, 2013) has also shown such a high level of negative ratio (29,7%).

We can conclude that in the period from 1972 to 2001, round-about ninety-five empirical evidences have been provided by Margolis and Walsh (2001) and Orlitzky *et al.* (2003) regarding CSR and financial performance. Many academics tried to analyze the relation between CSR and CFP. The results are not coherent neither conclusive. The literature review confirms the conclusions of Griffin and Mahon stated almost two decades ago; they underlined that "although numerous researches have explored the empirical relationship between SCP and CFP, no definitive consensus exists. The results have often been contradictory, even within a given analysis" (Griffin & Mahon, 1997: 6).

Comparing the results with the findings of the study relating the transition countries we can also see the heterogeneity of the CSR and CFP relationship. According to the research conducted by Djalilov (2015: 20) CSR activities may improve the financial performance of the banks of the transition countries in both, stable (2002-2005) and turbulent (2008-2012) periods. However, the researchers have found that the impact of Return of Assets and Return on Equity on CSR is negative in both periods, while they have found positive impact of CSR on Return on Assets as well as Return on Equity. To the other conclusions have come Asatryan R. & Březinová O. They found that there is a significant positive relationship between CSR initiatives and financial performance measures in the selected companies in Central and Eastern Europe, it means they found a positive relationship between Community Performance (CP), Environment Management System (EMS) and Employee Relations (ER) and the financial performance in terms of the ROE and ROA. Unfortunately, there is a lack of research relating the CSR-CFP in CEE countries, allowing for detailed and comprehensive analysis of this relationship.

Both in developed and developing countries there is still diversify and lack of an uniform understanding of CSR-CFP relations, which points to the need for the research that would order and synthetize the results as well as conclude on the CSR-CFP direction importance, its strength and dependence on the industry and size factor. There is also a need of the cohesive understanding of the influence of the CSR on the economic development in the micro and macro scale.

The interest in CSR among practitioners as well as academics is still growing and as it plays a distinctive role within the financial sector institutions the following analysis will focus on this sector.

4. Relation between corporate social responsibility (CSR) and corporate financial performance (CFP) – empirical research

4.1. Sample

The financial data has been obtained from audited consolidated financial statements derived from EMIS database. To the great extent the accounting-based measures have been used because the audited accounting data is likely to be authentic and credible and is not influenced by market perceptions or speculations, and is thus considered less noisy in comparison to market based indicators like stock returns, share prices, etc. (Lopez *et al.*, 2007). Market value was applied only as a control variable for size of companies. The data used to verify the hypotheses concerns listed companies which have the status of financial institution. Financial institutions in Poland are defined in the Code of Commercial Companies (Art. 4. § 1. 7) and comprise banks, investment companies, investment funds and trust funds, insurances, reinsurances, trusts, company pensions, retirement funds or brokerage houses, established in the Polish Republic or in a country belonging to the OECD.

The research embraced all the companies from the financial sector quoted on the Warsaw Stock Exchange in Poland. The analyzed period is 2012-2015. The collected data made it possible to calculate the change in earnings year on year. Then, the values obtained for each company separately for three consecutive years were treated as separate observations. In this way, the resulting study sample consisted of 298 observations. After removal of the observations for which there were missing data, calculations were performed on a sample of 257 observations.

4.2. Variables

CSR variable

CSR is difficult to measure. One of the approaches defines a socially responsible company as the one incorporated into one of the CSR indexes. The growth in the demand for ratings of CSR has resulted in a marked increase in the number of initiatives supplying CSR ratings to investors and customers (Marquez & Fombrun, 2005: 304). The examples are KLD index, The FTSE 4 Good, Dow Jones S.UI. Stoxx, Domini 400 and Respect Index (RI) introduced by Warsaw Stock Exchange. In many empirical works the definition of being socially responsible is likened to one of these indices memberships. Another approach defines socially responsible company as the one that communicates its CSR engagement disclosing CSR/sustainable report. In this study both approaches were applied and analyzed.

Financial Performance Measures variable

In this study the following measures of financial performance were considered and analyzed: book value, market value, ROA and ROE.

Control Variables

The control variable used in this research was the size of the company, based on the assumption that larger firms are likely to have higher profitability as they have greater resources for investing in profitable ventures. Other control variables used in this study are long-term debt to assets ratio as a proxy for risk, and - for the purpose of verifying hypothesis H1 - the dummy variable indicating companies incorporated into PL-WIG-BANKI index for banks. We introduce this variable assuming that banks are financial institutions subject to more stringent reporting requirements and generally better managed than other financial institutions.

4.3. Research model

The first model intends to examine the impact of the overall sustainability rating of the financial institution (independent variable - CSR) and CSR reporting on its financial performance (dependent variables – CFP).

H1: Corporate social performance and financial performance are related (positively or negatively) across the financial sector institutions

This research hypothesis is based on two other hypotheses:

1. social impact hypothesis (↑ CSR => ↑ CFP)
2. trade-off hypothesis (↑CSR => ↓ CFP)

To verify the research hypothesis about the impact of the publication of the CSR report and the impact of the fact that the company is listed in a RESPECT Index (RI) on the change of its financial result in the following reporting year we used an econometric model:

$$CFP_t = \alpha + \theta \cdot CSP_{t-1} + \sum_{i=1}^{I} \beta_i \cdot X_{i,t-1} + \varepsilon_t$$

where CFP_t means the change of financial performance at time t (or financial performance where it is justified), $X_{i,t}$ is control variable at the same time t and CSP_t (corporate social performance) is dummy variable indicating fact of publication the CSR report or the fact that the company is listed in *RI*.

Before we estimated model (1) we check if is there any correlation between CSR_t (or RI_t) and financial variables. We used standard Spearman's rank correlation coefficient. Second test was to show whether the average financial results differ between companies with different *CSR* (*RI*). We used Two-way Factorial ANOVA (analysis of variance).

The second model intends to examine the impact of financial results on the probability of publishing a CSR report and on the probability incorporating the company into RI.

H2: Financial results of financial institution impact (positively or negatively) the probability of its CSR reporting and the probability of incorporating the company into Respect Index

This hypothesis concerns two other hypothesis that may be found in the literature:

1. available funding hypothesis (slack resources hypothesis) (↑ CFP =>↑ CSR)
2. managerial opportunism hypothesis (↑CFP => ↓ CSR),

In order to verify the second research hypothesis we estimated binary logistic regression:

$$\pi_j = \Pr(CSP_{j,t} = 1 \mid X_i = x_i)$$

$$\log(\frac{\pi_j}{1-\pi_j}) = \alpha + \theta_1 \cdot FP_{j,t-1} + \theta_2 \cdot WIG_{j,t-1} + \sum_{i=1}^{I} \beta_i \cdot X_{i,t-1} + \varepsilon$$

where $CSPj,_t$ is response variable, equal 1 when company *j* published CSR report, or when company *j* was incorporated into RI, $WIG_{j,t}$ is dummy variable indicated companies incorporated into PL-WIG-BANKI index for banks and $X_{i,t}$ are the control variables.

4.4. Results of the analysis

The first analysis aimed to test the hypothesis about the impact of the CSR report publication and the impact of the company's presence on the RESPECT Index (RI) on the change in the financial results of the following reporting year.

Spearman's correlation coefficients results are presented in Table 3. Statistically significant correlation occurs between CSR variables (CSR reports / RI) and book value change, as well as between CSR variables and market value (capitalization). However, correlation coefficients do not show a clear relationship between these variables.

Table 3. Spearman correlation between financial data and CSR & RI from previous year

Spearman	ΔROA_t	ΔROE_t	*(Market value)* $_t$	Δ*(Net profit)* $_t$
CSR_{t-1}	-0.0589	-0.0496	0.367565 ***	0.06459
RI_{t-1}	-0.0693	-0.0989	0.43707 ***	0.01864

* p<0.1 ** p<0.05 ***p<0.01 ****p<0.001

The next stage of verification of the first research hypothesis is to check whether there are significant differences in the average value of the variables reflecting financial results for the following year between the companies that have published the CSR report and those that did not published it. In order to analyze it we use Two-way Factorial ANOVA.

The ANOVA test showed that the hypotheses about equality of vectors concerning mean value of changes in financial results between groups cannot be rejected (stat. F= 1,5926; p=0,1627). To verify whether the individual values are significantly different, one-dimensional results (Table 4) are checked.

Table 4. Two-way Factorial ANOVA of financial data for CSR (1 – publication of the report ; 0 – otherwise) **and RI** (1 – company in RESPECT Index; 0 – otherwise) as a treatment. Depend variables are change of financial data.

	ΔROA_t	ΔROE_t	*(Market value)* $_t$	Δ*(Net profit)* $_t$
Source	F - stat	F – stat	F – stat	F – stat
CSR_{t-1}	0.0348	0.2898	2.3429	1.8174
RI_{t-1}	0.0331	0.0086	72.115 ****	0.0207
CSR_{t-1}*RI_{t-1}	0.0264	0.5536	0.0639	1.3054

* p<0.1 ** p<0.05 ***p<0.01 ****p<0.001

The only statistically significant difference regarded the changes in the book value. A similar test was used for companies that were part of the RESPECT Index compared to other companies. For the vector of average change of the financial result between the analyzed groups, the hypothesis should be rejected (stat F = 16,2967; p <0.0001). In this case, for a one-dimensional result (Table 4), the statistically significant difference occurs between the average market valuation for RI companies and the rest.

In case of interaction effect study between CSR and RI it cannot be argued that the mean values of dependent variables are significantly different (stat. F = 0.2966; p = 0.9145). Since there are statistically significant differences between the average market value of the RESPECT Index companies and the others, as the next step the econometric model was applied to test the relationship between the market value and the RI variable (1 – company in the RESPECT Index; 0-otherwise). As control variables the employment size and the variable indicating the affiliation to the PL-WIG-BANKI index were used (1 - company in PL-WIG-BANKI; 0 - otherwise). The obtained model is shown in Table 5.

Table 5. Linear regression analysis for market value as depend variable

Dependent variable: (market value)$_t$	*Coefficients*	
Independent variable: RI_{t-1}	5228.723 ****	**3026.79** ****
Intercept	-222.736	-59.83
Control variables:		
PL-WIG-BANK index (0-1)	2026.756 ***	-2697.59 ****
Number of employees	1.48606 ****	
Dept/total assets	-208.691	27.27
Book value		1.90 ****
Stat. F=	514.88 ****	879.03 ****
R^2=	0.896	0.9319

* p<0.1 ** p<0.05 ***p<0.01 ****p<0.001

Using standard test we observe that the relationship between all independent variables in the model and the market value is statistically significant. Similarly, the fit of the model is high (R2 = 89.6%), the random component is not heteroscedastic Thus, the relationship between market value and RI can be indicated.

The second research hypothesis concerned the impact of the financial result on the company's probability to publish a CSR report and the impact of the financial result on the probability of the incorporation of the company to the Respect Index. In order to verify the hypothesis, logit models were constructed separately for the CSR report publication and RI variables. The results of the analysis are presented in Tables 6-9.

In each of the estimated models, the ROA and ROE values of the previous year were used as the financial result. At the same time, it was also verified whether the fact of being quoted within the PL-WIG-BANKI index of the largest banks quoted on the Warsaw Stock Exchange, influences the probability of the CSR report being published by the company and whether it increases the likelihood of incorporation into the RESPECT Index.

Table 6. Logit regression analysis using CSR (1 – publication of the report; 0 – otherwise) as depend variable and financial data from previous year as independent variables

Dependent variable: publication of the report	*Model 1*	*Model 2*	*Model 3*
Independent variable: ROA	7.668	7.911	7.657
Intercept	-9.492 ***	-9.431 ***	-9.538 ***
PL-WIG-BANK index (0-1)	2.167 ***	2.085 **	2.127 ***
Control variables:			
Dept/total assets	7.206 **	7.366 **	7.211 **
Book value	0.00003		
Market value		0.00002	
Number of employees			0.00004
Hosmer Lemeshow test:	0.9933	0.9954	0.9917
p =	0.4715	0.4949	0.4745
Nagelkerke R^2:	78,019	73.849	77.672
AIC:			

* p<0.1 ** p<0.05 ***p<0.01 ****p<0.001

Table 7. Logit regression analysis using CSR (1 – publication of the report; 0 – otherwise) as depend variable and financial data from previous year as independent variables

Dependent variable: publication of the report	*Model 1*	*Model 2*	*Model 3*
Independent variable: ROE	0.128 ***	0.279 ****	0.126 ***
Intercept	-6.41 ****	-6.388 ****	-6.412 ****
PL-WIG-BANK index (0-1)	2.47 ***	2.040 **	2.419 ***
Control variables:			
Dept/total assets	2.413	2.283	2.416
Book value	-0.00001		
Market value		-0.00005	
Number of employees			0.0000004
Hosmer Lemeshow test:	0.9182	0.9981	0.9917
p =	0.48396	0.5544	0.4745
Nagelkerke R^2:	76,587	67.108	77.672
AIC:			

* p<0.1 ** p<0.05 ***p<0.01 ****p<0.001

Table 8. Logit regression analysis using RI (1 – company in Respect Index; 0 – otherwise) as depend variable and financial data (ROA) from previous year as independent variables

Dependent variable: company in Respect Index	*Model 1*	*Model 2*	*Model 3*
Independent variable: ROA	-4.5651	-4.693	-4.519
Intercept	3.9043 ***	3.6968 **	3.503 ***
PL-WIG-BANK index (0-1)	0.8131	0.9185 **	1.1149 ***
Control variables:			
Dept/total assets	-1.3951	-1.289	-1.093
Book value	-0.0002 **		
Market value		-0.00008	
Number of employees		****	-0.00012 ***
Hosmer Lemeshow test:	0.5017	0.1377	0.5636
p =	0.4617	0.5018	0.4373
Nagelkerke R^2:	96.828	89.247	100.204
AIC:			

* p<0.1 ** p<0.05 ***p<0.01 ****p<0.001

Table 9. Logit regression analysis using RI (1 – company in Respect Index; 0 – otherwise) as depend variable and financial data (ROE) from previous year as independent variables

Dependent variable: company in Respect Index	*Model 1*	*Model 2*	*Model 3*
Independent variable: ROE	0.1447 ***	0.294 ***	0.151 ***
Intercept	-4.116 ****	-3.7867 ****	-4.060 ****
PL-WIG-BANK index (0-1)	1.917 **	1.543	2.440 ***
Control variables:			
Dept/total assets	-0.4726	-1. 3714	-0.6893
Book value	0.00098 *		
Market value		0.00019	
Number of employees			0.00006
Hosmer Lemeshow test:	0.4818	0. 6335	0.294
p =	0.4638	0. 5189	0.4466
Nagelkerke R^2:	89.993	80.291	92.560
AIC:			

* p<0.1 ** p<0.05 ***p<0.01 ****p<0.001

In all estimated models, it appears that the ROA value has no statistically significant impact either on the likelihood of a CSR report being published or on the likelihood of incorporation into the RESPECT Index (see Table 6 and Table 9).

Models in which the independent variable is ROA tend to generally model the probability of a dependent variable in a proper way. However, this is the result of other variables. In turn, the models in which the ROE is taken an independent variable have a significant effect on the probability of the dependent variable. The higher the ROE value, the greater the likelihood that the company will decide to publish a CSR report or that it will be included in the RESPECT Index the following year. In almost all models, the company's PL-WIG-BANK index participation has a significant impact on the probability of a dependent variable.

Apart from one case (Table 8, Model 1), this is the most important factor increasing the likelihood of a CSR report being published and increasing the probability of inclusion in the RESTECT Index. In all analyzed cases, the best results were obtained for Model 2, where the control variables are the debt ratio and the market value of the company. They have the lowest Akaike (1974) information criterion (AIC), and the highest R^2. Also based on the Hosmer-Lemeshow (2013) test there is no reason to reject the hypothesis that the observed and predicted values are equal.

5. Conclusions

CSR-related matters in CEECs has become "an important concept materializing in the accounting academic and practitioner literature, as well as in the practices of local companies" (Albu et all: 193). The 2008 financial crisis brought social responsibility to the important issues agenda in many financial institutions all over the world, including the CEE region. Applying more responsible attitude to the business running and communicating on that was treated as the way of re-establishing credibility and regaining legitimacy by financial sector.

The study presents the conducted analysis of the link between being socially responsible and achieving tangible financial outcomes in CEECs, on the example of Poland. The study attempted also to check if having financial sources influences the involvement in the socially responsible actions and reporting on that. The statistical results of the paper reveal that the publication of a CSR report has not influence the changes in the company's financial results; correlation coefficients have not shown that there is such a link. This results fall in line with the results obtained by Stouhal *et al.* (2015) that empirically proved no relationship between the disclosure of standalone CSR reports and financial performance in two other countries of CEE e.g. Czech and Estonia. On contrary to their study, our research showed a relatively weak relationship in case of a change in market value. The results of this analysis demonstrate also that the fact of publishing CSR report did not reveal significant differences in the financial performance compared to companies that do not publish this kind of report. This result falls in line with Djalilov and Hölscher (2016: 6), stating "where the business environment is not well-developed, markets do not reward banks engaged in social and environmental activities".

A similar analysis was carried out in the group of companies that were included in the RESPECT Index and the rest of companies. In case of companies listed in the RESPECT Index the results demonstrated however, that there is a clear correlation between the fact that the company is listed on that index and the market value. This means that companies included in that index tend to have higher market value. Also the average market value of companies in RESPECT Index is different from the average market value of other companies. We assume however that this may be caused also by the specific high requests concerning the inclusion of companies into this index that appeals not only to CSR engagement but also to the responsibility concerning financial measures themselves therefore the companies that are admitted into the index they already have a sound financial situation.

An econometric model presented in the paper was developed to explain the relationship between the RESPECT Index and the market value in the following year. In this model as the explanatory (independent) variable, apart from Respect Index variable (1 in the RESPECT Index; 0 - otherwise) the size of employment and the participation in the PL-WIG-BANKI index (embracing the largest listed banks in Warsaw) were taken into account. There was a statistically significant relationship between the market value and the three variables tested. These empirical results give grounds for rejecting the first research hypothesis. In the same way the social impact and the trade-off hypothesis are denied.

This is a clear sign that the market and the public is reluctant in considering the CSR importance of financial institutions. The results obtained from the first part of research highlight that the CSR activities do not impact the bottom line of the financial institutions or at least that the effects are not seen in the following year. It may be assumed that or CSR efforts are not focused properly, or they are not communicated effectively. We assume also that the factor of time is important, we may expect that the reaction of the public on the CSR activities, especially in case of the loss of trust, may be delayed. In this study one-year time-lag was applied. Maybe the public needs more time to recognize the CSR involvement that would contribute to the improvement of financial performance of socially responsible institutions. To rebuilt trust and credibility it takes time. One should also consider that the Polish financial market is still quite young therefore we may assume that the institutional factors and the development stage of this market influences the reaction of the public on the CSR initiatives and the degree to which CSR reports publications/ being listed on the Respect Index contributes to the financial bottom line.

In order to verify the second research hypothesis, the probability logit models were constructed, testing the probability of CSR report publishing and the probability of incorporating the company into the RESPECT Index depending on the financial result obtained in the preceding year. It has been shown that ROE is an important independent variable for both the likelihood of publication of the CSR report for the following year as well as for the probability of inclusion in the RESPECT Index. Similarly, the statistically significantly higher probability for the dependent variable was obtained with the variable informing about affiliation to the PL-WIG-BANKI index. On the other hand, ROA does not significantly influence the probability of a dependent variable. This is a result other than that obtained at work (Waddock & Graves, 1997), where the significant independent variable was ROA. We may therefore conclude that there is a will of companies from the financial sector to get involved in the CSR activities (and communicate on them) when the financial resources permit it. The involvement is surely related to the expectations of its positive results. This falls in line with the study of Kundid and Rogošić (2011) carried out the empirical research on all banks in Croatia and statistically confirmed that large and more profitable banks disclose more CSR activities. The results obtain in our study are however contrary to those achieved by Djalilov (2015) concerning mainly transition countries, where he found that banks with a lower level of profitability are more interested to engage in social projects. He also proved that CSR activities would improve the financial performance of the banks of the transition countries.

Contrary, our study proves that in Poland the awareness of positive impact of CSR is higher in the institutions that are willing to engage in the CSR than of the market and public that stills fails to react on the CSR efforts of financial institutions in the way it would translate into measurable results for the companies. We may deduct that there is a significant difference between CEE countries and other transitional countries. The result of this study fall in line with observations of Grigore and Candidatu (2009: 84) that while analysing the perception of CSR in Romania and Bulgaria state: “there is room for improvement in the perception of corporate social responsibility area, but good social and environmental practices are in place and they constitute the basis for further development of corporate social responsibility practices”. The results obtained confirm also the observations of Elms (2006: 206) concerning the stakeholders’ lack of activism in CEE and the low reaction on CSR. Elms indicated that “if stakeholders’ value responsibility, corporations will too”. Although more than 10 years passed since that study, still in Poland the clients do not value the CSR engagement.

The present study is subject to certain limitations. Firstly, the sample size is relatively small, however it covers all the public companies in the financial sector in Poland in 2012-2015. Secondly, the time frame of the research is fairly short (i.e. 4 years). Thirdly, the study ignores control variables like age of firm, growth of firm, capital intensity, leverage, risk, R&D intensity, industry type, etc. that may have significant influence on this relationship. Several control variables that were considered during data collection included the capital structure (including whether the company is part of an international financial corporation), the type of financial activity (banks, insurance companies, investment firms) or the fact that CSR report submitted to external audit. Due to incomplete data in the database or in some cases due to heterogeneous information contained in the databases used, these explanatory variables are also excluded. Another restriction concerns a variable that informs the CSR report as a variable informing about the applicable social responsibility policy. We do not have information on the standards that published CSR reports meet.

Therefore, the results of study should be interpreted in light of these limitations. The directions of future research could be an attempt to overcome those limitations. The cross-national comparison could also be valuable to better understand the specifics of the Polish financial market and CSR in the international context, especially in the CEE region. Future research could also focus on the analysis of the CSR activity on the CFP in much longer lag period, the reconstructed credibility and trust, if ever, may occur after many years and as a result of a very focused engagement in CSR supported by its effective communication.

Acknowledgement

The paper was presented during the conference *International Conference Accounting and Management Information Systems* (AMIS 2017). The paper was completed with the feedback received from conference participants, and also with the valuable comments from article`s reviewers.

References

ACCA (2013) *What do investors expect from non-financial information?*, http://www.accaglobal.com/content/dam/acca/global/PDF-technical/sustainability-reporting/tech-tp-wdir.pdf (access: 08.01.2017).

Aggarwal, P. (2013) "Impact of sustainability performance of company on its financial performance: a study of listed Indian companies", *Global Journal of Management and Business Research*, vol. 13, no. 11: 60-70

Akaike, H. (1974) "A new look at the statistical model identification", *IEEE Transactions on Automatic Control*, vol. 19 (6): 716-723

Albertini, E. (2012) "Does environmental strategy improve financial performance? a meta-analytical review", *Academy of Management Conference*, Boston USA.

Albu, C. N., Balsari, Ç & Krasodomska, J. (2016) "Introduction to the Special Issue on Corporate Social Reporting in Central and Eastern Europe", *Accounting and Management Information Systems*, vol. 15, no. 2: 193-205

Allouche, J. & Laroche, P. (2005) "A meta-analytical investigation of the relationship between corporate social and financial performance", *Revue de Gestion des Ressources Humaines*, vol. 57 (1): 8-41

Asatryan, R. & Březinová, O. (2014) "Corporate Social Responsibility and Financial Performance in the Airline Industry in Central and Eastern Europe", *Acta Universitatis Agriculturae et Silviculturae Mendelianae Brunensis*, vol. 62: 633-639

Barjaktarović, l., Paunović, M. & Ječmenica, D., (2013) "Development of the banking sector in cee countries – comparative analysis", *Journal of Central Banking Theory and Practice*, vol. 2: 93-114

Beck, T. (2006) *Creating an Efficient Financial System: Challenges in a Global Economy*, World Bank Policy Research paper WPS 3856

Belfo, F. & Trigo A. (2013) "Accounting information systems: tradition and future directions", *Procedia Technology*, vol. 9: 534-546

Bossone, B. (2000) "What makes banks special? a study of banking, finance, and economic development", *World Bank Policy Research Working Papers*, no. 2408.

Caroll, A.B., (1991) "The pyramid of corporate social responsibility: Toward the moral management of organizational stakeholders", *Business Horizons*, vol. 34, Iss 4, July-August: 39-48.

Centrum CSR, Mielechow, P. & Piskalski, G. (2009) "CSR and Polish Business on Foreign Markets. Preliminary research report", Friedrich Ebert Foundation – Warsaw Office 2009.

Clark, G. L., Feiner, A. & Viehs, M. (2015) "From the Stockholder to the Stakeholder: How Sustainability Can Drive Financial Outperformance", doi:10.2139/ssrn.2508281.

Cornett, M. Erhemjamts, O. & Tehranian, H. (2014) "Corporate social responsibility and the impact on financial performance: Investigation of U.S. commercial banks", Boston college, from https://www2.bc.edu/hassan-tehranian/CSR-Performance%20Relationship%20for%20Banks%20Jan%202014.pdf

Cowton, C. J. (2002) "Integrity, responsibility and affinity: three aspects of ethics in banking", *Business Ethics: A European Review*, vol. 11 (4): 393-400

Csafor, H., (2008) "Corporate social responsibility in Central and Eastern Europe", in M. Carmona, J. Szlavik and E. Zam., (Eds.) "Perdiodica Oeconomica – Regional Development and Competitiveness", pp. 115-126

Daniel, F, Lohrkeb, F. T., Fornaciari Ch. J. & Turner R. A. (2004) "Slack resources and firm performance: a meta-analysis", *Journal of Business Research*, vol. 57: 565-574

Decker, S. & Sale, C. (2009) "An Analysis of Corporate Social Responsibility, Trust and Reputation in the Banking Profession", in: S.O. Idowu, W.L., Filho (Eds.) *Professionals perspectives if corporate social responsibility*, Springer-Verlag, Berlin-Heidelberg.

Djalilov, K., Vasylieva, T., Lyonov, S. & Lasukova, A., (2015) "Corporate Social Responsibility and Bank Performance in Transition Countries", *Corporate Ownership and Control*, January: 1-25

Djalilov, K. & Hölscher, J. (2016) "Antecedents of corporate social responsibility in the banks of Central-Eastern Europe and in the countries of the former Soviet union", *BAFES – Bournemouth Accounting, Finance & Economic Series*, NO 05: 1-26

Dyczkowska, J., Krasodomska, J. & Waniak, J., (2016) "CSR in Poland Institutional context, legal framework and voluntary initiatives", *Accounting and Management Information Systems*, vol. 15, No. 2: 206-254

Elms, H., (2006) "Corporate (and stakeholder) responsibility in Central and Eastern Europe", *International Journal of Emerging Markets*, vol. 1(3): 203-211

Ernst & Young (2009) "Non-financial reporting", Retrieved Feb. 28, 2016, from http://www.ey.com/Publication/vwLUAssets/Nonfinancial_reporting/$FILE/Climate%20change_Non%20financial%20reporting.pdf

Feltham, S. (2016) "A Snapshot of CSR in Central and Eastern Europe", http://www.triplepundit.com/2016/10/snapshot-csr-central-eastern-europe/

Fijałkowska, J. (2012)„Społeczna odpowiedzialność wyzwaniem dla rachunkowości" [Corporate Social Responsibility as a Challenge for Accounting], *Przedsiębiorczość i Zarządzanie*, vol. 13(1): 141-154

Fijałkowska, J. & Zyznarska-Dworczak, B. (2017) "Społeczna odpowiedzialność biznesu a tworzenie wartości banków" [Corporate Social Responsibility and Value Creation of Banks], *The Journal of Management and Finance* (forthcoming).

Filatotchev, I., Buck, T., & Zhukov, V. (2000) "Downsizing in privatized firms in Russia, Ukraine, and Belarus", *Academy of Management Journal*, vol. 43(3): 286-304

Furceri, D. & Zdziencka, A. (2010) "Banking crisis and short and medium term output loses in developing countries: The role of structural and policy variables, MPRA", working paper 22078, Retrieved from http://mpra.ub.unimuenchen.de/22078/2/Banking_Crises_and_Short_and_Medium_Term_ Output_Losses_in_Developing_Countries_MRPA.pdff

Furrer, O., C. P. Egri, D. A. Ralston, W. Danis, E. Reynaud, I. Naoumova, M. Molteni, A. Starkus, F. L. Darder, M. Dabic, & Furrer-Perrinjaquet, A., (2010) "Attitudes toward corporate responsibilities in Western Europe and in Central and East Europe", *Management International Review*, vol. 50(3): 379-398

Friedman, M. (1970) "The social responsibility of business is to increase its profits", *New York Times Magazine,* September 13.

Gaultier-Galliard, S., & Louisot, J-P., (2006) "Risks to Reputation: A Global Approach", *The Geneva Papers*, vol. 31: 425-445

Gray, R., Owen, D. & Maunders, K. (1987) *Corporate Social Reporting*, Prentice-Hall, Englewood Cliffs, NJ.

Griffin, J.J. & Mahon, J.F. (1997) "The Corporate Social Performance and Corporate Financial Performance Debate: Twenty-Five Years of Incomparable Research", *Business and Society*, vol. 36(1): 5-31

Grigore, L.N. & Candidatu, C., (2009) "The Perception and Role Of Corporate Social Responsibility In Central And Eastern Europe", *Romanian Economics and Business Review,* vol. 4(4): 79-88

Hernaus, A. I. & Stojanovic, A. (2015) "Determinants of bank social responsibility: case of Croatia", *Ekonomie a Management,* vol. 18(2): 117-134

Hirigoyen, G. & Poulain-Rehm, T. (2015) "Relationships between corporate social responsibility and financial performance: What is the causality"?, *Journal of Business and Management*, vol. 4 (1): 18-43.

Hosmer, D. W., & Lemeshow, S. (2013) *Applied Logistic Regression*, New York: Wiley

Huang, XB & Watson L (2015) "Corporate social responsibility research in accounting", *Journal of Accounting Literature,* vol. 34(1): 1-16

Inglehart, R. & Welzel, C. (2005) *Modernization, cultural change, and democracy: The human development sequence*, New York: Cambridge University Press.

International Business Leaders Forum (IBLF) (2003) IBLF Members. http://www.iblf.org/csr/csrwebassist.nsf/content/g1.html, (access: 23.05.2015).

International Monetary Fund (2016) *Regional Economic Issues Central, Eastern, and Southeastern Europe How to Get Back on the Fast Track*, International Monetary Fund, May 16, https://www.imf.org/external/pubs/ft/reo/2016/eur/eng/pdf/rei0516.pdf, (access: 31.07.2017).

Ioannou, I. & Serafeim, G. (2010) "What Drives Corporate Social Performance?: International Evidence from Social, Environmental and Governance Sources", Harvard Business School.

ISO 26000 (2010) *Guidance Standard on Social Responsibility,* International Organization for Standardization's, http://www.cnis.gov.cn/wzgg/201405/P020140512224950899020.pdf, (access: 23.05.2015).

Kemmelmeier, M., Krol, G. & Kim, Y. H. (2002) “Values, economic, and proenvironmental attitudes in 22 societies”, *Cross-Cultural Research*, vol. 26(3): 256-285

Kleine, J., Krautbauer M. & Weller T. (2013) “Nachhaltige Investments aus dem Blick der Wissenschaft: Leistungsversprechen und Realität”, Research Center for Financial Services Steinbeis- Hochschule, Berlin.

Koleva, P., Rodet-Kroichvili, N., David, P. & Marasova, J. (2010) “Is corporate social responsibility the privilege of developed market economies? Some evidence from Central and Eastern Europe”, *The International Journal of Human Resource Management,* vol. 21(2): 274-293

Kundid, A. & Rogošić, A. (2011) “Bank Online Reporting: Comparative Advantage, Formalism of Fashion?”, *Global Business & Economics Anthology*, vol. 2(2): 500-518

Levine, R. (1997) “Financial development and economic growth: views and agenda”, *Journal of Economic Literature*, vol. 35: 688–726.

Levine, R. (2005) “Finance and growth: theory and evidence”, in: Aghion, P & Durlauf, S. (eds.), *Handbook of economic growth*, Elsevier Science, The Netherlands.

Lewicka-Strzalecka, A. (2006) “Opportunities and limitations of CSR in the postcommunist countries: Polish case”, *Corporate Governance*, vol. 6(4): 440-448

Llewellyn, D. (2005) “Trust and confidence in financial services: a strategic challenge”, *Journal of Financial Regulation and Compliance*, vol. 13(4): 333-346.

Lopez, M. V., Garcia, A., & Rodriguez, L. (2007) „Sustainable development and corporate performance: A study based on the Dow Jones Sustainability Index”, *Journal of Business Ethics*, vol. 75(3): 285-300

Margolis, J. D., Elfenbein H. & Walsh J.P. (2007) “Does it pay to be good? A meta-analysis and redirection of research on the relationship between corporate social and financial performance”, Working Paper, Ross School of Business - University of Michigan.

Margolis, J. D. & Walsh, J. P. (2001) “People and profits?: The search for a link between a company's social and financial performance”, Mahwah, N.J: Lawrence Erlbaum Associates.

Marquez A., & Fombrun, C.J. (2005) “Measuring Corporate Social Responsibility”, *Corporate Reputation Review*, vol. 7 (4): 304-308

McGuire, J. B., A. Sundgren, & T. Schneeweiss (1988) “Corporate Social Responsibility and Firm Financial Performance”, *Academy of Management Journal*, vol. 31 (4): 854-872

McWilliams A. & Siegel D. (2001) “Corporate social responsibility: A theory of the firm perspective”, *Academy of Management Review*, vol. 26 (1): 117-127

Merton, R.C. (1995) “A functional perspective of financial intermediation”, *Financial Management*, vol. 24(2): 23-41

Minor, D.B. (2009) *Corporate Social Responsibility as Reputation Insurance: Theory and Evidence*, Haas School of Business, UC Berkeley.

Mikołajewicz G. & Nowicki J. (2016) „Tworzenie wartości przedsiębiorstwa z uwzględnieniem aspektów środowiskowych i społecznych" [Creation of company value, with environmental and social aspects], in: Kochalski, C., *Zielony controlling i finanse. Podstawy teoretyczne* [*Greening and finance. Theoretical Foundations*], Wydawnictwo C.H.Beck, Warszawa, pp. 75-104

Moon, J. (2007) "The Contribution of Corporate Social Responsibility to Sustainable Development", *Sustainable Development*, vol. 15: 296-306

Nagelkerke, N.J.D. (1991) "A note on a general definition of the coefficient of determination", *Biometrika,* vol. 78: 691-692

Novokmet, A.K. & Rogošić, A. (2016) "Bank Sustainability Reporting within the GRI-G4 Framework", *Zeszyty Teoretyczne Rachunkowości*, vol. 88, no. 144: 109-123

Olsen, R. (2008) "Trust as risk and the foundation of investment value", *Journal of Socio Economics*, no. 37(4): 2189-2200

Olson M. W. (2006) "Are Banks Still Special?", Annual Washington Conference of the Institute of International Bankers, Washington, D.C., BIS Review, no. 20.

Orlitzky, M., Schmidt, F. L. & Rynes, S. L. (2003) "Corporate social and financial performance: A meta-analysis", *Organization Studies*, vol. 24 (3): 403-441

Peloza, J. (2009) "The challenge of measuring financial impacts from investments in corporate social performance", *Journal of Management*, vol. 35 (6): 1518–1541

Preston L.E. & O'Bannon D.P. (1997) "The corporate social-financial performance relationship: a typology and analysis", *Business and Society*, no. 36: 419-429

Rogošić A., Čaljkušić A. (2015) "Disclosure of the socially responsible activities of the banks in Croatia and Slovenia", Proceedings of the 3rd International OFEL Conference on Governance, Management and Entrepreneurship – The Quest for Organizational Identity, D. Tipurić, M. Daraboš (eds), Dubrovnik, Croatia, 17–18 April 2015, CIRU – Governance Research and Development Centre, pp. 313-324.

Rossier, J., (2003) "Ethics and Money: What is required of the banking professional", *La Lettre*, Geneva Private Bankers Association, no. 23, March.

Schanz, K. (2006) "Reputation and reputational risk management", *The Geneva Papers on Risk and Insurance,* vol. 31: 377-381

Scholtens B. (2009) "Corporate social responsibility in the international banking industry", *Journal of Business Ethics*, no. 86: 159-175

Seifert, B., Morris S.A. & Bartkus B.R. (2004) "Having, giving, and getting: Slack resources, corporate philanthropy, and firm financial performance", *Business & Society,* vol. 43(2): 135-161

Smith, N. C. (2002) "Arguments for and against corporate social responsibility", In: L. P. Hartman (Ed.), *Perspectives in business ethics*, New York: The McGraw-Hill Companies: 231-236.

Stansfield, G. (2006) "Some Thoughts on Reputation and Challenges for Global Financial Institutions", *The Geneva Papers*, no. 31: 470-479

Steurer, R. & Konrad, A. (2009) "Business-society relations in Central-Eastern and Western Europe: How those who lead in sustainability reporting bridge the gap in corporate (social) responsibility", *Scandinavian Journal of Management*, vol. 25: 23-36

Steurer, R. & Martinuzzi, A. (2012) "Public Policies on CSR in Europe: Themes, Instruments, and Regional Differences", *Corporate Social Responsibility and Environmental Management*, no. July: 206-227

Strandberg, C. (2005) "Best practices in sustainable finance", Standberg Consulting, from http://www.corostrandberg.com/pdfs/Sustainable%20Finance%20%20Best%20Practices.pdf.

Strouhal, J., Gurvits, N., Nikitina-Kalamae, M & Startseva, E. (2015) "Finding the Link between CSR Reporting and Corporate Financial Performance: Evidence on Czech and Estonian Listed Companies", *Central European Business Review*, vol. 4 (3): 48-59

UNDP (2007) Baseline study on CSR practices in the New EU Member States and Candidate Countries, http://www.acceleratingcsr.eu/uploads/docs/BASELINE_STUDY_ON.pdf.

UNEP (2004) "Finance and Stability in Central &Eastern Europe", http://www.unepfi.org/fileadmin/documents/ceetf_finance_sustainability_2004_01.pdf

Vaughan-Whitehead, D. C. (2003) *EU enlargement versus social Europe? The uncertain future of the European model*, Cheltenham: Edward Elgar.

Vynoslavska, O., McKinney, J. A., Moore, C. W. & Longenecker, J. G. (2005) "Transition ethics: a comparison of Ukrainian and United States business professionals", *Journal of Business Ethics*, vol. 61(3): 283–299

Waddock, S. A. & Graves, S. B. (1997) "The corporate social performance-financial performance link", *Strategic Management Journal*, vol. 303-319

Wang Q., Dou J. & Jia S. (2016) "A meta-analytic review of corporate social responsibility and corporate financial performance. The moderating effect of contextual factors", *Business & Society*, vol. 55 issue 8: 1083-1121.

World Economic Forum (2012) "The role of financial services in society a multistakeholder compact", from http://www3.weforum.org/docs/WEF_FS_RoleFinancialServicesSociety_Report_2013.pdf (20.03.2017).

Yilmaz, B., Yilmaz, O. & Akmese, H. (2016) "The role of accounting information system in business in terms of corporate governance and social responsibility of accounting in crisis periods and a research", *RSEP International Conferences on Social Issues and Economic Studies*

Zyznarska-Dworczak, B. (2016) "Determinanty rozwoju sprawozdawczości niefinansowej w świetle pozytywnej i normatywnej teorii rachunkowości" [The Development of Non-Financial Reporting in the Light of Positive and Normative Accounting Theories], *Prace Naukowe Uniwersytetu Ekonomicznego (AE) we Wrocławiu*, no. 436: 307-315

Živković, S. & Aktan, B. (2009) "Global financial crisis and VaR performance in emerging markets: A case of EU candidate states – Turkey and Croatia", *The Proceedings of Rijeka Faulty of Economics- Journal of Economics and Business*, vol. 27 (1): 149-170

[i] According to the classification of the International Monetary Fund (2016), the following countries are included in Central East Europe: Albania, Belarus, Bosnia and Herzegovina, Bulgaria, Croatia, Czech Republic, Estonia, Hungary, Kosovo, Latvia, Lithuania, Macedonia, Moldova, Montenegro, Poland, Romania, Russia, Serbia, Slovak Republic, Slovenia, Turkey, and Ukraine.

5

What explains changes in accounting divisional performance under liquidity shortage conditions?

Eleftherios Aggelopoulos [a1]

[a] *University of Patras, Greece*

Abstract: This is the first study which tests empirically to which extent the quality and the spread of consumer and small business loans are responsible for the increases or decreases in branch accounting performance, measured by the Residual Income (RI) performance indicator, over time. Moreover, given extreme liquidity shortage conditions the paper investigates to which extent the above factors are responsible for changes in RI. Unique accounting information derived from the Management Information System (MIS) of a Greek systemic commercial bank is utilized. The study finds that lending spreads for both types of loans are positively and statistically significant related to RI. The crisis increases the positive value effect of consumer lending spreads while reduces the value premium of small business lending spreads. The latter indicates that the upward repricing of small business credit lines during crisis years seems to destroy value due to the side effects that the repricing loan policy activates (i.e. reduces the repayment ability of borrowers). Moreover, the enormous increase of loan loss impairments during crisis exercises an extra negative impact on RI thus further accelerating shareholder value destruction, for both loan portfolios. The study provides useful information about the thorough understanding of the quality of banking performance at the retail level in bank-driven crisis economies.

Keywords: Divisional performance, lending operations, retail branches, spread and credit risk, crisis

---

[1] Adjunct Lecturer in Financial Accounting, Department of Business Administration, University of Patras, University Campus, 26504, Rio - Patras, Greece, , email: eaggelopoulos@upatras.gr

1. Introduction

According to Deville (2009), "Retail banking has always erred on the side of caution. The result of such practise has been the creation of inertia in branch management and performance evaluation". Indeed, the literature review reveals a significant proliferation of research on bank performance and efficiency (Garcia-Herrero *et al.*, 2009; Fiordelisi & Molyneux, 2010), but only few on branch performance where the unit of analysis is an individual branch of the bank. The main reasons include the lack of easy access to branch level data and the condition to have practical knowledge on the way the bank branch operates. Given that commercial banking is based on the operation of a network of bank branches and these branches are involved in all the crucial steps of modern banking like cost and risk management, the branch performance analysis is expected to have important implications for the bank management, policymakers and academics. The main research question that the paper attempts to answer is as follows: To which extent the quality of the loan portfolio and the lending spreads - which are two crucial value factors with important trade-offs between them - are responsible for changes in shareholder value creation at the branch level and how this value effect is associated with the type of the loan portfolio and external environmental changes? In particular, the paper measures the impact of credit risk and lending spreads, related to the consumer and small business loan portfolio, on the value creation process over time taking into account changes in the external environment in terms of liquidity. The analysis focuses on consumer and small business loans where their volumes are large and they generate substantial income and risks (i.e. mortgage loans are not incorporated into the analysis since provisions for these collaterized loans were somewhat fixed over time).

Generally, measuring the divisional performance of banks such as the performance of bank branches is of great importance since this bottom level performance analysis ensures that changes on shareholder value can be measured directly at their sources by also capturing the direct crisis effects immediately. Two are the crucial conditions as regards the effective measurement of divisional performance: the structure of the analysis and the homogeneity of the data set. The employed data set satisfies adequately these two conditions. Specifically, regarding the structure of the paper, the study uses internal data of bank branches of a specific banking institution. As the literature reports (see Gross, 2006), a research design in retail banking performance should be based on internal data of bank branches of a specific banking institution and not be performed across competing banking institutions since the definition of the retail segment considerably varies across banks. Moreover, the paper examines a strict homogeneous data set of branches in terms of their activity and size. In particular, a novel data set, derived from the monthly Profit and Loss (P&L)

statements of homogeneous retail branches of one of the four largest commercial banks in Greece, is utilized over the period January 2006 to December 2010. Subsequently, this period is divided into the credit boom period (Period A: January 2006- August 2008) and the first phase of the crisis period (Period B: September 2008 - December 2010). In total, the data sample is a balanced panel with 27 homogeneous retail branches spread across Greece and 1,620 monthly observations over the period from January 2006 to December 2010. The data set is representative as the Greek banking industry is very oligopolistic (i.e. there are four systemic Greek commercial banks: The National Bank of Greece, Piraeus Bank, Eurobank and Alpha Bank) and quite homogeneous operating in commercial banking, mainly retail banking.

A fixed-effects model specification is applied to the panel of retail branches which produces efficient estimates. It is worth noting, that since the study explores the liquidity shortage effects on lending spreads and credit risk quality where there is an exogenous shock to the banking sector, the results are expected to not suffer from endogeneity problems. For measuring shareholder value, the performance indicator of Residual Income is used (thus RI is the dependent variable). RI is an effective measure of shareholder value creation at bottom level (Koller *et al.*, 2005). In the same spirit other SHV banking studies (Fiordelisi & Molyneux, 2010, 2007) use the Economic Value Added (EVA) model adjusting accounting net operating profits by adding back loan loss impairments (considering that they used to manage earnings and smooth earnings overtime) and subtracting net charge offs. However, Gross (2006) reports that such adjustments to provisions may potentially no longer be needed since the provisions requirements under International Accounting Standard 39 (IAS 39), which are based on observable data, lead to more realistic figures and so they can be considered as cash cost. Overall, the study proposes that RI model and other SHV models such as EVA and Economic Profit (EP) are often identical in practice (see also Bodmer, 2001).

The results overall indicate that both the lending spread earned on consumer and small business loans and the credit risk-taking on these loans, are significantly associated with the RI, but with a different statistical sign. In particular, the lending spreads for both types of loans are positively and statistically significant related to RI. The crisis increases the positive value effect of consumer lending spreads while reduces the value premium of small business lending spreads. The latter is due to the negative value effects of the upward repricing credit policy that the small business loans segment followed in the crisis period. As regards the credit risk value driver, the occurrence of liquidity shortage increases the generally negative value effect of credit risk for both loan categories. The results have important implications for policymakers and bank managers (see the discussion section below). Generally, the study provides useful information about the quality of banking performance at the retail level in the “bank-driven” crisis economy of Greece which is characterized by sovereign debt and a relatively weak local financial market, as well as other

Mediterranean economies of the European region (e.g. Italy, Portugal, and Spain). In this way, this might offer useful lessons for those specific countries as well.

The rest of this paper is organized as follows: Section two illustrates the recent developments in the Greek banking sector. Section three presents the theoretical framework of the study along with the related literature review. Section four presents the methodology employed to construct the model. Section five describes the data set, the definition of variables used in the study, and it illustrates the empirical results. The last section concludes the study and discusses its main findings.

2. A brief overview of the Greek banking industry – the passage of the expansion period to the crisis period

Until the end of the 1980's the domestic banking sector was heavily protected and regulated (protectionism period). Since then the Greek banking industry has faced structural changes caused by liberalization and deregulation (liberalization period). The liberalization period is of particular interest for this research since the new environment has positively affected the performance of banking institutions in the local economy, especially their retail banking activities, and enabled banks to better serve the interests of shareholders with similar strategies. Up to 2008 the domestic banking market was steadily expanding (expansion period). In particular, the liberalization of the capital account in the 1990's which allowed Greek enterprises and individuals to borrow in lower yielding foreign currencies, triggered credit growth. Moreover, the abolition of various regulatory credit ceilings, the adoption of the Euro in 2001 with the subsequent decline in interest rates and the increased competition amongst financial institutions, boosted the demand for credit further. The fast growth of the Greek banking sector relied heavily on a wide distribution network, thus branch performance had a significant performance effect on the bank as a whole, as the number of branches increased by 24% during 2003-2008 (Bank of Greece, 2009).

The systematic global crisis that started in August 2007 in conjunction with high public debt of the Greek economy discontinued in 2008 the expansion process of the banking industry and threw the domestic financial market in deep crisis and afterwards the real economy[i]. Consequently, the crisis caused the drying up of liquidity in the domestic interbank market, and led to a substantial increase in deposit and lending rates. However, this crisis transmitted to the local banking system with a greater time lag if compared with most of the EU. The reason is that Greek banks have been focused on retail banking and not on investment banking activities, as in the case of other EU banks that caused huge marked to market losses related to toxic assets.

Since the study takes into account the first phase of the crisis and for the needs of our empirical research, the starting point of the crisis that marks the economic alteration should be determined. Exogenously it is observed that the average interest rates of time deposits for Greek banks increased markedly in September 2008 (Bank of Greece, 2009). Specifically, in that month the interest rates of time deposits jumped from 4.99% (August 2008) to 5.11% with an increasing trend until the end of December 2008, where the month rate was 5.36%. So, the structural point at which the crisis started with the form of liquidity shortage, is positioned on September 2008.

3. Literature review and determinants of value creation

3.1 Literature on determinants of shareholder value

There is a large amount of literature exploring generally how European banks are able to increase their performance and profitability. Studies like Dietrich and Wanzenried (2011), Athanasoglou *et al.* (2008), Brissimis *et al.* (2008), Lepetit *et al.* (2008) or Salas and Saurina (2003) investigate bank-specific variables that may have an impact on banking profitability measured by ROE or other efficiency measures. Their results vary since there are differences in studied time periods and sample countries. Also, the examination of the impact of crisis on bank profitability drivers is scarce. More specifically, Dietrich and Wanzenried (2011) analyze profitability determinants of 372 commercial banks in Switzerland during the pre-crisis period (1999 – 2006) and the crisis years (2007-2009). They find that the profitability effect of credit risk taking is negative and significant, only in the crisis period.

A gap is located on the empirical literature on measuring shareholder value creation as a proxy for bank performance and identify relevant value drivers. In particular, Fiordelisi and Molyneux (2010), examining several bank- and industry- and macroeconomic-specific determinants of SHV creation (measured by the EVA performance indicator which is identical in practise with the RI approach, see the introduction section) for a large sample of European banks between 1998 and 2005 (including Southern European Countries such as Spain, Portugal, Italy, Greece etc.) emphasize that such value factors often have both positive and negative effects on SHV creation. Their most important finding related to this study is the identification of a positive relationship between credit risk taking and SHV – as banks take on more credit risk they also boost their interest revenues. On the contrary, Gross (2006) examines determinants of SHV creation for the German banking sector during the period 1998-2003. The findings suggest that an increase in credit risk taking destroys value while an increase in cost efficiency creates it. The above limited SHV literature is applied at the bank level. To the best of my knowledge, no previous SHV study has been applied to the branch level and thus on retail banking, focusing at the same time on the simultaneous examination of the impact of credit risk and lending spreads on RI and taking also into account the effects of crisis and loan portfolio characteristics.

3.2 The effect of credit risk and lending spreads on value creation process

A bank branch creates value for its shareholders when the return on invested capital is greater than its opportunity cost (Feltham & Ohlson; 1995). A reliable accounting performance indicator is Residual Income (i.e. the difference between the allocated net operating income after taxes and the cost of allocated equity - the product of allocated equity and cost of equity-). According to Dermine (2009), equity allocation at branch level should be based on the risk taken at the branch level (that is essentially credit and operational risk) and to bank regulations on capital. Specifically, the equity employed to each branch is the sum of capital requirements for credit and operational risk according to Basel II capital rules (Gross, 2006; Uyemura *et al.*, 1996). The allocation of income to the branches is implemented through the concept of fund transfer pricing that allows interest income from lending and deposit transactions to be calculated in isolation for each branch (Gross, 2006)

Based on earlier shareholder value literature (Fiordelisi & Molyneux, 2010; Gross, 2006), this paper suggests that the credit risk taking activity is expected to have an interesting impact on RI. Also, granting loans with a high spread is considered a valuable driver (Dermine, 2009) for the income structure of the branch. In addition, the study recognizes the impact of crisis on the value effects of the above drivers. Thus, it is realistic to assume that when compared to the growth period that stimulates the influence of positive value factors the crisis hampers the SHV creation process, reducing the dynamic of the specific factors. The net effect (value creation in the growth period vs. value destruction in the crisis period) will finally show the overall contribution of the value determinants.

The following arguments shed some insights in this proposition discussing the uncertain impact of our independent variables on RI in a dynamic environment. The effect of higher credit risk on performance appears to be negative because of the relative rise of loan impairments (Athanasoglou *et al.* 2008; Brissimis *et al.,* 2008; Gross, 2006). Especially in the crisis period, a very high level of loan impairments, and consequently a bad quality of loan portfolio, may seriously threaten the survival of banking institutions. On the contrary, credit risk taking which lends to doubtful customers in terms of creditworthiness at high rates of interest may increase the loan volumes and thus the ability of the institution to generate interest income through market share expansion (Fiordelisi *et al.* 2011; Salas & Saurina, 2003). In the crisis period, a negative impact of credit risk taking on RI is expected due to the unfavorable economic environment.

In addition, profitability derived from lending taking business may be considered as potential value determinant (Dermine, 2010). From this point of view, it is expected that retail branches which charge higher lending spreads (i.e. difference between interest earned on loans before provisions and cost of funding –transfer price-) to their lending customers naturally present a higher value. However, high interest margins maybe hiding a relatively low quality loan portfolio. Such loan portfolios are usually related with higher credit risk in the period of crisis, with negative impact on SHV creation. Moreover, in the crisis period the chances of implementing a successful policy of higher spread seems to decrease due to reducing credit demand. This may be implemented through repricing the existing loan portfolio, especially the credit lines of the small business loan portfolio. In that case, a possible repricing policy might have side effects since the repayment ability of the borrower is decreased while at the same time the loan delays are increased given the negative economic environment.

Generally speaking, in a changing environment the uncertain impact of the aforementioned determinants requires that shareholder value creation can only be effectively investigated ex-post by empirical research.

4. Methodology

The divisional performance in retail branches, measured by RI (dependent variable), is linked to four independent variables related to interest income earnings and risk taking characteristics for each type of loan (consumer and small business loans). The RI is standardized by equity (RIOE) so that this ratio expresses the shareholder value created for any euro of capital invested by shareholders in the bank branch.

A linear panel model is specified to examine the determinants of shareholder value creation. As independent variables, the credit risk (CR) of consumer and small business loans relatively and the net interest spread on consumer and small business loans before provisions (S), are selected. For capturing the effect of value drivers on RI, given that liquidity shortage, a dummy variable d is introduced taking on the value of 1 in the period of the crisis and 0 otherwise. This dummy variable is multiplied separately with each of our four independent variables and thus four more variables included in our model, the coefficients of which show the supplementary impact of each independent variable on the performance in periods of credit crunch.

Below is illustrated the fixed-effects model specification assuming constant slope coefficients but intercepts that vary over time or individual branches (Baltagi, 2005).

$$RIOE_{it} = a + \mu_{\iota} + \lambda_{t} + b_1 Scon_{it} + b_2 CRcon_{it}$$
$$+ b_3 Ssbl_{it} + b_4 CRsbl_{it}$$
$$+ b_5 d * Scon_{it} + b_6 d * CRcon_{it} \quad (1)$$
$$+ b_7 Ssbl_{it} + b_8 CRsbl_{it} + u_{it}$$

Where, RIOE = Residual income on equity
α = Intercept.
i = 1,….. 27 , denoting retail branches.
t = 1, …..60 , corresponding months.
b_1..b_{11} = constant slope coefficients for independent variables.
μ_i = dummy variable coefficient for each branch i.
λ_t = dummy variable coefficient for each month t.
u_{it} = disturbance term varies with branches and time.
CRcons= Credit Risk on consumer loans
CRsbl= Credit Risk on small business loans
Scons = Net interest spread on consumer loans
Ssbl = Net interest spread on small business loans
d = Indicator dummy variable, 1 for the crisis and 0 otherwise.

In the above fixed effects model differences across branches are captured in differences in the constant term μ_i and differences over time in the constant term of λ_t. The branch specific effects and period specific effects are assumed fixed parameters to be estimated as coefficients of branch dummies and period dummies for each retail branch and for each period in the sample respectively. The estimations of the above two-way fixed effects specification are corrected for serial correlation and time varying variances in the disturbances by using the White (period) robust coefficient variance method (White, 1980). It is worth noting, that since the study explores the liquidity shortage effects on lending spreads and credit risk quality where there is an exogenous shock to the banking sector, the results are expected to not suffer from endogeneity problems. A possible limitation of the methodology is related with the risk of omitting other significant value drivers such as branch manager's skills, product diversification etc. However, the use of a panel data model with the incorporation of branch specific fixed effects captures adequately these omitted variables and thus reduces the omitted variable bias.

To test the fit of the above fixed-effects model to the data set, several tests are performed. It is worth pointing out that since the paper deals with fixed effects at the branch and year level, the omitted variables bias is reduced. Also, there are no endogeneity issues related to the results given that the paper investigates exogenous shock value effects to the banking industry. As regards the statistical tests (see below

Table 2, Panel B), initially a basic F-test is run for joint parameter insignificance. With an F-statistic of 284.1, the Ho at the 1% level is rejected and thus the model does not show a misspecification. The next step is to test that branch specific effects exist. An F-test is employed with the Ho that all the coefficients of branch dummies are redundant and equal to zero. With an F- statistic of 7.63 the Ho is rejected at the 1% level. Also, the null that all the coefficients of time-dummies are jointly equal to zero is rejected (F-statistic of 18.52), as well as all the coefficients of branch dummies and time dummies are jointly equal to zero (F - statistic of 15.28). Results therefore suggest that individual branch specific effects and time period effects exist and the appropriate model is the proposed fixed-effects model. The final test is to examine that the effects are fixed and not random. The Hausman test statistic (Hausman, 1978) with a value of 29.33 rejects the null hypothesis that independent variables are not correlated with the branch specific effect. In summary, the results of the above tests conducted suggest that the fixed effects model produces efficient coefficient estimates.

5. Data and empirical results

5.1 Data

As mentioned above the study's original data set is derived from a branch network of a systemic commercial bank spread across Greece for the period January 2006 to December 2010. The stepwise sampling process in order to form the observation set of homogeneous branches for this study is presented below: First, within the bank's entire branch network consisting of over 300 branches with different structure of their business, the paper focuses on almost 250 branches providing similar services to individuals and small sized enterprises (pure retail banking). Second, mature branches with an operation of more than six years, are selected. The intuition is that the age of branch substantially influences the calculation of loan loss impairments and, by extension, the quality of branch loans portfolio. After this adjustment, the data set is ended up with 130 branches. In addition, a sample restriction is introduced with respect to the usage of similar services (e.g. number of employees) from the selected branches. Small-sized branches (number of employees less than six according to the bank's definition) are excluded since they considered being less developed, thus 80 branches are remained. Since the aim of the paper is to conduct an extensive analysis of value drivers by manually gathering a series of monthly P&L statements in their original format, more than 30% of the bank's purely branch network by selecting through a random sampling technique 27 branches symmetrically spread across Greece (criterion of geographic dispersion), is decided to be analyzed. In total, the study's data sample is a balanced panel with 27 retail branches.

5.2 Definition of variables

As described above, the RI as a proxy for the shareholder value creation of the sample retail branches. Thus,

$$RI_{it} = (ROE_{it} - c_{et})xE_{i,t/t-1} \qquad (2)$$

Where:

RI_{it} = Residual income of bank branch i in month t.
ROE_{it} = Return on equity of branch i in month t.
c_{et} = Cost of equity of bank in month t.
$E_{i,t/t-1}$ = Average equity of bank branch i in month t and t-1.

The return on equity of bank branch i in month t, is defined as net operating income stemming from lending operations divided by the average allocated equity of bank branch i in month t and t-1. The equity employed by each branch is obtained by applying the capital requirements for retail exposures, against credit and operational risk (Basel II via Bank of Greece Governor's Act: No 2588 & No 2590, 20/08/2007). In particular, the capital requirement for credit risk is calculated by the sum of the risk weighted loans of each branch (weight 75% for mortgages, consumer, small business loans and credit cards) multiplied by the Basle capital ratio 8%. For the operational risk, the required capital is calculated by multiplying the three-year average operating income before taxes and loan provisions, by 12%.

Operating income from lending operations is derived if from income from consumer and small business loans we subtract costs and loan loss impairments for these types of loans. Loan's income is calculated as the sum of net interest income (interest revenue less interest expense) as reported in branches P&L statements. Net interest income from loans is defined as the difference between interest earned on loans and cost of funding (market price), multiplied by the loans balance. Total costs are comprised of staff costs and non-staff costs. To allocate costs to lending operation, the portion of loan's income to total branch income is considered. Loan loss impairments are the sum of loss impairments for consumer (include and credit cards) and small business loans. Impairment loss is an amount which has been created against identified credit losses and is calculated on a monthly basis. The bank of our study creates a loan loss provision on a portfolio basis using as observable data the day's payments loans and credit cards are overdue (IAS 39). Regarding the cost of equity at the retail branch, it is approximated it with the overall cost of equity of the bank (Gross, 2006; Dermine, 2009). The bank's cost of equity capital is calculated looking at the shareholders expected rate of return that is estimated by using the Capital Asset Pricing Model (CAPM) framework.

The descriptive statistics of the estimated dependent and independent variables are presented in Table 1 for both the total period, the expansion period and the crisis period respectively. The average monthly value created for any Euro of capital invested by shareholders in the bank branch for the total period is Euro 0.013 (i.e.

the average RIOE decreased substantially from 0.031 in the expansion period to a negative value -0.009 in the crisis period). Looking at the mean values for credit risk and lending spreads for both loan portfolios, it is observed generally for the total period that the spread of consumer loans (0.079) was almost twice than the corresponding spread of small business loans (0.043). The spread of consumer loans presented a marginal decrease during the crisis period (i.e. from 0.080 to 0.078) while the spread of business loans increased during the crisis period (i.e. from 0.040 to 0.048) because of the repricing policy that the business unit of small business loans adopted. As regards the risk structure of the studied branch network, the risk of consumer loans (0.458) in the expansion period was higher than the risk of small business loans (0.0271). This is logical since consumer loans are unsecured and this is reflected to their higher rates. The coming of the crisis increased substantially both the credit risk of consumer and small business loans portfolio thus covering totally the monthly generated interest income. Finally, the model was checked for multicollinearity problems through estimating correlation coefficients between the independent variables (i.e. they found less than 15%)

Table 1. Descriptive statistics of the dependent and independent variables (monthly average data for the total period, the expansion period and the crisis period)

	RIOE	SPREAD CONC	RISK CONS	SPREAD SB	RISK SB
Entire period (January 2006 – December 2010)					
mean	0.013	0.079	1.111	0.043	0.926
max	0.130	0.126	12.682	0.105	26.061
min	-0.130	0.027	0.000	0.005	0.000
std dev	0.032	0.010	1.589	0.009	1.980
Expansion period (January 2006 – August 2008)					
	RIOE	**SPREAD CONC**	**RISK CONS**	**SPREAD SB**	**RISK SB**
mean	0.031	0.080	0.458	0.040	0.271
max	0.072	0.126	1.608	0.105	3.562
min	-0.048	0.027	0.000	0.005	0.000
std dev	0.013	0.007	0.251	0.007	0.327
Crisis period (September 2008 – December 2010)					
	RIOE	**SPREAD CONC**	**RISK CONS**	**SPREAD SB**	**RISK SB**
mean	-0.009	0.078	1.856	0.048	1.674
max	0.130	0.107	12.682	0.074	26.061
min	-0.130	0.041	0.006	0.026	0.003
std dev	0.033	0.013	2.074	0.008	2.690

Notes: RIOE: residual income on equity employed, as an indicator of shareholder value created for any euro of capital invested by shareholders in the bank; Risk CONS: Credit Risk on consumer loans; Risk SB: Credit Risk on small business loans; Spread CONS: Net interest spread on consumer loans; Spread SB: Net interest spread on small business loans

5.3 Econometric results

In Table 2 are presented the efficient coefficient estimates of the fixed-effects model (Panel A) and the redundant fixed effects tests (Panel B).

Table 2. The association of RIOE with the independent drivers of Greek retail branches estimated with a fixed effects model and the results of the redundant fixed effects tests.

***Panel A**: regression results*

Variable	Coefficient	t-statistic
Constant	-0.0170	2.010**
Spread on Consumer Loans (Scon)	0.1445	2.879 ***
Credit risk on Consumer Loans (CRcon)	-0.0049	-4.413***
Spread on Small Business Loans (Ssbl)	0.5258	4.202 ***
Credit risk on small business loans (CRsbl)	-0.0010	1.667*
d*Scon	0.3548	2.973***
d*CRcon	-0.0042	-2.105**
d*Ssbl	-0.3439	-2.170**
d*CRsbl	-0.0023	-2.010 **
R^2	0.7378	
χ^2 statistic (Hausman test)	29.33	
Probability (Hausman test)	0.0000	

***Panel B** : redundant FEs tests*

Effects test	Statistic	Probability
Cross – section F	7.632	0.000
Cross – section χ^2	198.041	0.000
Period F	18.526	0.000
Period χ^2	875.070	0.000
Cross- section/period F	15.288	0.000
Cross-section/period χ^2	998.013	0.000

***Notes**: Dependent variable: RIOE*
Number of cross-sections used: 27
Number of time- periods: 60
Total panel (balanced observations): 1,620.
*RIOE: residual income on equity employed, as an indicator of shareholder value created for any euro of capital invested by shareholders in the bank; CRcons: Credit Risk on consumer loans; CRsbl: Credit Risk on small business loans; Scons: Net interest spread on consumer loans; Ssbl: Net interest spread on small business loans; d :dummy variable, 1 for the crisis and 0 otherwise d*CRcon, d*CRsbl, d*Ssbl, ,d*Scon: the coefficients of these variables*

measure the supplementary impact of each independent variable on the inefficiency score given the crisis occurred.
*Statistical Significance Index: *** at 1%, **at 5%, * at 10%; The model is estimated on the basis of a two-way Fixed Effects specification and the estimates are corrected for serial correlation and time varying variances in the disturbances by using the White (period) robust coefficient variance method. The reported R-squared (estimated by e-views which is based on the difference between the residual sums of squares form the estimated model and the sums of squares from a single constant only specification, not from a fixed effects only specification) describes the explanatory power of the entire specification including the estimated fixed effects.*

Looking at the results, firstly the impact of spread on Consumer Loans on RI is analyzed. This specific earning factor related to the consumer loan portfolio creates value as shown by the positive and statistically significant coefficient (+ 0.1445) at the 1% level. The crisis causes an increase of the value of the coefficient by 0.354, bringing the total effect to + 0.4985 (0.1445 + 0.354).

Regarding the impact of credit risk of consumer loans on value creation is found that higher credit risk destroys value as shown by the negative and statistically significant coefficient (- 0.0049) at the 1% level. The crisis period destroys value more, increasing the value of that specific coefficient by – 0.0042 (statistically significant at the 5%), bringing the total effect to – 0.0091 ((-0.0049 + (- 0.0042)).

Moreover, an increase in spread of small business loans creates shareholder value as shown by the positive and statistically significant coefficient (+ 0.5258) at the 1% level. The crisis period decreases the effect of that factor by – 0.3439, bringing the total effect to + 0.1819 (0.5258-0.3439).

Finally, an increase in credit risk from granting small business loans destroys shareholder value as shown by the negative and statistically significant coefficient (- 0.0010) at the 10% level. The crisis period destroys value more, increasing the value of that specific coefficient by – 0.0023 (statistically significant at the 5%), bringing the total effect to – 0.0033 ((-0.0010 + (- 0.0023)). Table 3 summarizes the above relationships.

Table 3. Summary of the results (impact on value determinants on RIOE, taking into account the financial crisis)

	Variable	Policy field	Total period		Crisis period		Incremental impact of each factor in the crisis period (2)	
			sign	St. sign. (1)	sign	St. sign. (1).	Non Statistical significant	Statistical significant
1	Consumer loans income/Consumer loans balance	Spread of Consumer loans (earnings)	+	***	+	***		↑***

	Variable	Policy field	Total period		Crisis period		Incremental impact of each factor in the crisis period (2)	
			sign	St. sign. (1)	sign	St. sign. (1).	Non Statistical significant	Statistical significant
2	Consumer loan loss impairments/Consumer loans income	Credit risk (Quality) of Consumer loans	-	***	-	*		↑*
3	Small business loans income/Small business loans balance	Spread of Small Business Loans (earnings)	+	***	-	**		↓***
4	Small business loans impairments/Small business loans income	Credit risk (Quality) of Small business loans	-	***	-	***		↑***

Notes: (1) Statistical Significance Index: *** at 1%, **at 5%, * at 10%.

(2) Denotes the incremental impact (increase or decrease) of each factor on RIOE - given that the crisis occurs- along with its statistically significance.

6. Discussion and conclusions

The main research objective of the paper was to investigate what explains changes on performance of banks over time exploiting the advantages of a unique monthly data set. In particular, the paper analyzed for the first time to which extent is the quality and the spread on consumer and small business loans, responsible for the increases or decreases in branch performance ((measured by the reliable RI approach (Fiordelisi & Molyneux, 2010; Gross, 2006)), over time. Also, it is tested under liquidity shortage conditions, where it is expected the loans spread to be increased and the quality of loans to be decreased, to which extent the above drivers were responsible for the decrease or increase in RI. Due to the non-existence of higher quality secondary data, the non-published monthly P&L statements of 27 retail branches of one of the four systemic commercial banks in Greece were utilized. Generally, a research design in retail banking performance should be based on internal data of bank branches of a specific banking institution and not be performed across competing banking institutions since the definition of the retail segment considerably varies across banks (Gross, 2006). Obviously, to conduct a comparative study is unrealistic because of the difficulty to get access to more than one bank. Nevertheless, this limitation does not necessarily prevent generalization of findings from a certain case study since strategic players within retail banking industry are basically similar thus their branches are very comparable. Thus, the data set is representative as the Greek banking industry is very oligopolistic and quite homogeneous operating in commercial banking, mainly retail banking.

The paper finds that the lending spread earned on consumer and small business loans and credit risk-taking on these loans, are all significantly associated with the RI, but with a different statistical sign. In particular, it is found that the value driver of spread of consumer and small business loans increased RI significantly, confirming the findings of Gross (2006), Fiordelisi and Molyneux (2010) and Dermine (2010). This finding reveals that the effect of higher interest income related to higher spreads for both the small business loan and consumer portfolio seems to over compensate the risk that high interest margins may lead to a decrease on credit quality. Also, the positive effect of the spread of small business loans on RI, was found to be higher than the spread of consumer loans. Regarding the external environmental change effects, the crisis increases even more the positive value effect of the spread of consumer's loans. However, lending spreads on small business loans lose their dynamic during the crisis period causing a statistical significant reduction in RI. This destructive value effect of lending spreads during the crisis indicates that the adoption of a repricing policy to the small business loans portfolio (i.e. as it explained analytically in the theoretical framework section above) seems to not be the appropriate due to the side effects that repricing loan policy activates. In particular, the credit policy to increase contractual loan rates of credit lines seems to reduce the repayment ability of small business loan borrowers thus exacerbating even more the accumulation of loan loss impairments, given and the unfavorable external environment under which loan delays -by definition- increase substantially.

Regarding the impact of credit risk taking on value creation, it is observed that higher credit risk destroys value for both loan portfolios. This result stands in line with the results of Fiordelisi and Molyneux (2010) and Gross (2006). Moreover, (in the crisis period) the enormous increase of loan loss impairments relative to the income of loans (credit risk) exercises an extra negative impact on RI thus further accelerating shareholder value destruction, for both loan portfolios. Combining the empirical results for both value drivers as regards the consumer loan portfolio, the paper concludes that the crisis increases the positive value effect of the spread factor while increases even more the negative value effect of credit risk due to the unstable economic environment. On the contrary, for the small business loan portfolio, the crisis decreases the generally positive value effect of the spread factor while increases even more the negative value effect of credit risk. On average, the negative value effect of credit risk for small business loans was higher than consumer loans, (almost doubled), relative to their pre-crisis value effects levels. These differences in the empirical results can be explained by the different strategic policies that two bank business units (i.e. consumer loans business unit and small business loans business unit) followed during crisis in their attempt to minimize the negative consequences of the unfavorable environment. The business unit of consumer loans followed a strategic policy of restructuring immediately its portfolio through securing loans with collateral (reducing in some cases the loan rates), while the small business banking segment followed a different policy through proceeding to an upward repricing of small business loans with low rates, reflecting in this way the higher banks cost funding. Therefore, it is demonstrated that the policy of restructuring directly the loan portfolio held back the expected increase in loan loss provisions for consumer loans (due to loan delays), while at the same time the repricing policy on small business loans resulted in multiple shareholder value destruction through the negative effect of credit risk and lending spread.

The study findings have important strategic implications: Firstly, in the crisis period, it appears that the strategic priority for the bank management should be the reorganization of loan portfolios given the negative value impact of credit risk. This finding stresses the importance of setting rules to manage credit risk, hence supporting the post-crisis initiatives taken by policymakers in the EU (European Banking Authority -EBA-, 2014) for the effective management of NPL and arrears, attempting to achieve a single evaluation approach of credit portfolios by European banks. Secondly, the destructive value effect of lending spreads during the crisis indicates that the adoption of a repricing policy to the small business loan's portfolio is not appropriate and seems to reduce the repayment ability of borrowers. Overall, the empirical findings can have important implications for the assessment of the quality of bank performance and the change of its dynamic in the turbulent crisis environment, for both the bank managers and the policymakers. Given the similarities of the Greek Economy with other bank-driven European economies, the empirical results offer useful lessons to other EU peripheral crisis economies such as Italy, Spain, and Portugal with contiguous banking operations (e.g. pure retail banking) revealing the important role of crisis in the total value creation process. Future research in branch networks of these countries would be of interest in order to check for any possible similarities and differences in the factors that influence shareholder value.

References

Athanasoglou, P., Brissimis, S. & Delis, M. (2008) "Bank specific, industry specific and macroeconomic determinants of bank profitability", *Journal of International Financial Markets, Institutions and Money*, 18: 121-136

Baltagi, B. (2005) *Econometric Analysis of Panel Data*, 3rd Edition, John Wiley&Sons

Bank of Greece (June 2009) *Financial Stability Report*, Bank of Greece, Athens

Bank of Greece (July 2010) *Financial Stability Report*, Bank of Greece, Athens. Available at: http://www.bankofgreece.gr/BogEkdoseis/fstability201007_en.pdf

Bank of Greece, Governor's Acts No 2588, 2589, 2590, 20/08/2007. Bank of Greece, Athens

Beccalli, E., Casu, B. & Girardone, C. (2006) "Efficiency and stock performance in European banking", *Journal of Business Finance and Accounting*, 33: 218–235

Brissimis, S., Delis, M. & Papanikolaou, N. (2008) "Exploring the nexus between banking sector reform and performance: Evidence from newly acceded EU countries", *Journal of Banking and Finance,* 32: 2674- 2683

Dermine, J. (2009) *Bank Valuation and Value – Based Management*, 1st Edition McGraw – Hill

Dermine, J. (2010) "Bank valuation with an application to the implicit duration of non-maturing deposits", *International Journal of Banking, Accounting and Finance*, vol. 2, no. 1: 1-30

Deville, A. (2009) "Branch Banking Network Assessment Using DEA: A Benchmarking Analysis — A Note", *Management Accounting Research*, 20, 252-261

Dietrich, A., & Wanzenried, G. (2011) "Determinants of bank profitability before and during the crisis: Evidence from Switzerland", *Journal of International Financial Markets, Institutions and Money,* 21: 307-327

European Banking Authority –EBA-. (February 2014) A final draft: Implementing of technical standards on Supervisory reporting on forbearance and non-performing exposures under article 99(4) of Regulation (EU) No 575/2013. Available at: https://www.eba.europa.eu/documents/10180/449824/EBA-ITS-2013-03+Final+draft+ITS+on+Forbearance+and+Non-performing+exposures.pdf

Feltham, G. & Ohlson, J. (1995) "Valuation and Clean Surplus Accounting for Operating and Financial Activities", *Contemporary Accounting Research*, vol. 11: 689-731

Fiordelisi, F. (2002) "Shareholder Value and the Clash in Performance Measurement: Are Banks special?", *Working paper* at the University of Wales Bangor

Fiordelisi, F. (2007) "Shareholder value efficiency in European banking", *Journal of Banking and Finance*, 31: 2151-2171

Fiordelisi, F. & Molyneux, P. (2007) "Value Creation in Banking", *working paper*. Available at https://papers.ssrn.com/sol3/papers2.cfm?abstract_id=965441

Fiordelisi, F. & Molyneux P. (2010) "The determinants of shareholder value in European banking", *Journal of Banking and Finance,* vol. 35: 1189-1200

Fiordelisi, F., Marquez – Ibanez, D. & Molyneux, P. (2011) "Efficiency and risk-taking in European banking", *Journal of Banking and Finance,* vol. 35: 1315-1326

Garcia-Herrero, A., Gavila, S. & Santabarbara, D. (2009) "What explains the low profitability of Chinese banks?", *Journal of Banking and Finance*, 33: 2080-2092

Goddard, J., Molyneux, P. & Wilson, J. (2004) "The profitability of European Banks: a cross sectional and dynamic panel analysis", The Manchester School, vol. 72: 363-381

Gross, S. (2006) *Banks and Shareholder Value. An overview of Bank Valuation and Empirical Evidence on Shareholder value for Banks,* 1st Edition DUV Gabler Edition Wissenschaft

Hausman, J. (1978) "Specification Tests in Econometrics", *Econometrica*, vol. 46:1251 -71

Hsiao, C. (2003) *Analysis of Panel Data*, 2nd edition, Cambridge

Koller, T., Goedhart, M. & Wessels, D. (2005) *Measuring and Managing the Value of Companies*, 4th edition, Mc Kinsey & Company

Lepetit, L., Nys, E., Rous, P. & Tarazi, A. (2008) "Bank income structure and risk: an empirical analysis of European Banks", *Journal of Banking and Finance*, vol. 32: 1452-1467

Mundlak, Y. (1978) "On the Pooling of Time Series and Cross Section Data", *Econometrica*, vol. 46: 69-85

Salas, V. & Saurina, J. (2003) "Deregulation, market power and risk behavior in Spanish Banks", *European Economic Review*, vol. 47: 1061-1075

Uyemura, D., Kantor, C. & Pettit, J. (1996) "EVA for Banks: Value creation, Risk Management and Profitability Measurement", *Journal of Applied Corporate Finance*, vol. 9: 94-113

White, H. (1980) "A Heteroskedasticity- Consistent covariance matrix estimator and a direct test for heteroscedasticity", *Econometrica*, vol. 48: 817-838

[i] This adverse environment negatively affected the performance of the Greek banking system. The number of non-performing loans increased gradually from 2008 onwards. In particular, the overall NPL ratio of Greek banks rose to 7.7% in 2009, from 5.0% in 2008 and more than doubled in 2010 from its 2008 levels (Bank of Greece, 2010).

6

Impression management in the letters to shareholders of listed entities

Maria-Silvia Săndulescu[a,1] and Cătălin-Nicolae Albu[a]

[a] *The Bucharest University of Economic Studies, Romania*

Abstract: There is recent increased interest in investigating the way corporate reports are used to convey management's view of organizational performance. While previous research was mainly conducted in developed economies, the case of emerging economies in Southeast Europe provides new insights as these countries are characterized by poorer corporate governance mechanisms, a lack of transparency and higher ownership concentration. We fill this gap in literature by investigating the letters to shareholders issued by OMV Petrom, the largest oil and gas producer in Southeast Europe. Using content analysis, we evaluate the tone used by managers in their disclosures in order to identify any reporting biases via impression management techniques. Even though OMV Petrom is perceived in literature as a benchmark for reporting transparency, our results provide evidence of promotional aspects used in corporate narratives.

Keywords: impression management; content analysis; financial performance; tone; corporate narratives; emerging economies.

[1] *Corresponding author:* Department of Accounting and Auditing, The Bucharest University of Economic Studies, Piața Romană no. 6–8, sector 1, București, Romania. ; email: maria.sandulescu@cig.ase.ro

1. Introduction

In this paper we analyse the letters to shareholders issued by OMV Petrom, a Romanian entity listed on the Bucharest Stock Exchange (ro. Bursa de Valori Bucureşti-BVB), to detect any reporting biases via impression management (IM) techniques. IM has recently become a favourite research topic, as literature shows that the purpose of corporate narratives is not always to increase the transparency by reducing the information asymmetry between the managers and actual and potential investors (Clatworthy & Jones, 2006; Merkl-Davies & Brennan, 2007; Rutherford, 2005). While most IM research has been conducted in western developed settings, little is known about such behaviours potentially affecting organizational reporting in emerging economies, particularly geographically located in Southeast Europe (SEE).

OMV Petrom is the largest Romanian company and the largest oil and gas producer in SEE. The company is part of the OMV Group, and its main shareholders (as stated on the company's website as of 31 December 2017) are OMV Aktiengesellschaft (holding 51 % of the shares), the Romanian State through the Ministry of Energy (20.6% of the shares), Fondul Proprietatea (9.9% of the shares), and the rest being held by other shareholders. In 2004 the former Romanian company Petrom was subject to a contested privatization (Lupu & Sandu, 2017). The company was profitable until 2015, when it incurred its first time ever loss. This short period is characterized by a deep contrast, as OMV Petrom obtained in 2013 the highest profit ever recorded in Romania (Musgociu, 2014). Consequently, we are looking at the letters to shareholders issued by OMV Petrom between 2012 and 2015, which gives us an opportunity to reflect potential IM practices and identify any differences that may arise between profit and loss periods.

The increasing interest in understanding the communication process between companies and its stakeholders has heightened the need for analysing the IM strategies used by managers to favourably portray the investment image (Brennan & Merkl-Davies, 2013). From an economic perspective, rooted in the agency theory, IM may arise when managers (as rational decision makers) take advantage of the information asymmetry that exists between them and the shareholders (who are subject to bounded rationality) (Krische, 2005; Merkl-Davies & Brennan, 2011; Schrand & Walther, 2000). The managers' inherent motivation is the maximization of their own wealth (Merkl-Davies & Brennan, 2011; Yekini *et al.*, 2016). Therefore, as negative organizational outcomes may generate conflicts of interest between the principal and the agent, „management has economic incentives to disclose messages that convey good performance more clearly than those conveying bad performance" (Rutherford, 2003: 189). This reporting bias concerning the companies' financial performance will further result in short-term capital misallocations (Merkl-Davies & Brennan, 2007). Also, IM strategies may be as subtle as to be imperceptible (Henry, 2008), hence one must be careful as they may contradict the faithful representation of information (Beattie & Jones, 2000; Clatworthy & Jones, 2003, 2006; Guillamón-Saorín & Martínez-López, 2013).

Even if narratives may be partly used to build brands and manage impressions, some research supports the incremental value of the information disseminated by companies (Baginski *et al.,* 2000; Dainelli *et al.,* 2013; Yekini *et al.,* 2016; Yuthas *et al.,* 2002) by underlining the contribution of narratives to the reduction of informational asymmetries (Yekini *et al.,* 2016). In addition, it is considered that companies' reputation (Yekini *et al.,* 2016), share price and cost of capital (Merkl-Davies & Brennan, 2011) can be negatively impacted as a result of a possible identification of biased disclosures by users (Rutherford, 2005; Yekini *et al.,* 2016; Yuthas *et al.,* 2002). Evidence is therefore mixed in terms of the context and outcome of potential management attempts to manage impressions as reflected in company reports.

Although considerable research has been devoted to the study of IM in the context of developed economies such as the United States of America (e.g. Allee & DeAngelis, 2015; Henry, 2008; Price *et al.,* 2012; Yuthas *et al.,* 2002) and the United Kingdom (e.g. Clatworthy & Jones, 2003, 2006; Rutherford, 2005; Yekini *et al.,* 2016), less attention has been paid to emerging economies. Understanding whether and how these strategies may be used by entities located in the SEE countries may be extremely fruitful since they are in the pursuit of economic development, experiencing higher growth rates and profitability. It is thus a contribution of this paper that we are evaluating the way and the extent to which IM may differ in the context of emerging countries of SEE. While transparency is highly neglected by companies in the Central and Eastern European (CEE) region (Gîrbină *et al.,* 2012), OMV Petrom is perceived as being „a model of good practices" (Albu *et al.,* 2014b: 337). However, Cho et al. (2012: 35) highlight that in these conditions, users of accounting information may „fail to realize the inherent biases in the reporting, and continue to laud the practice as evidence of increased corporate transparency and accountability". We are thus mobilizing the case of OMV Petrom as an example of how corporate reporting may be influenced by management in an under-researched context, via the case study of a very large, internationally-owned entity, acting in a sensitive domain (oil and gas) and with of great national and regional importance.

From a methodological standpoint, we evaluate the tone used by management in corporate narratives in order to identify any potential reporting biases. In this respect, we identify positive and negative words as suggested in the Loughran and McDonald (2011) dictionary and Henry's (2008) wordlist in OMV's letters to shareholders issued between 2012 and 2015. Examples of such words are „efficiency", „favourable", „great", „successfully", „enhance"; examples of negative words are „decline", „failed" or „losses". Because 2015 was the first year when the company recorded a loss, it is probable that opportunistic practices may be identified (Clatworthy & Jones, 2003; Merkl-Davies & Brennan, 2011; Rutherford, 2005). Overall, we find a decreasing number of both positive and negative words used in the letters to shareholders from 2012 to 2015, correlated with a similar decrease in the lengths of the letters. Following previous research (e.g., Merkl-Davies & Brennan, 2011) we had anticipated a different number of words used in 2013 as compared to 2015. However, contrary to prior literature, our results also highlight a steep decrease in the number of both positive and negative words between 2012 and 2013 (40% decrease). This finding is surprising since 2013 was the year when the company recorded the highest profit after privatization, and there was no apparent reason to mislead the users of accounting information.

Our results also provide evidence consistent with the Pollyanna effect (Henry, 2008; Rutherford, 2005). Particularly, we identify a tendency to present the company's outcomes in a positive light, both in profit and loss periods. A lack of objectivity is therefore reflected in the use of positive relative to the use of negative keywords.

We contribute to literature in several ways. First, as foreshadowed before, we provide evidence of manipulating behaviour from an emerging economy, and the largest oil and gas company in SEE. We thus contribute to a nascent literature (e.g. Hadro *et al.,* 2017) on IM behaviour in an under-researched region of the European Union (i.e. Central and Southeast Europe), which is quite significant in size and raised increased economic interest. Second, we use a case study approach (Yin, 2014), a research method that allows for in-depth understanding of the issues under consideration. We are thus able to explore the context of a company that is representative of the reporting practices in SEE. The results of our research should therefore be useful for researchers interested in the effect of the implementation of Western-inspiration reforms in SEE; for accounting professionals and management, who should be interested in how companies' reports are looked at by users of financial information; for investors, to understand the context of rapid growth of the SEE countries; and for regulators of financial reporting and stock exchanges, who should seek evidence about the organizational financial reporting practices and how these can shape and induce unwanted investor behaviour.

The remainder of this paper is organized as follows. A review of the relevant literature is presented in section 1, while the research background is described in section 2. Section 3 sets out the methodology we applied for the purpose of this study. Results are presented in section 4. The paper concludes with a discussion of the contributions, implications and future research directions.

2. Literature review

IM has recently become a favourite research topic, as literature shows that the purpose of corporate narratives is not always to increase the transparency by reducing the information asymmetry between the managers and actual and potential investors (Clatworthy & Jones, 2006; Merkl-Davies & Brennan, 2007; Rutherford, 2005). From an economic perspective this opportunistic behaviour may be the result of the managers' intentions to maximize their remuneration (Merkl-Davies &

Brennan, 2011; Yekini *et al.,* 2016) by taking advantage on the limited rationality of the shareholders (Krische, 2005; Merkl-Davies & Brennan, 2011; Schrand & Walther, 2000). Consequently, the narrative segments of the annual reports may be used to favourably portray the financial performance of the company (Clatworthy & Jones, 2001, 2006; Riley & Luippold, 2015). This reporting bias entitles the tendency to conceal negative information and enhance positive results (Beattie & Jones, 2000; Brennan *et al.,* 2009; Merkl-Davies & Brennan, 2007, 2011). As Clatworthy and Jones (2001: 311) argued, „management may well seek to manage their narratives just as they manage other features of the annual report such as earnings".

Adverse effects, such as short term capital misallocations (Brennan & Merkl-Davies, 2013; García Osma & Guillamón-Saorín, 2011; Leung *et al.,* 2015; Merkl-Davies & Brennan, 2007) may arise especially because the annual reports are widely used in the decision making process (Clatworthy & Jones, 2003; Breton & Taffler, 2001 cited by Davison, 2008). In other words, „both lay and expert readers are open to persuasive devices and unconscious signals" (Davison, 2008: 794). As a result, knowing the IM strategies is the first step that has to be taken on the way toward understanding and interpreting the inherent purposes of the information disclosed by companies (Rutherford, 2005). Although the efficiency of these practices cannot be generalized (Rutherford, 2005), „any investor can neglect relevant aspects of information, without fully realizing that their attention is imperfect" (Hirshleifer & Teoh, 2003 cited by Krische, 2005: 265).

Previous studies (Henry, 2008; Rutherford, 2005) have argued that the tone used by companies in their disclosures may influence the users of accounting information. This IM strategy is generally referred to in the literature as thematic manipulation (e.g. Brennan *et al.,* 2009; García Osma & Guillamón-Saorín, 2011; Guillamón-Saorín & Martínez-López, 2013; Merkl-Davies & Brennan, 2007). As Yekini et al. (2016, 418) notes,

> influence is conceptualized as a cumulative series of signals in the text that, when read by the actor, gradually brings about cognitive structure change and a change in attitude (...) the more often positive tone expressions are mentioned in the text, the more likely it is that they will be influential.

Moreover, a lack of objectivity has been noticed in the use and abuse of positive words (Clatworthy & Jones, 2003, 2006; Guillamón-Saorín & Martínez-López, 2013; Rutherford, 2005) known as the Pollyanna principle (Matlin & Stang, 1978 cited by Rutherford, 2005). However, according to Rutherford (2005: 375), IM may reach its efficiency by using „a level of positive charging that users might not be expecting and thus might not allow for appropriately".

So far, IM research was mainly conducted in developed economies and it is currently still unclear whether differences may appear in emerging countries. A research background such as SEE offers several opportunities for in depth analysis since this area is characterized by poor corporate governance mechanisms (Berglöf & Pajuste, 2005), a lack of transparency, ownership concentration and less demanding users of information (Albu & Gîrbină, 2015). Significant amount of change manifested in the SEE countries after the fall of communism in the region in the late 1980s – early 1990s (Zecchini, 2013). The countries were left without any equity markets and with weak banking sectors (Mueller & Peev, 2007) and high levels of perceive corruption and discontent with government efficiency (Djankov *et al.,* 2016). However, significant pressure from international funding institutions such as the International Monetary Fund (IMF) or the World Bank (WB) has prompted sustained actions to reform the countries' political, economic and social institutions and practices. Currently, such countries enjoy one of the fastest economic growth in the European Union, have modernized their written laws and regulations, and have improved the functioning of their markets (World Economic Forum, 2016). In this context, it would be interesting to investigate the potential opportunistic management behaviour apparent in the companies' reports on the way to attracting investors or consolidate management's perception.

The IM literature in emerging economies is scarce at best. One notable exception is Hadro et al. (2017), looking at the IM practices of Polish listed firms. By using content analysis, the authors find patterns of IM techniques used by management of Polish listed firms. Results underline the importance of ownership concentration, where companies with more concentrated ownership tend to write shorter letters, particularly where there are many insiders holding shares.

We thus contribute to this literature by seeking to answer the following research question: Are corporate narratives informative or do they play a promotional role? While a promotional role will be reflected in a tendency to maintain a positive tone both in periods of profit and loss, an informational purpose will involve an objective perspective (Henry, 2008; Rutherford, 2005).

3. Research background

3.1 Romania as an emerging economy

In this study we provide evidence from Romania, a country in the pursuit of economic development, after a prolonged exposure to the negative effects of a communist ideology (Albu *et al.,* 2014a; Deaconu & Cuzdriorean, 2016). Although the economy is under the influence of European Union (EU) Directives and International Financial Reporting Standards (IFRS) (Albu & Albu, 2017) due to the EU membership, (reporting) deficiencies (and not only) still prevail. The stock market is still characterized by a low level of liquidity (Albu *et al.,* 2014a), while corporate governance principles are not properly enforced (Albu & Gîrbină, 2015). Romania has a population of almost 20 million inhabitants, making it the largest SEE member of the EU (WB, 2016a). After the fall of communism in 1989, the Romanian economic setting underwent a major reform process which involved the change from a socialist to a capitalist economy (Dobre, 2010; Piątek *et al.,* 2013). In this respect, a significant impact had the application for EU membership in 1993 (Albu & Albu, 2012; Ionaşcu *et al.,* 2014). Moreover, the WB and IMF requested several conditions to be met in order to grant the loan that could further support the economic development of the country. The subsequent results were reflected in an increase in GDP from US$ 37.4 billion (in 2000) to US$ 208.2 billion (in 2008) (WB, 2016b). Although the crisis caused a recession of around 7%, positive values were once again recorded in 2011, the current level being 4.8% (Eurostat, 2016a). This positive view is further confirmed by the declining trend of unemployment and inflation rates (Eurostat 2016b, 2017).

In a code-law country, International Accounting Standards/IFRS implementation was therefore the result of the conditions imposed by the WB, being perceived as a useful tool to influence the perception of foreign investors (Albu & Albu, 2012). Framing a positive image was necessary in a local environment where accounting is highly influenced by taxation requirements (Albu *et al.,* 2011). This situation resides in the dominant position exerted by Romania's accounting regulator, namely the Ministry of Public Finances (Albu *et al.,* 2014a). The process of implementation began in 2001 but after 2007, when Romania became an EU member, IFRS became mandatory only for consolidated listed companies and credit institutions. Although previous literature (e.g. Albu & Albu, 2017) document a good level of convergence between IFRS and the local regulations, „one cannot say that IFRS are fully understood and implemented by the Romanian companies even today, since merely imposing some standards is not enough to have them applied" (Albu *et al.,* 2011: 94). Even though the inherent benefits of IFRS are acknowledged by local users of accounting information, practitioners are still influenced by the „routines established in the pre-IFRS period" (Feleagă & Feleagă, 2016: 402).

Another condition of the WB concerned the development of the financial market (Albu & Albu, 2012). Established in 1995, the BVB still has a low level of liquidity. As stated on the BVB' website, only 86 companies are currently listed on the main regulated market and have a significant percentage of foreign or institutional investors (such as pension or investment funds). In 2001 BVB issued the first Corporate Governance Code that was further replaced by a new one in 2008. Although the formal requirements exist, the inefficient enforcement generates a low level of transparency (Albu & Gîrbină, 2015; Feleagă *et al.,* 2011). Moreover, prior literature documents the Romanian companies' tendency to „indicate compliance where it is not the case in practice" (Albu & Gîrbină, 2015: 102).

3.2 OMV-Petrom as the case firm

OMV Petrom holds a leading position in the oil and gas industry in Romania and the SEE region. The privatization of the company was part of Romania's transition from a centralized towards a market economy. The practice of Initial Public Offering (IPO) that was adopted by the CEE countries (Păun *et al.*, 2010) was also used in the case of Petrom. Although the privatization process began in 1995, the IPO prospectus was released in 2001, while the contract between the Romanian Government and the Austrian group OMV was signed in 2004 the. Since then, the contract became the main source of dispute, its conditions being highly contested by both politicians and the media. To this point, Lupu and Sandu (2017: 542) outline not only the „unfortunate and unfavourable conditions for Romania but also on the negative consequences of its high and unjustified price hikes and creation of national dependency with regards to the security of the country's energy supply". The contract was also scrutinized in the 2014 report of the Romanian Court of Accounts (Romanian Court of Accounts). According to this report, the buyer (OMV), failed to respect the Decision issued in 2009 to increase the share capital by considering the revalued amount of the lands at the moment when the privatization contract was signed. Nonetheless, OMV benefited from the write-off of several existing liabilities of Petrom's, and small royalties that the company has to pay for the Romanian natural resources (Dimitriu, 2006).

Petrom was listed for the first time on BVB in 2001 and, on the London Stock Exchange in 2016, following the secondary public offering. Petrom's free float increased from 6.62% in November 2012 to 18.3521% in September 2017, being the largest company listed on the BVB. Despite this fact, „a successful privatization from a financial and economic point of view does not automatically equate to social acceptability and legitimacy" (Lupu & Sandu, 2017: 560).

On the other hand, OMV Petrom is perceived in literature as a benchmark for reporting transparency (Albu *et al.*, 2014b; Albu *et al.*, 2011). However, Cho et al. (2012: 35) argue that in these conditions users of accounting information may „fail to realize the inherent biases in the reporting, and continue to laud the practice as evidence of increased corporate transparency and accountability". OMV Petrom thus makes a very useful and instrumental case company, one able to shed light on the reporting practices of a large entity that was transformed from a not-so-profitable state-owned institution into a very successful major player on the international oil and gas market.

4. Research methodology

This study was designed to evaluate the tone used by managers in their letters to shareholders. In this respect, the suitability of a case study is reflected in the

„opportunity to study the changes in disclosure by one company without possible contamination through the integration of different corporate values, strategies and personnel" (Tilling & Tilt, 2010: 66). Accordingly, we have gathered the corporate annual reports issued by OMV Petrom between 2012 and 2015 (4 reports) from the company's website. We considered the English version of the annual reports (and therefore the letters to shareholders) in order to ensure reproducibility (Krippendorff, 2004) and facilitate comparison with prior literature.

The period was chosen with the view of identifying potential contrasts in the reporting behaviour between high profit and loss years. While OMV Petrom's financial performance has increased during the first two years included in our analyses, the company was very negatively affected by the oil crises in the following ones. Over this period, the oil barrel price hit $49.87 (in March 2015), only to become even lower ($29.67 in January 2016), 10-year lowest price (Macrotrends, 2018). The period under consideration is however characterized by consistency regarding the company's Chief Executive Officer (CEO), Chief Financial Officer and auditor (Ernst & Young). Moreover, 2012 was the first year following privatization when the members of the supervisory board were not changed. At that time the board had 9 members, and Gerhard Roiss was the president of the Board of Directors of OMV Petrom as well as OMV's CEO. He had been a member of the board since 2004 when the company was privatized and became the new president since April 2011. He was replaced in 2015 by Rainer Seele as a result of the poor financial results incurred by OMV and OMV Petrom (Petrescu, 2014). OMV Petrom's CEO between 2006 and 2018 was Mariana Gheorghe. She was a member of the new board of directors that was appointed in 2004, when the privatization contract was signed. Starting with 2006 she has been the company's CEO and is one of the most powerful businesswoman in the world (Fortune, 2012–2014). In 2010 Mariana Gheorghe received 100 shares that were distributed free of charge, while her husband owns 60,000 shares.

Table 1 gives an overview of the characteristics of the letters to shareholders investigated (no. of pages, no. of paragraphs, no. of words) As noted from Table 1, the total length of the letter to shareholders (measured as the number of words) has significantly decreased from 2,048 words in 2012 to 1,239 in 2013 (40% decrease) and maintained a declining trend until 2015.

Table 1. Characteristics of the letters to shareholders analysed

	2012	2013	2014	2015
Pages	4	2	2	2
Paragraphs	19	11	17	11
Words	2048	1239	1233	1052

In line with prior literature (Melloni, 2015; Melloni *et al.,* 2015), manual content analysis was performed to evaluate the disclosure tone by analysing the language used in reporting. A classification of positive and negative keywords was done by using Loughran and McDonald (2011) dictionary available on the authors' website. It includes 354 positive words and 2,329 negative words that were identified by examining language in a large sample of 10-K fillings (50,115 observations consisting of 8,341 unique firms) submitted to the Securities and Exchange Commission. Examples of positive words are „efficiency", „favourable", „great", „successfully", „enhance"; examples of negative words are „decline", „failed" and „losses". This dictionary was used in accounting and finance literature for measuring the tone of the business communication (Allee & DeAngelis, 2015; Davis *et al.,* 2015; Feldman *et al.,* 2010).

Moreover, we used the positive and negative wordlists developed by Henry (2008) for analysing financial text. This wordlist includes 105 positive and 85 negative keywords, being the first one developed in the literature for financial text analysis (Loughran & McDonald, 2016). Although the number of words is smaller relative to the Loughran and McDonald (2011) dictionary, the Henry (2008) list includes 46 positive and 35 negative words that are not classified as positive or negative by Loughran and McDonald (2011). Examples of positive unique words are: „certain", „increase", „rise", „more", „record"; examples of negative unique words are: „risk", „down", „decrease", „drop". Its specificity and utility was demonstrated in previous studies that measured tone in earnings conference calls (Davis *et al.,* 2015; Price *et al.,* 2012).

In order to overcome the limitations of a computer-aided analysis, we identified the keywords in context (Krippendorff, 2004). We did not count the positive word „growth" when it was used to mention the percentage of „economic growth", or the word „up" when it was part of a phrasal verb. We also adjusted for negation and we eliminated negative words such as „lost", „injury", „unemployment", „fatalities" when they were followed by the word „rate". At this stage, a total number of 18 words were excluded. Finally, we investigated directional keywords such as „decreased", „increased", „higher" or „lower", because they can be affected by ambiguity (Henry, 2008). Disambiguation entails „distinguishing the positive versus negative context-dependent affect of the specific words" (Henry, 2008, 399). Therefore, analysing these words in context gave us the possibility to determine whether they were used in a positive or negative sense. Following Clatworthy and Jones (2003), the assessment was done from a shareholder perspective and as a result, 14 negative and 5 positive keywords were eliminated in the process of disambiguation.

We have further computed a tone measure by using the Henry (2008) formula: positive words less negative words over the sum of positive and negative words. Therefore, the tone measure is a continuous variable that takes values between -1 and 1; the closer this measure is to 1, the more positive is the tone used in the document analysed. In this respect, previous studies that have used this formula in assessing tone reported mean values of 0.568 (Henry, 2008), and 0.64 (Price *et al.*, 2012). Following previous literature, we expect the accounting narratives to be biased toward the positive especially in the two years (2014 and 2015) when the financial performance of the company started to decrease (Clatworthy & Jones, 2003; Merkl-Davies & Brennan, 2011; Rutherford, 2005).

5. Results and discussions

We identified a total number of 78 positive and 45 negative keywords in the sample period, using the wordlists developed by Loughran and McDonald (2011) and Henry (2008) (see Table 2). We found 48% of the positive words from Henry's (2008) list in the reports we used. Although Henry's (2008) wordlist comprises 105 positive words, compared to Loughran and McDonald (2011) dictionary of 354 positive words, the former has an increased specificity and applicability than the latter. However, the length of the Loughran and McDonald (2011) dictionary proved its usefulness in the analysis of negative keywords. In this respect, 27 unique keywords were identified and this offered the opportunity to analyse in depth the frequency of their occurrences.

Table 2. Number of positive and negative keywords identified

	Total	Loughran & McDonald (2011)	Henry (2008)	Both
Positive	78	28	25	25
Negative	45	27	12	6

Table 3 illustrates the frequency of positive and negative keywords identified in the sample period. An overall decrease year on year may be observed, evolution consistent with the decreasing number of total words used in the company's narratives over the same period. Following previous research (e.g. Merkl-Davies & Brennan, 2011), we anticipated a different number of words used in 2013 as compared to 2015. Even if our results confirm our expectation (a 15% decrease in the number of words used), we also note an even bigger decrease between 2012 and 2013 (i.e. 40%). This finding is surprising since 2013 was the year when the company recorded its highest profit after privatization, and there was no apparent reason to mislead the users of accounting information.

Table 3. Frequency of positive and negative keywords

	2012	2013	2014	2015
Positive	97	73	69	60
Negative	31	20	22	18
Length	2048	1239	1233	1052

Note: Length is expressed as the number of words in the letters to shareholders.

We now turn to the examination of the tone and the company's financial performance indicators. Table 4 highlights the fact that the tone was maintained positive across the entire period of analysis, with almost constant and increased values that are comparable with previous findings in the literature (Henry, 2008; Price *et al.,* 2012). In 2013 both EBIT and profit increased with 5.2% and 22.2% respectively, while the tone measure had a similar evolution (10.5 % increase). However, in 2014, when these two performance indicators decreased by almost 50%, the tone measure was reduced only to a similar but still higher value than the one in 2012. These results are further emphasized in 2015, when although the company recorded a loss, the tone measure actually increased reflecting Pollyannaish tendencies (Henry, 2008; Rutherford, 2005).

Table 4. Analysis of the tone used in the letter to shareholders and key performance indicators

	2012	2013	2014	2015
Tone	0.5156	0.5699	0.5165	0.54
EBIT	5,662.00	5,957.86	3,338.30	-529.75
Profit	3,946.10	4,824.04	2,099.67	-689.65

Notes: Tone is measured as a continuous variable taking values between -1 and 1, calculated as positive words less negative words over the sum of positive and negative words. EBIT and Profit figures are expressed in million RON. 1 EUR=4.6 RON (as of 24 October 2017).

The following quote shows how OMV Petrom's CEO presents the financial performance of the company in direct contrast with the conditions provided by the economic environment in which the company operates. The emphasis of the positive results is not surprising since in 2013 EBIT and profits increased by 5% and 22% respectively compared to 2012. The same ascending trend can be observed for the tone measure.

> In 2013, Petrom performed very well and *delivered strong* financial and operating results, in spite of *persistent* macroeconomic *challenges* in our area of operations (OMV Petrom, 2013) (emphases added).

It can be noticed how the positive keywords were linked with the image of the company, while the negative word „challenges" was used to describe the environment. This observation determined us to compare and contrast the narratives from 2013 and 2015 in order to analyse the way in which language is used in relation to the company or the environment. Table 5 provides an illustration of the most frequently used keywords in this period. We can easily remark the similarities between the two lists and the fact that only positive words are included in this ranking. Although the frequency of positive keywords slightly decreased in 2015, the choice of words is inappropriate in this period of sharp contrast between the highest profit ever recorded and the first loss after the privatization.

Table 5. Comparative analysis of the keywords used to describe the company in profit vs. loss years

2013 (profit)	Frequency	Company	2015 (loss)	Frequency	Company
Growth	7	6	Higher	6	3
Increased	4	4	Deliver	3	3
Strong	4	4	Delivered	3	3
Achieve	3	3	Efficiency	3	3
Delivered	3	3	Improved	3	3
Efficiency	3	3	Strong	3	3
High	3	3	Growth	3	2
More	3	3	Achieved	2	2
Progress	3	3	More	2	2
Achieved	3	2	Successfully	2	2

In addition, Table 6 confirms the aforementioned observation, as around 80-89% of the positive words are attributed to the company. This result is in direct contrast with the overall performance in 2015, when the financial results were negative. Consequently, we can confirm previous research that supports Pollyannaish effects (Henry, 2008; Rutherford, 2005). As shown in our case, the tone measure increased from 2014 to 2015 although the financial performance of the company decreased drastically; this positive tone is mainly used to favourably portray the company.

Table 6. Attribution of positive and negative keywords

Panel A. 2013	Total	Company		Environment	
Positive	73	65	89%	8	11%
Negative	20	5	25%	15	75%
Panel B. 2015	**Total**	**Company**		**Environment**	
Positive	60	48	80%	12	20%
Negative	18	5	28%	13	72%

Moreover, we note from Table 6 that, in relation to the company's environment, the number of positive words used in 2015 is almost similar to the number of negative words used in the same year. If the economic conditions were neutral, Petrom's 2015 negative result may be attributed to the company, although the CEO highlights mainly positive results.

Whether this bias was effective or not may be observed by analysing the context of the company. The same underperformance also manifested at the group's level. As a result, OMV's CEO Gerhard Roiss was replaced, leading to his subsequent replacement as President of Petrom's supervisory board. However, neither Petrom's CEO nor its CFO were affected by this unfavourable outcome, despite both having held executive positions in the company. At this point it becomes relevant to link with our analysis the following statement made in 2015 by Gerhard Roiss, which illustrates his overall perspective on OMV Petrom:

> If we hadn't taken over Petrom, it would have been very difficult to survive in the current climate (Romania-insider, 2015).

While this quote highlights the real value of the company that was underestimated at the moment when the privatization contract was signed, it also contributes to a better interpretation of our observations. Assuming Petrom's importance for OMV, we consider that an earlier replacement of Mariana Gheorghe would have further affected the image of Petrom, signalling an overall instability. While the company is highly scrutinized in the Romanian environment, this perspective would have damaged the idea of a successful privatization.

Considering the aforementioned arguments, our results do not support the economic perspective on IM which argues that this opportunistic behaviour may be the result of the managers' intentions to maximize their remuneration (Merkl-Davies & Brennan, 2011; Yekini *et al.,* 2016) by taking advantage of the information asymmetry that exists between them and the shareholders (Krische, 2005; Merkl-Davies & Brennan, 2011; Schrand & Walther, 2000). While this may be applicable in a diffused ownership, it is not relevant when the ownership is concentrated. Even if the tone of the narratives was positive across the entire period of analysis, the negative results of OMV Petrom triggered the replacement of the president of the supervisory board. In addition, following Fondul Proprietatea's decision to sell part of its stock, the Extraordinary General Meeting of Shareholders approved the secondary listing of OMV Petrom on the London Stock Exchange.

However, our case study suggests that IM may prove its efficiency in order to build, consolidate and eventually restore the image of a successful privatization in a highly scrutinized environment. This finding is supported by the positive tone that was kept constant across the entire period of analysis. Another incentive for using IM can also be the need to frame a favourable investment image (Brennan & Merkl-Davies, 2013) in the context of a secondary public offering. Using a positive tone to express stability even when the results of the company are negative still represents opportunistic behaviour, albeit it may be accepted by the shareholders.

6. Conclusions

In this paper we explored the tone used by the managers of OMV Petrom in their letters to shareholders in order to identify potential reporting biases. We considered the choice of positive and negative words, the frequency and context in which they were used in the letters to shareholders issued from 2012 to 2015. The results highlight the opportunistic tendency to present the company's outcomes in a positive light, both in profit and loss periods. This behaviour is consistent with the Pollyanna effect identified in prior literature (Henry, 2008; Rutherford, 2005).

The paper extends the body of work on IM (Allee & DeAngelis, 2015; Clatworthy & Jones, 2003, 2006; Feldman *et al.,* 2010; García Osma & Guillamón-Saorín, 2011; Henry, 2008; Price *et al.,* 2012; Rutherford, 2005; Yekini *et al.,* 2016; Yuthas *et al.,* 2002), by providing a new perspective from an emerging economy characterized by lack of transparency and low ownership concentration (Albu & Gîrbină, 2015).

On the one hand, individual and institutional investors may benefit from the results of this study because they „need to adopt a healthy scepticism" (Clatworthy & Jones, 2006: 506) in reading corporate narratives and not „to laud the practice as evidence of increased corporate transparency and accountability" (Cho *et al.,* 2012: 35). On the other hand, this paper will be useful for researchers, since it provides insights from an insufficiently explored research background, i.e. the case of emerging economies in SEE. Finally, accounting policy-makers and professional bodies should try to prevent and detect this opportunistic behaviour because its manifestation contradicts the faithful representation of information (Beattie & Jones, 2000; Clatworthy & Jones, 2003, 2006; Guillamón-Saorín & Martínez-López, 2013), possibly leading to capital misallocations (Merkl-Davies & Brennan, 2007).

This study is subject to inherent limitations of the methods employed. Hand-collecting data may be subject to limitations; however, the subjectivity was mitigated when identifying positive and negative words, due to the use of wordlists previously developed in the international literature. However, the number of positive and negative keywords was limited to those provided by the two dictionaries used, namely Loughran and McDonald (2011) and Henry (2008). Also, since the paper is a single-company study, results may be difficult to extrapolate in different contexts.

Future research may further investigate other IM strategies, such as causal attributions of performance outcomes. Comparisons could be performed between companies situated in several SEE countries, possibly within the same industry, to assess any country variation in IM practices. Also, an investigation of more listed companies from various industries within the same country may allow inference of conclusions at the country level. Moreover, the potential impact of managers' opportunistic behaviour on the decisions made by users of the accounting information can be explored in an experimental setting.

Acknowledgements

The authors acknowledge the guidance of the editor in chief of JAMIS and the helpful comments of Sebastian Hoffmann from University of Edinburgh Business School. An earlier version of this paper was presented at the International Conference Accounting and Management Information Systems at the Bucharest University of Economic Studies in 2017 and at the International Conference Financial Reporting and Auditing: Challenges and Opportunities for Accounting Researchers and Educators at the Cracow University of Economics in 2017. This paper was co-financed by The Bucharest University of Economic Studies during Maria-Silvia Săndulescu's PhD program.

References

Albu, C.N. & Albu, N. (2017) „The role and current status of IFRS in the completion of national accounting rules - Evidence from Romania", *Accounting in Europe,* vol.14: 177-186.

Albu, C.N., Albu, N. & Alexander, D. (2014a) „When global accounting standards meet the local context - Insights from an emerging economy", *Critical Perspectives on Accounting,* vol. 25, no. 6: 489-510.

Albu, C.N. and Gîrbină, M.M. (2015) „Compliance with corporate governance codes in emerging economies. How do Romanian listed companies 'comply-or-explain'?", *Corporate Governance: The International Journal of Business in Society,* vol. 15, no. 1: 85-107.

Albu, N. & Albu, C.N. (2012) „International Financial Reporting Standards in an emerging economy: Lessons from Romania", *Australian Accounting Review,* vol. 22, no. 4: 341-352.

Albu, N., Albu, C.N., Bunea, Ş., Calu, A.D. & Gîrbină, M.M. (2011) „A story about IAS/IFRS implementation in Romania", *Journal of Accounting in Emerging Economies,* vol. 1, no. 1: 76-100.

Albu, N., Lupu, I. & Sandu, R. (2014b) „Multinationals as vectors of corporate governance improvement in emerging economies in Eastern Europe: A case study", in Boubaker, S. and Nguyen, D. K. (Eds.), *Corporate Governance in Emerging Markets. CSR, Sustainability, Ethics & Governance*, pp. 331-349, Springer-Verlag Berlin Heidelberg.

Allee, K.D. & DeAngelis, M.D. (2015) „The structure of voluntary disclosure narratives: Evidence from tone dispersion", *Journal of Accounting Research,* vol. 53, no. 2: 241-274.

Baginski, S.P., Hassell, J.M. & Hillison, W.A. (2000) „Voluntary causal disclosures: Tendencies and capital market reaction", *Review of Quantitative Finance and Accounting,* vol. 15, no. 4: 371-389.

Beattie, V. & Jones, M.J. (2000) „Impression management: The case of inter-country financial graphs", *Journal of International Accounting, Auditing & Taxation,* vol. 9, no. 2: 159-183.

Berglöf, E. & Pajuste, A. (2005) „What do firms disclose and why? Enforcing corporate governance and transparency in Central and Eastern Europe", *Oxford Review of Economic Policy,* vol. 21, no. 2: 178-197.

Brennan, N.M., Guillamón-Saorín, E. & Pierce, A. (2009) „Impression management: Developing and illustrating a scheme of analysis for narrative disclosures - A methodological note", *Accounting, Auditing and Accountability Journal,* vol. 22, no. 5: 789-832.

Brennan, N.M. & Merkl-Davies, D.M. (2013) „Accounting narratives and impression management", in Jack, L., Davison, J. and Craig, R. (Eds.), *The Routledge companion to accounting communication*: 109-132, Abingdon: Routledge.

Cho, C.H., Michelon, G. & Patten, D.M. (2012) „Impression management in sustainability reports: An empirical investigation of the use of graphs", *Accounting and the Public Interest,* vol. 12: 16-37.

Clatworthy, M.A. & Jones, M.J. (2001) „The effect of thematic structure on the variability of annual report readability", *Accounting, Auditing and Accountability Journal,* vol. 14, no. 3: 311-326.

Clatworthy, M.A. & Jones, M.J. (2003) „Financial reporting of good news and bad news: Evidence from accounting narratives", *Accounting and Business Research,* vol. 33, no. 3: 171-185.

Clatworthy, M.A. & Jones, M.J. (2006) „Differential patterns of textual characteristics and company performance in the chairman's statement", *Accounting, Auditing and Accountability Journal,* vol. 19, no. 4: 493-511.

Dainelli, F., Bini, L. & Giunta, F. (2013) „Signaling strategies in annual reports: Evidence from the disclosure of performance indicators", *Advances in Accounting, incorporating Advances in International Accounting,* vol. 29, no. 2: 267-277.

Davis, A.K., Ge, W., Matsumoto, D. & Zhang, J.L. (2015) „The effect of manager-specific optimism on the tone of earnings conference calls", *Review of Accounting Studies,* vol. 20, no. 2: 639-673.

Davison, J. (2008) „Rhetoric, repetition, reporting and the 'dot.com' era: words, pictures, intangibles", *Accounting, Auditing and Accountability Journal,* vol. 21, no. 6: 791-826.

Deaconu, A. & Cuzdriorean, D.D. (2016) „Accounting and the state in post-communist Romania", *African Journal of Accounting, Auditing and Finance,* vol. 5, no. 1: 59-93.

Dimitriu, S. (2006) „Contractul de privatizare 'Petrom' - sfatul înțelepților' [The privatization contract of 'Petrom'- wise men counsel]", *Bursa*, 4 December, available on-line at http://www.bursa.ro/energia-contractul-de-privatizare-petrom-sfatul-inteleptilor-2358&s=companii_afaceri&articol=2358.html (Accessed 7 November 2017).

Djankov, S., Nikolova, E. & Zilinsky, J. (2016) „The happiness gap in Eastern Europe", *Journal of Comparative Economics,* vol. 44, no. 1: 108-124.

Dobre, A.M. (2010) „Europeanization and new patterns of multi- level governance in Romania", *Southeast European and Black Sea Studies,* vol. 10, no. 1: 59-70.

Eurostat (2016a) „Real GDP growth, 2006-2016", available on-line at http://ec.europa.eu/eurostat/statistics-explained/index.php/File:Real_GDP_growth,_2006-2016_(%25_change_compared_with_the_previous_year;_%25_per_annum)_YB17.png (Accessed 7 November 2017).

Eurostat (2016b) „Unemployment rate 2005-2016", available on-line at http://ec.europa.eu/eurostat/statistics-explained/index.php/File:Unemployment_rate_2005-2016_(%25)_new.png (Accessed 7 November 2017).

Eurostat (2017) „HICP - inflation rate", available on-line at http://ec.europa.eu/eurostat/tgm/table.do?tab=table&init=1&language=en&pcode=tec00118&plugin=1 (Accessed 7 November 2017).

Feldman, R., Govindaraj, S., Livnat, J. & Segal, B. (2010) „Management's tone change, post earnings announcement drift and accruals", *Review of Accounting Studies,* vol. 15, no. 4: 915-953.

Feleagă, L. & Feleagă, N. (2016) „Romania. Shifting to IFRS: The case of Romania", in Didier, B. and Praquin, N. (Eds.), *IFRS in a Global World*: 393-404, Cham: Springer.

Feleagă, N., Feleagă, L., Dragomir, V.D. & Bigioi, A.D. (2011) „Corporate governance in emerging economies: The case of Romania", *Theoretical & Applied Economics,* vol. 18, no. 9: 5-16.

Fortune (2012) „50 most powerful women in business", 8 October, available on-line at http://archive.fortune.com/magazines/fortune/most-powerful-women/2012/global/ (Accessed 7 November 2017).

Fortune (2013) „The International Power 50: Fortune's Most Powerful Women", 10 October, available on-line at http://fortune.com/2013/10/10/most-powerful-women-the-international-power-50/ (Accessed 7 November 2017).

Fortune (2014) „The Most Powerful Women of Europe, the Middle East and Africa", 18 September, available on-line at http://fortune.com/2014/09/18/most-powerful-women-emea/ (Accessed 7 November 2017).

Garcia Osma, B. & Guillamón-Saorín, E. (2011) „Corporate governance and impression management in annual results press releases", *Accounting, Organizations and Society,* vol. 36, no. 4: 187-208.

Gîrbină, M.M., Albu, N. & Albu, C.N. (2012) „Corporate governance disclosures in Romania", in Boubaker, S. and Nguyen, D.K. (Eds.), *Board Directors and Corporate Social Responsibility*: 122-141, Palgrave Macmillan UK.

Guillamón-Saorín, E. & Martínez-López, F.J. (2013) „Corporate financial communication and the internet: Manipulating investor audiences?", *Online Information Review,* vol. 37, no. 4: 518-537.

Hadro, D., Klimczak, K. & Pauka, K. (2017) „Impression management in letters to shareholders: Evidence from Poland", *Accounting in Europe,* vol. 14, no. 3: 305-330.

Henry, E. (2008) „Are investors influenced by how earnings press releases are written?", *Journal of Business Communication,* vol. 45, no. 4: 363-407.

Ionaşcu, M., Ionaşcu, I., Săcărin, M. & Minu, M. (2014) „IFRS adoption in developing countries: the case of Romania", *Accounting and Management Information Systems*, vol. 13, no. 2: 311-350.

Krippendorff, K. (2004) *Content analysis. An introduction to its methodology*, 2nd ed., Thousand Oaks: Sage.

Krische, S.D. (2005) „Investors' evaluations of strategic prior-period benchmark disclosures in earnings announcements", *The Accounting Review,* vol. 80, no. 1: 243-268.

Leung, S., Parker, L. & Courtis, J. (2015) „Impression management through minimal narrative disclosure in annual reports", *The British Accounting Review,* vol. 47: 275-289.

Loughran, T. & McDonald, B. (2011) „When is a liability not a liability? Textual analysis, dictionaries, and 10-Ks", *Journal of Finance,* vol. 66, no. 1: 35-65.

Loughran, T. & McDonald, B. (2016) „Textual analysis in accounting and finance: A survey", *Journal of Accounting Research,* vol. 54, no. 4: 1187-1230.

Lupu, I. & Sandu, R. (2017) „Intertextuality in corporate narratives: A discursive analysis of a contested privatization", *Accounting Auditing & Accountability Journal,* vol. 30, no. 3: 534-564.

Macrotrends (2018) „Crude Oil Prices - 70 Year Historical Chart", available on-line at http://www.macrotrends.net/1369/crude-oil-price-history-chart (Accessed 7 November 2017).

Melloni, G. (2015) „Intellectual capital disclosure in integrated reporting: An impression management analysis", *Journal of Intellectual Capital,* vol. 16, no. 3: 661-680.

Melloni, G., Stacchezzini, R. & Lai, A. (2015) „The tone of business model disclosure: An impression management analysis of the integrated reports", *Journal of Management & Governance,* vol. 20, no. 2: 295-320.

Merkl-Davies, D.M. & Brennan, N.M. (2007) „Discretionary disclosure strategies in corporate narratives: Incremental information or impression management?", *Journal of Accounting Literature,* vol. 26, no. 1: 116-194.

Merkl-Davies, D.M. & Brennan, N.M. (2011) „A conceptual framework of impression management: New insights from psychology, sociology and critical perspectives", *Accounting and Business Research,* vol. 41, no. 5: 415-437.

Mueller, D.C. & Peev, E. (2007) „Corporate governance and investment in Central and Eastern Europe", *Journal of Comparative Economics,* vol. 35, no. 2: 414-437.

Musgociu, Ș. (2014) „Petrom a obținut în 2013 un profit record pentru o companie românească" [Petrom reached in 2013 a record profit for a Romanian company], *Gândul, 19* February, available on-line at http://www.gandul.info/financiar/petrom-a-obtinut-in-2013-un-profit-record-pentru-o-companie-romaneasca-12111875 (Accessed 7 November 2017).

OMV Petrom (2013) *2013 Annual Report*, available on-line at http://www.omvpetrom.com/SecurityServlet/secure?cid=1255758867089&lang=en&swa_site=&swa_nav=&swa_pid=&swa_lang (Accessed 7 November 2017).

Păun, C., Miclăuș, P. & Ungureanu, S. (2010) „Initial public offering underpricing effect in case of Eastern European capital markets", *Transformations in Business & Economics,* vol. 9, no. 1: 289-305.

Petrescu, R. (2014) „Gerhard Roiss pleacă de la şefia OMV cu doi ani mai devreme şi lasă grupul austriac, acționarul majoritar al Petrom, 'într-o situație extrem de dificilă'[Gerhard Roiss leaves OMV two years earlier and leaves the Austrian group, the major shareholder of Petrom, 'in an extremely difficult situation']", *Ziarul Financiar*, 16 October, available on-line at http://www.zf.ro/profesii/gerhard-roiss-pleaca-de-la-sefia-omv-cu-doi-ani-mai-devreme-si-lasa-grupul-austriac-actionarul-majoritar-al-petrom-intr-o-situatie-extrem-de-dificila-13394391 (Accessed 7 November 2017).

Piątek, D., Szarzec, K. & Pilc, M. (2013) „Economic freedom, democracy and economic growth: A causal investigation in transition countries", *Post-Communist Economies*, vol. 25, no. 3: 267-288.

Price, S.M., Doran, J.S., Peterson, D.R. & Bliss, B.A. (2012) „Earnings conference calls and stock returns: The incremental informativeness of textual tone", *Journal of Banking & Finance,* vol. 36: 992-1011.

Riley, T.J. & Luippold, B.L. (2015) „Managing investors' perception through strategic word choices in financial narratives", *The Journal of Corporate Accounting & Finance,* vol. 26, no. 5: 57-62.

Romania-insider (2015) „How did Romania's Petrom save Austria's OMV?", 18 June, available on-line at https://www.romania-insider.com/how-did-romanias-petrom-save-austrias-omv/ (Accessed 7 November 2017).

Romanian Court of Accounts (2014) „Raportul public pe anul 2014" [Public report for the year 2014], available on-line at http://www.curteadeconturi.ro/Publicatii/Raport_public_2014.pdf (Accessed 7 November 2017).

Rutherford, B.A. (2003) „Obfuscation, textual complexity and the role of regulated narrative accounting disclosure in corporate governance", *Journal of Management & Governance,* vol. 7, no. 2: 187-210.

Rutherford, B.A. (2005) „Genre analysis of corporate annual report narratives: A corpus linguistics-based approach", *Journal of Business Communication,* vol. 42, no. 4: 349-378.

Schrand, C.M. & Walther, B.R. (2000) „Strategic benchmarks in earnings announcements: The selective disclosure of prior-period earnings component", *The Accounting Review,* vol. 75, no. 2: 151-177.

Tilling, M.V. & Tilt, C.A. (2010) „The edge of legitimacy. Voluntary social and environmental reporting in Rothmans' 1956-1999 annual reports", *Accounting, Auditing & Accountability Journal,* vol. 23, no. 1: 55-81.

World Bank (2016a) „World Development Indicators: Population", available on-line at https://data.worldbank.org/indicator/SP.POP.TOTL (Accessed 7 November 2017).

World Bank (2016b) „World Development Indicators: GDP", available on-line at https://data.worldbank.org/indicator/NY.GDP.MKTP.KD (Accessed 7 November 2017).

World Economic Forum (2016) „The Global Competitiveness Report 2016-2017", available on-line at http://www3.weforum.org/docs/GCR2016-2017/05 FullReport/TheGlobalCompetitivenessReport2016-2017_FINAL.pdf (Accessed 7 November 2017).

Yekini, L.S., Wisniewski, T.P. & Millo, Y. (2016) „Market reaction to the positiveness of annual report narratives", *The British Accounting Review,* vol. 48: 415-430.

Yin, R.K. (2014) *Case Study Research: Design and Methods*, 5th ed., Thousand Oaks: Sage.

Yuthas, K., Rogers, R. & Dillard, J.F. (2002) „Communicative action and corporate annual reports", *Journal of Business Ethics,* vol. 41, no. 1: 141-157.

Zecchini, S. (2013) *Lessons from the Economic Transition: Central and Eastern Europe in the 1990s*, New York: Springer Science & Business Media.

7

Accounting by SMEs – Evidence from Slovenia

Mateja Jerman[a,1]

[a] *University of Primorska, Slovenia*

Abstract: The paper aims to investigate the characteristics of financial reporting and management accounting by Slovenian Small and Medium-sized Entities (SMEs), which represent 99.8% of all Slovene enterprises. The paper examines the most important legal bases for external financial reporting of SMEs, rules in national accounting standards and their close linkage with taxation. The paper highlights how Slovenia adopted the relevant European Union (EU) Directives and emphasizes the particularities of the Slovenian environment that demonstrate diversity at the international level. The paper raises issues concerning lenient requirements on accounting practitioners' qualifications and a lack of supervision of financial statements. We then provide a literature review of relevant studies in the field of financial and management accounting. The financial accounting literature seems to be more developed than that of management accounting. Studies reviewed in this paper mainly focused on the link between financial accounting and taxation, indicating that the use of accounting discretion is motivated by the effort to minimize taxation.

Keywords: SMEs, financial reporting, financial accounting, management accounting, Slovenia

1. Introduction

The Slovenian economy is influenced by the continental European accounting system in which capital is mainly provided by the banking sector, law provides detailed accounting rules, financial accounting is closely connected with taxation, the primary users of financial statements are creditors and tax authorities, and there

[1] *Corresponding author:* University of Primorska, Faculty of Management, Cankarjeva 5, 6101 Koper, Slovenia; E-mail address: mateja.jerman@fm-kp.si

is a tendency towards limiting the extent of disclosures (Haller & Walton, 2003). Slovenia is interesting in this regard for several reasons. Since the country became independent in 1991 the business environment has been characterized by the privatization process (ownership transformation), followed by internationalization and the access of Slovenia into the EU (2004). All these circumstances have affected the development of the corporate reporting system.

Small and medium-sized entities (SMEs) are essential to the Slovenian economy. They represent 99.8% of all national enterprises, their share in employment amounts to 70% and 66.8% of total revenues (SI-STAT, 2016). Thus, it is important how they report their financial information, what kind of information they provide to external users of financial statements, and how well they manage their accounting for purposes of internal reporting.

The paper examines legal provisions and rules in accounting standards concerning financial reporting of SMEs in Slovenia. A comparative analysis of national rules with EU Directives and full International Financial Reporting Standards (IFRS)/IFRS for SMEs highlights how Slovenia adopted the relevant EU Directives and emphasizes the particularities of the Slovene regulatory framework. The paper also provides a literature review of evidence from financial and management accounting studies made on samples of Slovenian SMEs.

Findings show that recent changes of the Companies Act and national accounting standards simplified the corporate reporting of small and especially micro-enterprises. Despite the fact that the Slovenian Companies Act states that Slovenian Accounting Standards (SAS) shall not be contrary to IFRS, the comparative analysis performed in the paper shows that there are indeed certain differences between them. The paper also raises issues concerning lenient requirements for accounting practitioner qualifications and a lack of supervision of financial statements. The literature review of relevant studies from the field of financial and management accounting shows characteristics and particularities of the accounting of SMEs in Slovenia.

The present paper contributes to the literature in emerging economies (for more details see for example Garrod & Turk, 1995; Novak, 2008; Hopper *et al.*, 2009; Odar *et al.*, 2015; Novak & Valentinčič, 2017) by examining the development of accounting in an emerging country. Particularities of the Slovenian environment will illustrate international diversity and as such could be of interest to an international readership. Many Slovenian studies have been written in the Slovenian language and as such unavailable to the international public (e.g. Kavčič *et al.*, 1998; Kavčič *et al.*, 2003; Kavčič *et al.*, 2004a; Kavčič *et al.*, 2004b; Odar *et al.*, 2009; Kavčič *et al.*, 2010; Prusnik, 2013; Kavčič *et al.*, 2013; Kavčič *et al.*, 2014). The review of the studies will enable international audience to learn about the characteristics of accounting in Slovenia.

The structure of the paper is as follows. In the first section, we illustrate the content of annual reports, the required audit of financial accounts, the relationship between financial statements for financial reporting and tax purposes, professional rules in accounting standards and their key changes and the accounting profession in Slovenia. The second section concludes with a presentation of the relevant studies from financial accounting by SMEs from Slovenia. The third section is devoted to reviewing the results of studies in management accounting from Slovenia. The conclusions along with suggestions for improvements are presented in the final section.

2. Characteristics of external financial reporting of Slovenian SMEs

In 2015, there were in total 191,963 active enterprises, employing 837,454 persons and recording € 95.299 billion in revenues (SORS, 2016). Most of these enterprises employed one person (73.5%), followed by micro-enterprises with 2-9 employees (21.5%) (SI-STAT, 2016). The importance of SMEs for the Slovenian economy is presented more in detail in table 1 below.

Table 1. Importance of SMEs for the Slovenian economy

	Micro enterprises	Small enterprises	Medium-sized enterprises	Total
% of total enterprises	95.1%	3.7%	1%	99.8%
% of total employment	29.6%	16.8%	23.6%	70%
% of total revenues	20.7%	20%	26.1%	66.8%

Source: SI-STAT, 2016

Requirements regarding external financial reporting depend not only upon enterprises' size but also by their legal form. In 2015, among all Slovenian enterprises 45.7% were legal entities and 54.3% natural persons. The most numerous of all were "samostojni podjetniki [sole traders]", whose share was 48.0%. The majority of legal entities are "družbe z omejeno odgovornostjo [limited liability companies]" (SORS, 2016). Taken together, sole traders and limited liability companies total 79.8% of Slovenian enterprises.

Slovenian companies take one of the following legal forms (Companies Act, 2006): a) "osebna družba [partnership]": "družba z neomejeno odgovornostjo [unlimited company]" or "komanditna družba [limited partnership]"; or b) "kapitalska družba [company limited by shares]": "družba z omejeno odgovornostjo – d.o.o. [limited liability company]", "delniška družba – d.d. [public limited company]", "komanditna delniška družba [partnership limited by shares]" or "evropska delniška družba [European public limited-liability company]".

The legal basis for external financial reporting is provided by the Companies Act (2006). It delineates general rules on accounting, auditing, public announcement of annual reports, the content of the annual report and the general rules concerning the valuation of items in financial statements. The Companies Act refers to accounting standards, requiring that companies and entrepreneurs keep books of accounts and complete them annually in accordance with the act and the SAS or IFRS.

Companies whose securities are traded on one of the organized securities markets in the Member States of the European Community and are subject to consolidation have to report in accordance with IFRS. IFRS is applied by banks, insurance companies, and other companies if the general meeting so decides (in this case, the enterprise has to use IFRS for at least five years). From 2015 IFRS are also used for consolidated financial statements. Medium-sized and small companies are not obliged to use IFRS, unless they are classified among the previously mentioned groups of companies. Most of the Slovene SMEs report in accordance with SAS. SAS 2016 is effective since 1 January 2016. This is the third revised version of SAS. The first SAS were adopted in 1993, followed by SAS 2002, SAS 2006 and SAS 2016.

In accordance with the Companies Act, companies must prepare the annual report for each financial year within three months after the end of the financial year (Companies Act, 2006). The annual report must be submitted to the Agency of the Republic of Slovenia for Public Legal Records and Related Services (AJPES). AJPES must publish an annual report in computerized form on its website (Companies Act, 2006). The obligation of annual report publication did not change after the implementation of EU Directive 2013/34. Slovenia has not exempted from mandatory reporting the smallest enterprises.

Entrepreneurs who are taxed on the basis of profit, taking into account "normirani odhodki [flat-rate expenses]", are not obliged to submit annual reports for publication (Companies Act, 2006). More details about the system of flat-rate expenses are presented in section 2.3.

Annual reports of medium-sized "kapitalska družba [company limited by shares]" (most common are: "družba z omejeno odgovornostjo [limited liability company]", and "delniška družba [public limited company]") and "dvojna družba [double partnership]" must include the auditor's report since they have to be audited. The annual reports of these companies must be transmitted to AJPES within eight months after the end of the financial year for the purpose of public announcement.

2.1 The content of the annual report

The content of annual reports of Slovenian enterprises depends upon their size and legal form. Annual financial statements of small "kapitalska družba [company limited by shares]" whose securities are not traded on a regulated market are composed of minimum required statements defined by the Directive 2013/34 (i.e. a balance sheet, income statement and notes to the financial statements). As permitted by the Directive 2013/34 Slovenia requires more numerous financial statements for enterprises other than small enterprises. In accordance with Slovenian Companies Act medium-sized "kapitalska družba [company limited by shares]" and "dvojna družba [double partnership]" have to prepare (Companies Act, 2006): a balance sheet, income statement, cash flow statement, statement of changes in equity, notes to the financial statements and the management report. They must also draw up the statement of comprehensive income or other comprehensive income. The statement of comprehensive income may be presented as a separate statement or as part of the income statement.

In Slovenia, the number of required annual financial statements differs between companies and entrepreneurs of the same size. In accordance with SAS (SAS 2016, 30.1) medium-sized entrepreneurs have to prepare all previously mentioned financial statements as medium-sized "kapitalska družba [company limited by shares]", with the exception of statement of comprehensive income. The latter is obligatory only for companies which are audited. However, on December 31, 2016 there were no active large entrepreneurs and only one medium-sized (GVIN, 2017).

On the other hand an entrepreneur whose business meets the criteria for a small or micro-company, has to compile (Companies Act, 2006): a balance sheet and income statement. Entrepreneurs are not required to prepare notes to financial statements. Moreover, entrepreneurs are not required to keep books of accounts and draw up the annual report, if he/she is taxed on the basis of the profit, taking into account flat-rate expenses (Companies Act, 2006). On the other hand, companies (legal entities) which are taxed on the basis of this system do not have any simplifications in terms of keeping books of accounts.

Given the structure of Slovenian enterprises' sizes and legal forms, the majority of Slovenian enterprises for the purpose of external financial reporting prepare only a balance sheet and income statement. Moreover, many entrepreneurs do not compile annual reports for external reporting purpose (because they have the option not to do so, if they are taxed by taking account of flat-rate expenses). The latest data show that currently approximately 31% of natural persons engaged in business use this kind of option (Delo, 2016).

The structure of the balance sheet and income statement for external financial reporting purposes is delineated by the Companies Act. The breakdown is different for large, medium-sized and small companies. The breakdown does not differ between small and micro companies. As permitted by the Directive 2013/34 Slovenian small and micro-entities are required to draw up abridged financial statements compared with medium-sized entities. Differences in the layout of financial statements are greater among medium-sized and small/micro companies, in comparison to the differences between legal entities and natural persons engaged in business of the same size. SAS additionally simplifies the layout of financial statements for external reporting of the smallest entrepreneurs (i.e. micro-entrepreneurs).

In Slovenia, enterprises use the vertical layout of the balance sheet (Directive 2013/34 allows two options), while enterprises have the option to choose between two layouts of income statement permitted by the Directive (i.e. by nature of expense or by function of expense). SAS suggests the second type of layout. The exception are micro-entrepreneurs who have to compile the income statement presenting expenses by their nature (SAS 2016, 30.4). SAS additionally defines the structure of the cash flow statement and the statement of changes in equity.

An important difference between the medium-sized and small (micro) enterprises in the volume of reported information refers to the volume of the notes to the financial statements. SAS lists the required disclosures for enterprises that are committed to audit (including medium-sized enterprises). Small and micro-enterprises are not supposed to provide disclosures required by SAS but must prepare only information required by the Companies Act which are in line with notes required by the Directive 2013/34 for all undertakings. This information is most frequently the predominant part of all notes provided by Slovenian small businesses (in addition to the information in the financial statements).

In accordance with the possibilities given by the Directive 2013/34 regarding exceptions for micro-undertakings the Companies Act introduced a special regimen for micro-companies in 2015. Micro "kapitalska družba [company limited by shares]" that do not measure assets in accordance with the principle of fair value, but in accordance with the principle of historical cost, are not obliged to compile all notes that are required by the Companies Act for small companies, but must disclose only a part of them (the requirements are in conformity with those listed in the Directive). The required information for this kind of micro-entities is the following (Companies Act, 2006):

1. the total amount of contingent financial liabilities which are not included in the balance sheet,
2. if that information is important for assessing the financial position of the company, the amount of any obligations that are secured (lien, etc.),
3. advances and loans made by the company or its subsidiaries to members of management, supervisory board members, other employees of the company and contract employees not subject to the tariff part of the collective agreement,
4. if a company has own shares during the financial year.

Slovenia exempted small and micro-enterprises from the obligation to prepare management reports. A management report of medium-sized companies and medium-sized entrepreneurs, must include at least (Companies Act, 2006): a fair presentation of the development and results of company's operations and its financial position, including a description of the principal risks and uncertainties to which the company is exposed. Fair view should be a balanced and comprehensive analysis of the development and performance of the company and its financial position, which corresponds to the extent and complexity of its operations. The analysis must, to the extent necessary for understanding the development and performance of the company and its financial position, contain the financial, and other indicators, including information related to environmental protection and employees.

In the management report companies must also show all major business events that occurred after the end of the financial year. If this is important the management report shall also include the objectives and measures of financial risk management, and the company's exposure to price, credit, liquidity risks and risks related to cash flow (Companies Act, 2006).

Companies subject to audit (including medium-sized companies) must include in their annual reports a corporate governance statement which has to include a reference to the corporate governance code, a description of the main features of internal controls and risk management. Contents of the management report are in a large part in conformity with EU Directives.

2.2 Audit of annual reports

An audit of annual reports is required for large and medium-sized companies and those reports of small companies whose securities are traded on a regulated market. Recently the Companies Act introduced the "preiskava računovodskih izkazov [examination of financial statements]" for certain small enterprises. Previously, small and micro-enterprises were not forced to inspect their financial statements. From and including 2016 onwards, the auditor should carry out an examination of the annual financial statements for those small "kapitalska družba [company limited by shares]" that measure property and plant assets at revalued values, investment property at fair value, or have in their accounts financial instruments for which no quoted price on regulated markets is available, including financial derivatives. The examination of the financial statements must be done within six months after the end of the financial year.

Since neither the Companies Act nor SAS require that the fair value measurement has to be performed by a certified appraiser, we believe that this type of examination has enhanced the quality of financial data, as previously this type of measurements in small "kapitalska družba [company limited by shares]", were not subject to verification.

In Slovenia, a licence to carry out the tasks of a certified auditor is issued by the "Slovenski inštitut za revizijo [Slovenian Institute of Auditors]". Compulsory auditing (defined by the Companies Act) can be performed only by auditors who meet the conditions laid down by the EU Directive (adequate educational qualifications, examination of professional competence). In accordance with the current Slovene Auditing Act a person shall also have a minimum of five years of work experience (the Directive 2014/56 requires a minimum of 3 years), with a minimum of three years of experience in auditing in the six years prior to submission of the application for the issue of the license (Auditing Act, 2008, Article 48). A person who had a license for carrying out the tasks of a certified auditor withdrawn in the past lost the license permanently. In addition to these conditions an individual must have a high level of proficiency in the Slovenian language. The license to carry out the tasks of a certified auditor is valid two years from the date of issue. The validity of the license can be renewed every two years at the holder's request, provided that he/she undergoes additional professional training in accordance with applicable rules (Auditing Act, 2008, Article 48). At the end of 2016 there were 52 active auditing firms in Slovenia (The Slovenian Institute of Auditors, 2016). Supervision of the quality of auditing is performed by the Institute of Auditors and the Agency for the Public Oversight of Auditing in accordance with their competencies pursuant to the Auditing Act (Auditing Act, 2008, Article 6). Due to the adoption of Directive 2014/56 and Regulation 537/2014, in 2015 in Slovenia began the process of drafting the Auditing Act 3. The latter will transpose the provisions of the aforementioned EU legislation. The process remains ongoing.

For the year 2015, 155,842 annual reports for the purpose of public announcement were submitted to AJPES. Of these, only 1,671 were audited (AJPES, 2016), which represents 1% of total annual reports. If a company is not listed and is not a corporation subject to external audit, then there is no other direct official financial reporting enforcement authority apart from the tax authorities.

2.3 Connection between financial accounting and taxation

In accordance with the "Zakon o davku od dohodkov pravnih oseb – ZDDPO-2 [Corporate Income Tax Act]" (2006) the determination of profit for tax purposes is grounded on recognized income and expenses found in the income statement prepared in accordance with established accounting standards. The income tax rate in 2016 was 17%, in 2017 it rose to 19%.

Taxable income is based on commercial income from the individual entity income statement, which is for tax purposes modified according to specific tax rules. Law on Corporate Income Tax defines certain categories which are recorded differently than in accounting standards. In addition to the adjustments of certain expenses and revenues the Law on Corporate Income Tax allows "davčne olajšave [tax relief]". These allowable deductions from the tax base are (Law on Corporate Income Tax,

2006): for investment in research and development; for investment in equipment and intangible assets; employment; for voluntary supplementary pension insurance; for grants; and on employment and investment in certain regions.

The alternative to the calculation of taxable income based on commercial income is the system of flat-rate expenses. Some taxpayers, if they fulfill conditions defined by the law, can determine the tax base by taking account of actual revenues reduced by 80% of flat-rate expenses (calculated as 80% of recorded revenues). Taxable income is thus equal to 20% of recorded revenues. Such taxpayers are not able to use tax reliefs and expenses actually incurred.

Natural persons engaged in business more commonly use (approximately 31%) the system of flat-rate expenses in comparison with legal persons. The latest data show that in 2015 only approximately 1% of legal persons chose this option (Delo, 2016).

Among the legal entities and natural persons engaged in business, there is a difference in books of accounts if their income tax base is determined by taking account of flat-rate expenses. For legal persons, this status does not affect the requirements regarding bookkeeping and reporting. On the other hand, natural persons engaged in business with such a status have very little obligations regarding financial reporting. They are not required to keep records of expenses and the costs of their operations. To determine the tax base they are not required to keep books of accounts, but only the required tax evidence. For many entrepreneurs, this law simplified their obligation of mandatory financial reporting and keeping books of accounts. These kinds of entrepreneurs are not required to submit financial statements for public announcement.

For natural persons engaged in business, the taxation of profits is determined by the Personal Income Tax Act (2006) by: 1) taking into account actual revenues and expenses, or 2) by taking account of flat-rate expenses. Profit is in their case taxed progressively. Currently, the scale of five grades of tax rates from 16% to 50% is in use. The exception are persons who qualify and opt for taxation on the basis of flat-rate expenses who apply a tax rate of 20%.

In addition to "davčne olajšave [tax relief]" that may be taken into account by legal persons, natural persons engaged in business can also take into account the general allowance, deduction(s) for dependents and relief for voluntary supplementary pension insurance premiums.

Slovenia is characterized by a close relationship between financial accounting and taxation. Income statements for tax purposes result from the income statements prepared for the purpose of external financial reporting. Tax authorities are an indirect general enforcement authority for accounting standards (Jerman & Novak, 2014). In 2015, there were 191,863 companies actively operating. At the same time, as of December 31st, 2015 the number of tax inspectors in the Financial Administration of the Republic of Slovenia was 434 (Ministry of Public Administration, 2016). Clearly, the number of tax inspectors is relatively low. As a result, the number and extent of inspections is rather limited. This is the only form of control for the majority of small and micro organizations.

2.4 Accounting rules in "Slovenski računovodski standardi – SRS [Slovenian Accounting Standards – SAS]"

The first SAS were issued in 1993, and began to be used on 1 January 1994. The first revision followed in 2001 with the issuance of the SAS 2002. The revised standards were striving for the use of fair value principle, particularly with regard to the presentation of assets and liabilities. Since Slovenia joined the European Union, the European Directives had to be introduced into Slovenian law. For this reason the revised SAS were published in 2005 (for more details about the historical development of SAS see Garrod & Turk, 1995; Novak, 2008; Jerman & Novak, 2014; Novak & Valentinčič, 2017). The last revision followed in 2015, when SAS 2016 were issued (in force from 1 January 2016). SAS 2016 transferred into the Slovenian law contents of the new accounting directive 2013/34.

SAS 2016 were adapted in particular for preparation of separate financial statements of medium, small and micro entities. In addition to changes that were made as a consequence of EU law transfer into SAS, other changes were completed in the direction of accounting simplification.

The current SAS 2016, unlike previous versions, contain only the rules of financial accounting and reporting, not the solutions for internal reporting (previously an integral part of the standards). SAS 2016 are complemented by so-called »Good accounting practice rules« (Pravila skrbnega računovodenja - PSR), which contain solutions for: bookkeeping, budgeting, financial control, financial analysis, financial reporting and consolidation. The PSR are not mandatory, since they are only an addition to the SAS. A large part of the current PSR was in the earlier version of the SAS included in separate sections in standards (SAS 20–23 and SAS 28–30). The application of these SAS was not obligatory, but was recommended primarily in the case of internal reporting. These SAS were called accounting standards for mere formal reasons (SAS, 2006).

SAS 2016 are divided into the following sections: Introduction to SAS and the framework of the SAS, SAS considering the accounting of economic categories that are observed in accounting (Standards I), standards of external financial reporting (Standards II) and standards that define accounting solutions for organization of specific activities (Standards III). The SAS framework contains the following chapters (SAS 2016, Introduction):

- Basic accounting assumptions and qualitative characteristics of accounting.

- Recognition of economic categories in financial statements and accounting records.
- Measurement of economic categories in financial statements and accounting records.
- The revaluation of economic categories in financial statements and accounting records.
- Changes in accounting estimates, changes in accounting policies and corrections of errors.
- Business combinations (mergers).
- Deferred tax assets and deferred tax liabilities.
- Joint Arrangements.
- A group of organizations.

The central part of the standards contains disclosure requirements of individual financial categories. These disclosures are required for organizations whose annual reports shall be examined by an auditor (in this set, medium-sized enterprises). Small and micro organizations, must reveal only statutory information and data.

Standards I deal with professional rules for the accounting of certain types of assets and liabilities, costs, expenses and revenues. The standards eliminated accounting solutions related to consolidation. In accordance with the amendments of the Companies Act from the year 2015, the consolidated financial statements are now prepared using IFRS (previously companies could use SAS or IFRS). The group of Standards II includes the presentation of the balance sheet, income statement, cash flow statement and statement of changes in equity for external reporting purposes.

What is new in SAS 2016 is that the rules for recognizing, measuring, evaluation and disclosure were set out for all entities, irrespective of legal status and form. The set of standards III deals only with the particularities of accounting in various entities. Previously they also contained specific rules regarding the recognition, de-recognition, measurement and evaluation of economic categories.

Unlike SAS 2006, SAS 2016 no longer refers to IFRS. The SAS 2016 are now completely independent standards. To this end, the authors of SAS complemented some SAS solutions with those from IFRS; therefore, SAS does not rely on them anymore. SAS 2016 is based on the provisions of the Directive 2013/34 and those of the Slovenian Companies Act. Where the Directive 2013/34 or Companies Act does not provide otherwise, SAS 2016 follows the fundamental accounting rules of IFRS.

Although the Slovenian Companies Act (2006) states that SAS shall transpose the content of Directive 2013/34 and their concept must not be contrary to IFRS, there are certain differences between SAS and IFRS. Key differences between SAS and IFRS in terms of recognition, measurement and valuation are presented in more detail in the following section.

2.5 Changes of SAS 2016 and their comparison with IFRS and IFRS for SMEs

SAS 2016 introduced some significant changes in terms of recognition, measurement and valuation of economic categories. The most important are as follow:

- In the case of property, plant and equipment (PP&E), SAS 2016 in contrary to SAS 2006 does not permit revaluations of equipment.
- There were also some changes in relation to the revaluation surplus. In accordance with SAS 2006 a revaluation which affected the value of equity was presented in the balance sheet in one single item. The layout of the balance sheet in accordance with SAS 2016 changed. Currently, two separate items are presented: i.e. revaluation reserve (showing revaluation of PP&E) and fair value reserve (showing effects of all other revaluations, especially those of financial assets).
- SAS 2016 allows only one possible reversal of the revaluation reserve. The revaluation reserve is reversed to retained earnings when the revalued recognition of PP&E is derecognized. In accordance with the EU Directive 2013/34 no part of the revaluation reserve may be distributed, either directly or indirectly, unless it represents a gain actually realized. Previous SAS 2006 allowed that some of the surplus could be transferred as the asset was used by the entity.
- SAS 2016 does not allow anymore revaluations of intangible assets. Previous SAS allowed intangibles to be revalued to fair value if they had an active market (SAS 2006, 2.30).
- In SAS 2016 goodwill is treated as an intangible asset with a definite useful life. When the useful life cannot be reliably determined, goodwill is amortized using the straight-line method over five years (SAS 2016, 2.26). Previously the goodwill could be classified as an intangible asset with an indefinite useful live. In accordance with SAS 2006 goodwill was not subject to amortization, only tested for impairment (SAS 2006, 2.26).
- Changes to SAS 2016 relate also to the field of financial investments. The revised standards contain more detailed provisions about the methods of identifying impairments and the rules of accounting in relation to hedging.

SAS 2016 introduced certain simplifications for micro organizations. Micro entities that are not subject to audit, may decide that the deferred tax will not be accounted for (SAS 2016, Introduction). Simplification also applies to provisions for jubilee awards and severance pay upon retirement. Even these micro-entities are not obliged to account for. In accordance with SAS 2006 deferred taxes, provisions for jubilee awards and severance pay upon retirement were not recorded if this kind of information was not material. Many small companies did not present them. Since SAS 2016 is in use small companies do not have this option anymore. For many small companies this represents an additional administrative burden.

SAS is in a large part in conformity with IFRS. However, there are some differences between them. In relation to the aforementioned changes of SAS 2016, we present the most important differences between rules in SAS 2016 and those of IFRS and IFRS for SMEs (table 2).

In accordance with IFRS/IFRS for SMEs all items of PP&E can be revalued. On the other hand, users of SAS 2016 cannot apply the revaluation model for equipment. Reversals of the revaluation reserve differ between SAS 2016 and full IFRS, while IFRS for SMEs do not provide detailed guidance. SAS 2016 and IFRS for SMEs do not permit the revaluation of intangibles, while IFRS permits revaluations if there is an active market for these assets. Goodwill is in accordance with SAS 2016 amortized (and tested for impairment) in its useful life. If the useful life cannot be determined, it is written off over the period of five years. Similar are the rules in IFRS for SMEs with the only difference that goodwill has to be written off over the period of ten years if its useful life cannot be determined. On the other hand full IFRS require goodwill to be tested for impairment. The comparative analysis of selected accounting rules shows that SAS 2016 is more in conformity with IFRS for SMEs than full IFRS.

Table 2. Comparative analysis of selected accounting rules in SAS 2016 with those of IFRS and IFRS for SMEs

Rules in accounting standards	SAS 2016	IFRS	IFRS for SMEs
Revaluation of PP&E	Equipment cannot be revalued	All items of PP&E can be revalued	All items of PP&E can be revalued
Reversal of the revaluation reserve	One option – when the revalued recognition of PP&E is derecognized	Two options – a) the surplus can be transferred as the asset is used by the entity or b) is transferred when the revalued recognition of PP&E is derecognized	Detailed guidance not provided
Revaluation of intangible assets (other than goodwill)	Not permitted	Permitted	Not permitted
Goodwill	Amortized in its useful life. If the useful life cannot be determined, it is written off over the period of five years	Goodwill is tested for impairment	Amortized in its useful life. If the useful life cannot be determined, it is written off over the period of ten years

Moreover, IFRS and IFRS for SMEs do not prescribe the form of financial statements for external financial reporting. Slovene Companies Act and SAS 2016 precisely prescribe the form of the balance sheet and income statements for external reporting purposes (SAS additionally defines the structure of the cash flow statement and the statement of changes in equity). The format is exactly prescribed for different sizes of organizations.

We expect that the extent of differences between SAS and IFRS will increase in time, since the frequency of IFRS changes is greater than those of SAS.

2.6 Accounting profession in Slovenia

Due to particularities regarding the regulation of the accounting profession in Slovenia, we also present the characteristics related to the profession of accountants in this emerging economy. Accounting practitioners are not required to have any professional qualification nor a professional certificate. There are no requirements for mandatory registration. Professional certificate can be obtained on a voluntary basis. The Slovenian Institute of Auditors performs the training process for "preizkušeni računovodja [qualified accountant]", while the Chamber of Commerce and Industry of Slovenia offers the title "Strokovni vodja računovodskega servisa [Expert Manager of (external) Accounting Services]".

The bookkeeping process and the preparation of annual reports can be performed by accountants who are employed in the organization (internal accountants) or by external firms providing accounting services. For the latter, Slovenian law does not require any particular criteria that should be met for conducting business. As stated by Slapničar *et al.* (2013), practitioners working in accounting firms have various educational backgrounds and experiences. The latest data show that in 2015 there were 3,661 companies operating as accounting firms employing 4,095 employees (Chamber of Commerce and Industry of Slovenia, 2016).
Typically, large and medium-sized companies have internal accountants (they work in an internal accounting department), while many small companies and especially micro-companies often use external accounting service providers. The number of firms operating as accounting service providers in Slovenia is relatively high.

The legislature should consider establishing minimum professional qualifications for accountants in Slovenia and their mandatory registration, since there are currently no minimum requirements and anyone can pursue this profession.

2.7 Review of research of Slovenian SMEs from the field of financial accounting

Little research has been done in the field of financial accounting involving Slovenian SMEs. To date research is mainly focused on large companies, especially those whose securities are traded on a regulated market. The reason for this is probably the fact that small and micro-enterprises disclose a limited extent of information to external users of financial statements and thus their analysis is rather difficult. Another simple reason for the limited number of studies on samples of Slovenian companies is there are few researchers in the field of accounting in Slovenia.

To date studies from the field of financial accounting indicate that Slovenian SMEs use discretion in accounting standards for tax minimization purposes. Non-tax costs and benefits also seem to be important drivers of their choices. One of the few studies on a sample of Slovenian SMEs was published by Garrod *et al.* (2008). The work explores economic incentives that drive small private companies operating in Slovenia to record revaluations of current and fixed assets (sample of 23,455 companies). Selected companies are characterized by the absence of agency problem. They find that more profitable companies are more likely to write-off assets and the write-off magnitude is greater. They also find a positive association of company size with the probability to write-off, and negative association with its magnitude. Kosi and Valentinčič (2013) provide further evidence that firms exploit discretion in accounting standards that results in tax savings. Moreover, the results indicate that non-tax costs and benefits are also important drivers when companies choose accounting policies. Their analysis was made on a large sample of 20,505 small private companies.

Mörec (2012) analyzed earnings distribution among Slovenian companies in the period 2008-2010. The results of her analysis shows that earnings shifts occurred more often among micro and small companies in comparison to medium-sized and large companies. The results show statistically significant discontinuity of net earnings' distribution around zero. Micro and small companies that recorded operating loss recognized significantly higher financing income compared to profit making micro and small companies.

Prusnik (2013) studied the link between the tax burden and accounting choice. His sample includes companies of all sizes from the activities of construction, trade and manufacturing. These companies accounted for 51% of all Slovenian companies. Most of the companies in the sample are micro and small companies. Prusnik (2013) finds that the company's' size (measured by number of employees) affects the propensity of companies to manage profit and thereby to reduce tax liability. Profits are more managed by smaller companies (than large companies) and by companies with a higher effective tax rate. He also notes that companies tend more to manage earnings in times of recession in comparison to times of economic growth. The author also investigated the methods that companies use to manage earnings. He finds that the amount of tax base and the level of taxation of companies is most often affected by the write-downs of assets and manipulations of purchases and sales, which are reflected in changes of short-term receivables and liabilities.

At this point it should be useful to summarize the key characteristics of external financial reporting of Slovenian SMEs (Table 3).

Table 3. Key characteristics of external financial reporting of Slovenian SMEs

Characteristic	Description
Legal system	Companies Act provides detailed accounting rules.
Accounting standards	SMEs mostly use the Slovene national standards, exceptions are consolidated accounts which have to be prepared in line with IFRS.
Frequency of financial reporting	Annually. The exceptions are companies that are listed in the security market, which must also prepare interim financial statements.
Publication of annual reports	Financial reports for external reporting are publicly available at the website of AJPES. The exception are annual reports of entrepreneurs who are taxed on the basis of profit, taking into account flat-rate expenses. They are not obliged to submit annual reports for publication.
Tax reports	Mutual influence of taxation and financial accounting.
Preparers of financial reports	Accounting practitioners are not required to have any professional qualification nor a professional certificate. Professional certificates are obtained on a voluntary basis.
Auditing	Annual reports of medium-sized companies are audited. Mandatory audit is not required for annual reports of small companies (the only exceptions are small publicly listed companies). New in 2016 – "preiskava računovodskih izkazov [examination of financial statements]" of certain small companies.
Harmonization of national standards with IFRS	After the latest revision of SAS, the extent of harmonization with IFRS decreased.
Quality of accounting data	Studies indicate mixed results in terms of firms' size and accounting discretion. Further evidence is needed.
Discretionary accounting choice	Research indicates that discretion choice in accounting is motivated by tax minimization reasons.

3. Review of research of Slovenian SMEs from the field of management accounting

Although in the field of management accounting contributions about Slovene SMEs to scientific journals are also limited, the papers from this area of accounting are more numerous and include a quite comprehensive analysis of the development of management accounting among Slovenian companies. The first survey was conducted in 1996 and covered the situation in 1995. The survey was repeated in 2002 (considering the situation at the end of 2001), 2007 and 2008 (addressing the situation at the end of 2006) and 2012 (addressing the situation at the end of 2011)

(Kavčič *et al.*, 2002; Kavčič *et al.*, 2013). The survey was repeated in order to determine the extent of accounting development and the influence of a variety of socio-economic factors that were present during the analyzed period of time. The study partly covers the area of financial accounting, but is mainly focused on management accounting. The survey was conducted in joint cooperation between the Slovenian Institute of Auditors, the Association of Accountants, Treasurers and Auditors of Slovenia and the Faculty of Economics, University of Ljubljana (Kavčič *et al.*, 2002; Kavčič *et al.*, 2013).

The questionnaire consisted of 133 questions, divided into several themes. Research was repeated using the same methodology; therefore, the results of the study are comparable. The researchers excluded from the analysis companies with a number of employees lower than 20. They assumed that in the majority of micro-enterprises accounting is narrowed to bookkeeping, and thus most companies of this kind could not answer a number of the survey questions (Kavčič *et al.*, 2013).

The questionnaire included in addition to some general questions about the company questions about the organization of accounting, methods of valuation of economic categories, information provided for decision-making, information for the purpose of performance measurement analysis and areas of responsibility (Kavčič *et al.*, 2013). In 1995, this was the first comprehensive study in the field of accounting since Slovenia became independent. None yet has been more comprehensive. Table 4 presents the number of companies included in the survey and the number of companies obliged to prepare annual reports for whole period of their analysis.

Table 4. Number of companies included in the survey and the number of companies obliged to prepare annual reports

	1995	2001	2006	2011
Companies in the survey	286	320	173	161
Companies obliged to prepare annual reports	33,609	37,210	45,330	57,798

Source: Kavčič *et al.* (2013)

As can be noticed, the number of respondents decreased over time, since companies are not willing to fulfill long questionnaires. Nowadays companies can hardly devote time to answering the questionnaires of this kind. In the first two surveys 10% of the sample was represented by small enterprises, in 2006 30%, and in 2011 34%. In the case of medium-sized enterprises the proportion ranged from 30% to 34%. In 2001, the share of large enterprises was the largest, amounting to 59%. In 2006 and 2011 it fell to 36% (Odar *et al.*, 2009; Kavčič *et al.*, 2013).

Their data show that the accounting department has gained in importance. Companies where the accounting department represents a predominant source of information for decision making amounted to 49% in 1995 and rose to 64% in 2011 (Kavčič *et al.*, 2013; Kavčič *et al.*, 2014).

In 1995, only 60% of companies prepared different information for different levels of decision-making. The results do not differ significantly by firm size (Kavčič *et al.*, 1998). In 2011, the situation had improved, yet the percentage was still only 68% (Kavčič *et al.*, 2014). These data show that the management accounting system in Slovenia is not highly developed. As suggested by the theory we would expect that different hierarchical levels of decision-makers would receive information appropriate to specific needs (for details see Gorry & Scott Morton, 1971).

Among the companies there are substantial differences between the information that the accounting department provides on a daily, weekly and monthly basis to management (Kavčič *et al.*, 2003; Kavčič *et al.*, 2010; Kavčič *et al.*, 2014; Odar *et al.*, 2015). Kavčič *et al.* (2014) found that the information most frequently reported to management is about liquidity. The authors found that the extent of information that the accounting department provides to management increased, especially in the period of crisis (Kavčič *et al.*, 2014; Odar *et al.*, 2015). In times of crisis, compared to the year 2006, management was willing to receive more information about cash and liquidity (Odar *et al.*, 2015).

The most interesting findings of the survey as regards information about specific basic business functions are (Kavčič *et al.*, 2004a; Kavčič *et al.*, 2004b; Kavčič *et al.*, 2013):

- Budgeted balance sheet was prepared by 47% of companies in 1995, by 2011 the share rose to 70%, indicating a significant improvement.
- The budgeted cash flow statement was prepared by 66% of the companies in 2006, in 2011 the share increased to 77%.
- Before 2006 accounting departments only rarely made budgets or monitored their deviations.
- In 1995, 35% of enterprises had no responsibility centers, 48% in 2011%. Data show that the decentralization of decision-making in Slovenian medium-sized and small companies is relatively rare. Among those companies that have responsibility center(s), the majority established cost centers of responsibility.

Within the survey, the authors asked about the form of income statement used by the respondents. The most commonly used method of income statement is that which classifies the expenses on a natural basis. Its importance in time increased from 75% in 1995 to 80% in 2011 (Kavčič *et al.*, 2013). SAS suggests the use of an income statement that classifies expenses on a functional basis, but both are permitted.

Odar *et al.* (2012) analyzed in detail the performance measurement systems used by large, medium and small Slovenian companies. Their analysis was made on a sample of 167 companies, of which 36.5% are large companies, 33.5% medium, and 30% small-sized companies. They found that Slovenian companies predominately use traditional performance measurement techniques, while contemporary techniques are used rarely. The research further explored the use of different groups of ratios which were defined by the SAS 2006. The analysis reveals no statistically significant difference in their use between companies of different size in the case of leverage ratios, while it shows statistically significant difference in the case of liquidity and turnover ratios. Smaller companies use fewer ratios than larger companies. The authors found that the majority of small companies from the sample (64%) for performance evaluation purposes use comparison of the current results with the previous years' results and plan. Odar *et al.* (2012) found that economic performance measurement methods (like EVA) are used only rarely. They performed an additional test, analyzing whether there are significant differences between those companies that have an internal accounting department and those which use external providers of accounting services. Authors could not find significant differences between these two groups. Their findings also suggest that accounting practitioners in small companies perform bookkeeping activities almost exclusively. Their study confirms findings of Haldma and Lääts (2002) and Hopper *et al.* (2009) which have shown that transitional and less developed economies have management accounting systems that are less developed than those in traditional market economies.

The results of these comprehensive studies over a period of 16 years provide important information about the development of accounting in Slovenia. Unfortunately, the research does not consider micro companies, a significant share of Slovenian companies. As Kavčič *et al.* (2013) points out, the majority of micro organizations narrow accounting to bookkeeping.

The surveys from the field of management accounting in Slovenia show that solutions from developed market economies were quickly introduced at the level of theory. However, a gap has emerged between theory and practice (Milost, 1998; Kavčič *et al.*, 2013).

4. Conclusions

We find that the majority of small and micro-enterprises (representing almost 99% of total Slovene enterprises) compile only a balance sheet and income statement for external reporting purposes. Approximately a third of sole traders (which represent almost a half of all enterprises in Slovenia) do not submit annual reports for publication, because they have the option not to do so if they are taxed using the system of flat-rate expenses. Since 2015, when the legislature increased the proportion of normalized expenses, the number of enterprises which have opted for this type of taxation (and therefore those that do not submit annual reports for publication) increased. We expect that their number will increase in the future as well.

In accordance with the fact that accounting professionals in Slovenia are not required to have any professional certificate and that the supervision of financial statements in the case of most small and micro-enterprises is rather limited, the tax authority (as an indirect general enforcement authority for accounting standards), should consider increasing the number of tax inspectors, which currently number relatively few.

SAS 2016 no longer refers to IFRS. SAS are now completely independent standards. Although the Slovenian Companies Act states that SAS shall not be contrary to IFRS, there are certain differences between them. After the latest revision of SAS, the extent of harmonization with IFRS actually decreased. We expect that the extent of differences between SAS and IFRS will increase in time, as the frequency of IFRS changes is greater than those of SAS. The latest version of SAS was introduced 10 years after the preceding one. Therefore, the legislature should eliminate the provision from the Companies Act requiring that the SAS must not be contrary to the IFRS.

We found that since the EU Directive 2013/34 was implemented into Slovenian law, corporate reporting of small and especially micro enterprises was simplified. We believe that future changes of SAS will be also tailored toward further simplifications of accounting for SMEs.

Studies from the field of financial accounting in Slovenia reviewed here were mainly focused on the linkage between financial accounting and taxation. The use of accounting discretion is motivated by the effort to minimize taxation. Studies indicate mixed results in terms of firms' size and accounting discretion. Further evidence is needed.

The literature review from the field of SMEs in Slovenia shows that there are numerous possibilities for further research. Studies of small, especially micro, companies are few. More studies are needed to investigate the quality of accounting data prepared for the purpose of external financial reporting. To date, there remains a lack of research investigating whether the application of revised versions of national accounting standards are associated with increased quality of accounting information. This issue is important, since most of the SMEs report in accordance with SAS.

In the field of management accounting possibilities for future studies are numerous. Studies could focus on cost allocation processes in use, approaches to budgeting, management control systems design and performance measurement systems. To date little is known especially in regard to the micro enterprises that are so numerous in Slovenia. We have shown that in Slovenia there are relatively numerous external accounting service providers, which assist small and micro-companies almost exclusively. Future studies could investigate the extent of management accounting information prepared by these kinds of organizations. Thus, more research is needed both from the field of financial and management accounting. SAS is in a large part in conformity with IFRS, thus the Slovenian environment has integrated contemporary accounting solutions.

References

AJPES (Agency of the Republic of Slovenia for Public Legal Records and Related Services) (2016) "Public Posting of Annual Reports", available online at https://www.ajpes.si/jolp/ (on-line access: November 23rd 2016)

Auditing Act (Zakon o revidiranju) (2008), available online at http://www.pisrs.si/Pis.web/pregledPredpisa?id=ZAKO5273 (on-line access: March 19th 2017)

Chamber of Commerce and Industry of Slovenia (2016) "Development and representation of NACE 69.200 for 2015", available online at https://www.gzs.si/zbornica_racunovodskih_servisov/vsebina/Za-podjetja/Prikaz-dejavnosti/Razvoj-in-%C5%A1tevil%C4%8Dni-prikaz-panoge-2015 (on-line access: December 3rd 2016)

Companies Act (Zakon o gospodarskih družbah) (2006), available online at http://www.pisrs.si/Pis.web/pregledPredpisa?id=ZAKO4291 (on-line access: November 24th 2016)

Corporate Income Tax Act (Zakon o davku od dohodkov pravnih oseb – ZDDPO-2) (2006), available online at http://www.pisrs.si/Pis.web/pregledPredpisa?id=ZAKO4687 (on-line access: November 24th 2016)

Delo (2016) "Flat tax displaces other forms of work", available online at http://www.delo.si/gospodarstvo/finance/pavsalna-obdavcitev-izriva-druge-oblike-dela.html (March 21st 2017)

Garrod, N. & Turk, I. (1995) "The development of accounting regulation in Slovenia", *The European Accounting Review*, vol. 4, no. 4: 749-764

Garrod, N., Kosi, U. & Valentinčič, A. (2008) "Asset Write-Offs in the Absence of Agency Problems", *Journal of Business Finance & Accounting*, vol. 35, no. 3-4: 307-330

Gorry, G.A. & Scott Morton, M.S. (1971) "A Framework for Management Information Systems", *Sloan Management Review*, vol. 13, no. 1: 55-70

GVIN (Financial data) (2017), available online at http://www.bisnode.si/produkt/gvin/ (on-line access: January 6th 2017)

Haldma, T. & Lääts, K. (2002) "Contingencies influencing the management accounting practices in Estonian manufacturing companies", *Management Accounting Research*, vol. 13, no. 4: 379-400

Haller, A. & Walton, P. (2003) "Country differences and harmonization?", in P. Walton, A. Haller & B. Raffournier (Eds.), *International Accounting*, pp. 1-34), London: Thomson

Hopper, T., Tsamenyi, M., Uddin, S. & Wickramasinghe, D. (2009) "Management accounting in less developed countries: what is known and what needs knowing", *Accounting, Auditing & Accountability Journal*, vol. 22, no. 3: 469-514

Jerman, M. & Novak, A. (2014) "IFRS application in Slovenia", *Accounting and Management Information Systems*, vol. 13, no. 2: 351-372

Kavčič, S., Koželj, S. & Odar, M. (2004a) "Development of Management Accounting in Slovene Companies", *Revizor [Auditor],* vol. 15, no. 2: 54-95

Kavčič, S., Koželj, S. & Odar, M. (2004b) "Development of Management Accounting in Slovene Companies", *Revizor [Auditor],* vol. 15, no. 3: 26-63

Kavčič, S., Koželj, S. & Odar, M. (2010) "Development of accounting in Slovene companies", *Revizor [Auditor]*, vol. 21, no. 2: 29-64

Kavčič, S., Koželj, S. & Odar, M. (1998) "Development of accounting in Slovenian companies", *Revizor [Auditor],* vol. 9, no. 3: 40-57

Kavčič, S., Koželj, S. & Odar, M. (2002) "Development of accounting in Slovene companies: first findings of research by the Slovenian Institute of auditors and the Faculty of Economics of the University of Ljubljana", *Revizor [Auditor],* vol. 13, no. 11: 71-87

Kavčič, S., Koželj, S. & Odar, M. (2003) "State of development of management accounting in Slovene companies", *Revizor [Auditor],* vol. 14, no. 11: 58-87

Kavčič, S., Odar, M. & Koželj, S. (2013) "Development of accounting in Slovenian companies - presentation and first research results", *Sirius*, vol. 1, no. 6: 110-134

Kavčič, S., Odar, M. & Koželj, S. (2014) "Development of Management Accounting in Slovene Companies – Information for the first and the second decision-making levels", *Sirius*, vol. 2, no. 5: 117-143

Kosi, U. & Valentinčič, A. (2013) "Write-offs and Profitability in Private Firms: Disentangling the Impact of Tax-Minimisation Incentives", *European Accounting Review*, vol. 22, no. 1: 117-150

Milost, F. (1998) "Development of accounting theories", *Revizor [Auditor],* vol. 9, no. 2: 50-59

Ministry of Public Administration (2016) "Annual report of the Inspection Board for the year 2015", http://www.mju.gov.si/fileadmin/mju.gov.si/pageuploads/JAVNA_UPRAVA/SOUS/mnenja/Letno_porocilo_Inspekcijskega_sveta_za_leto_2015.pdf (January 12th 2017)

Mörec, B. (2012) "Do small companies have superior financial expertise or are they just managing earnings?", *International Business & Economics Research Journal*, vol. 11, no. 12: 1289-1298

Novak, A. (2008) "Harmonization of Slovene accounting standards with International financial reporting standards", in Kandžija, V., Kumar, A. (eds.) *50 years of European Union = L'Union Éuropéenne a 50 ans: research monograph.* Rijeka: University of Rijeka, Faculty of Economics: 511-520

Novak, A. & Valentinčič, A. (2017). "The Role and Current Status of IFRS in the Completion of National Accounting Rules – Evidence from Slovenia", *Accounting in Europe*, vol. 14, no. 1-2, 187-198

Odar, M., Kavčič, S. & Jerman, M. (2012) "Performance measurement systems: empirical evidence from Slovenia", *Economic Research*, vol. 25, no. 2: 445-464

Odar, M., Kavčič, S. & Jerman, M. (2015) "The role of a management accounting system in the decision-making process: evidence from a post-transition economy", *Engineering Economics*, vol. 26, no. 1: 84-92

Odar, M., Kavčič, S. & Koželj, S. (2009) "Organisation of accounting in Slovene companies", *Revizor [Auditor],* vol. 20, no. 4: 63-81

Personal Income Tax Act (Zakon o dohodnini – ZDoh-2) (2006), available online at http://www.pisrs.si/Pis.web/pregledPredpisa?id=ZAKO4697 (November 25th 2016)

Prusnik, M. (2013) "Correlation between tax burden and accounting choice: Slovenian example, PhD Thesis", available online at http://www.cek.ef.uni-lj.si/doktor/prusnik.pdf (January 16th 2016)

SAS 2006 (Slovene Accounting Standards 2006) (2006) Ljubljana: Association of Accountants, Treasurers and Auditors of Slovenia

SAS 2016 (Slovene Accounting Standards 2016) (2016) Ljubljana: The Slovenian Institute of Auditors

SI-STAT (2016) "Enterprises by industry (SKD 2008) and their size, Slovenia", available online at letnohttp://pxweb.stat.si/pxweb/Database/Ekonomsko/14_poslovni_subjekti/01_14188_podjetja/01_14188_podjetja.asp (December 7th 2016)

Slapničar, S., Zaman Grof, M. & Štumberger, N. (2013) "Does professional accounting qualification matter for the provision of accounting services?" In C. N. Albu & R. V. Mustata (Eds.), *Accounting in Central and Eastern Europe* (pp. 255-277), Bingley: Emerald Group Publishing Limited

SORS (Statistical Office of the Republic of Slovenia) (2016) "Enterprises, Slovenia, 2015", available online at http://www.stat.si/StatWeb/prikazi-novico?id=6328&idp=16&headerbar=14 (December 7th 2016)

The Slovenian Institute of Auditors (2016) "List of auditing firms", available online at http://sis.si-revizija.si/public/registry/revcompanylist (December 11th 2016)

8

Corporate Social Responsibility and accounting in Poland

Halina Waniak-Michalak [a,1], **Małgorzata Macuda** [b,2] **and Joanna Krasodomska** [c,3]

[a] *Lodz University, Poland*
[b] *Poznań University of Economics and Business, Poland*
[c] *Cracow University of Economics, Poland*

Abstract. Corporate Social Responsibility (CSR) has become a popular research stream across scientific disciplines as indicated by the number of publications increasing world-wide. At the same time, this is a very much country-specific notion. In Poland, as in other CEE countries, the development of CSR has been influenced by the communist past and the economic situation. The paper presents an overview of Polish literature on CSR and accounting themes. Our findings result from quantitative (2000-2015) and longitudinal qualitative (1984-2016) analyses of Polish publications. An analysis of the content of BazEkon and EBSCO databases, as well as the search performed using the Google Scholar have demonstrated a growing interest of Polish academia in CSR issues since 2001. However, a significant increase in the number of publications on the topic has been observed only since 2005. In order to present the key debates in the area of CSR disclosures, we have analyzed 67 papers. We discovered that most papers published by Polish researchers concentrated on the content of CSR reports and on the integrated reporting concept. The most frequently used methods were literature review and content analysis. Only a few researchers applied statistical tools or conducted interviews or surveys. The interests of Polish researchers in the area of CSR reporting focus on factors influencing CSR reporting and the quality of CSR reports. Because CSR and reporting on CSR are in the early stages of development in Poland, it would be valuable to repeat the performed literature analysis in a few years' time. It can be expected that the CSR concept will gain in popularity and more research sources (like CSR or integrated reports) will be available to Polish academics, which will be reflected in the topics of their studies and the methods used.

---

[1] *Corresponding author (1)*: Department of Management Accounting, Lodz University, Matejki Str. 21/23, 90-237 Lodz, e-mail: hwaniak@uni.lodz.pl

[2] *Author (2)*: Department of Accounting, Poznań University of Economics and Business; al. Niepodległości 14, 61-875 Poznań; ; e-mail: malgorzata.macuda@ue.poznan.pl

[3] *Author (3)*: Department of Financial Accounting, Cracow University of Economics; Rakowicka Str. 27, 31-510 Cracow; e-mail: joanna.krasodomska@uek.krakow.pl

Keywords: corporate social responsibility, CSR, social responsibility accounting, integrated reporting, Poland, literature review

1. Introduction

Companies are required to earn a profit which continues to be their defining characteristic. However, it matters how the profit is made as it is a part of a wider process which takes into consideration the companies' relationships with a wide range of individuals, groups and institutions. Corporate social responsibility (CSR) can be understood as the way in which a company is consciously responsible for its action(s) and non-action(s) and the impact of these on society and the environment. The concept refers to the approach used by companies to integrate social, environmental and economic concerns into their values, culture, decision making, strategy and operations in a transparent and ethical manner. The CSR idea has been evolving since the 19th century, when it emerged in the United States, and the stage of the development of the concept is different in various regions. According to Hopkins (2015), Europe is now ahead of most countries and followed by the USA, while the developing countries are on the first rung of CSR.

CSR in Poland is a relatively new concept. After many years of the communist system and expropriation of private capital, companies' responsibility for their actions was not the subject of scientific discussion in Poland. During the communist period, all problems connected with social welfare, as well as social and environmental issues were the State's responsibility. After the fall of communism in 1989, Polish market started to change following the model of the developed markets.

First public discussion on CSR took place in Poland in 1999 and was organized by Business Leaders' Forum. Since then, different actions have been undertaken to foster the development of CSR and CSR reporting as business concepts in Polish enterprises. One of the many initiatives is a CSR reports contest organized by the Responsible Business Forum (a non-profit organization which works for the development of the CSR concept) and SGS (an organization selling business supporting services). In 2007, only 11 companies took part in this competition while in 2015, a total of 37 CSR reports were judged. The increase in the number of contestants can be seen as an evidence of the change in the Polish companies' attitude towards CSR that has occurred over the last few years. It is expected that the trend toward implementing the CSR in the companies' strategies will prevail, mostly due to the adoption by Polish business of best practices used by foreign companies operating in Poland.

Along with the growing interest in the CSR notion on the part of practitioners, there has been an increase in the popularity of the concept as a subject of studies carried out by the Polish academia. Basing, to a large extent, on the achievements of foreign scholars, researchers in Poland explore the CSR theme and related notions from various perspectives, such as management, marketing, philosophy or accounting. This paper discusses the main views on the CSR concept which are driven mainly by the related accounting themes. It should be noted that although the CSR concept has been present in public discourse in Poland since 2000, the first publications of authors representing the accounting discipline and referring to additional obligations (social and environmental) of companies appeared in the mid-1980s. The aim of the paper is to provide an overview of literature on CSR and its relation to accounting, and to present some of the key debates in this area.

The paper is organized as follows. The second section presents general issues concerning the CSR concept which can be encountered in Polish publications on the subject of accounting and reporting. In the third section we concentrate on the number of studies referring to these issues which have appeared in Polish literature over the last 15 years. The fourth section takes us back in time to 1984, to the pioneer papers in the field of CSR disclosures, and presents the development of the Polish authors' studies since that time till the present day. In conclusion we summarize the findings, indicate the limitations of the paper and suggest future research possibilities.

2. Polish accounting academia and the CSR concept

There is no definite definition of CSR – neither in the literature of respective fields nor in practice (Bartkowiak, 2011). The way it is understood and implemented differs greatly for each company and country. In general, it is about encouraging companies to be more aware of the impact of their business on the society and the environment. There are numerous CSR synonyms, the most popular of which are: business ethics, corporate citizenship, sustainability or sustainable development, corporate environmental management, business and society, business and governance, business and globalization, and stakeholder management. Therefore, CSR is viewed as an umbrella concept, which includes corporate citizenship, corporate sustainability, stakeholder management, environmental management, business ethics and corporate social performance.

Polish authors referring to the CSR issues, such as Pogodzińska-Mizdrak (2010) and Dyląg and Puchalska (2014), stress its interdisciplinary character – as it is explained by a number of different studies and practice, such as: business ethics, law, ecology, management and accounting. Nakonieczna (2008), Paszkiewicz and Szadziewska (2011), Roszkowska (2011) as well as Żemigała (2007) agree that CSR concept combines the elements of economic sciences, social sciences and philosophy. The subject of social responsibility, distinguished by Stępień (2001) are: man-worker (human capital, also called intellectual capital), physical resources (economic capital) and natural resources (environment, i.e. natural capital). CSR results from the fact that all these resources are made available (shared) to the company, which operates within the society on a contract basis („legitimacy") in order to conduct business activity.

CSR is often treated as an implementation of sustainable development politics and understood as an effective management strategy, which through social dialogue, contribute to shape the conditions for sustainable social and economic development (Bernatt *et al.,* 2011; Broniewska, 2012; Brzozowski, 2011; Dołęgowski, 2005; Dyląg & Puchalska, 2014; Gabrusewicz, 2010; Gołaszewska-Kaczan, 2010). It is very often defined in the Polish literature as an integration on a voluntary basis of social and environmental concerns in business operations and in interaction with stakeholders of a company in long-term perspective (Marcinkowska, 2006; Bernatt *et al.*, 2011; Bielińska-Dusza & Pająk 2012; Mizdrak & Pogodzińska-Mizdrak, 2013; Różańska, 2014; Macuda *et al.*, 2015b). Some authors stress the moral responsibility of the company to give an account for its activities (accountability) before internal and external stakeholders (Jarugowa, 1984; Zbiegień-Maciąg, 1996; Bernatt *et al.*, 2011). Moreover, Gasparski (2007) describes CSR as a two-level concept. On the one hand, it is the responsibility of the assigned tasks, namely achieving a desired result (responsibility), on the other hand, it is the readiness to be evaluated – presenting the results of business activity and the associated consequences (accountability).

CSR means to take actions that go beyond legal requirements. It is an idea of constructing a long-term strategy by a company that voluntarily takes into account the social, ethical and ecological aspects in its business operations. Such a company takes responsibility for the decisions that it made and the activities that it undertook, which have an impact on the local community and the environment, and also leads a dialogue with the internal and external stakeholders (Macuda *et al.*, 2015b: 118). Wykrzykowski (1986) treats CSR as taking care of the interests of the whole society, and therefore, it can ensure the implementation of specific, legitimized interests of the general public, organized in a particular form, while respecting the freedom of the individual.

Expanded around the world the idea of CSR shows that there must be no conflict between achieving by companies strictly economic objectives and simultaneously pursuing their activities related to society and the environment (Mizdrak & Pogodzińska-Mizdrak 2013: 54). Moreover, precisely those companies which manage to reconcile these two aspects, build their reputation, improve their image (competitive advantage by responding to societal signals), as well as gain financially and developmentally, and are very attractive to investors. Business cannot succeed in societies that are failing – whether this is due to social or environmental challenges, or governance problems. CSR concept is spread non only in companies, but also in specific entities, such as shale gas producers (Galimska, 2015) or hospitals (Macuda, 2013). A particular attention is paid to environmental accounting (Stępień, 2003; Chojnacka, 2014; Dyląg & Puchalska, 2014; Macuda, 2015).

In recent years the idea of CSR became an important and worldwide subject, also in Poland. Therefore the role of accounting in implementation of this concept became a topic of frequent discussions. Socially responsible accounting (social responsibility accounting / social accounting / social and environmental accounting / sustainability accounting) is a manifestation of the development of accounting theory and practice arising from economic and social changes. Accounting, just like any other system, is constantly developing, adapting its solutions to dynamic changes and the level of complexity of company management processes. As a crucial informative system of a company, it evolves in line with new ideas and challenges related to management tasks and instruments (Macuda *et al.*, 2015b: 119). The potential of accounting system for adaptation (adaptability) to the objectives and situational determinants of the measurement has been already verified in its history (Burzym, 2008: 78).

CSR may be seen as one such idea that requires the adoption of a new set of solutions within the area of accounting, in particular its ethical and environmental aspects. CSR appears to be a complex and multidimensional organizational phenomenon, which consists on re-evaluating and recalibrating the relationship between the company and its wider context. Socially responsible accounting aims to identify, measure and present CSR issues – namely to report about activities in the social, environmental and economic areas related to the functioning of the company. According to Matuszak (2013: 106), in the context of implementation of CSR, the purpose of accounting is to create reliable, clear, credible and comparable financial and non-financial information based on the True and Fair Value principle, which will make it possible to materialise the responsibility of companies in relation to their stakeholders.

Burzym (1993: 6-7) underlines that the role of socially responsible accounting is to provide information to stakeholders in order to enable monitoring and evaluation of the company's activities from the point of view of compliance of its objectives with the social objectives and its contribution to social welfare. Thus, socially responsible accounting should (1) constitute an integrated system of economic measurement capable of acquiring information in three dimensions: economic, environmental and social; (2) provide a numerical basis for a systematic assessment of environmental and social impact of the company' activities; (3) assist management team in decision-making processes through the appropriate measurement of environmental and social costs and benefits associated with the influence of the company on the environment; (4) report relevant and reliable information (related to CSR issues) allowing to make the right decisions by different stakeholder groups; and (5) create the conditions for independent audits of reports containing CSR information in terms of their usefulness.

Mizdrak and Pogodzińska-Mizdrak (2013: 53) claim that economic sciences deal with systems that should have an appropriate social resonance and should adapt to the environment. According to Pogodzińska-Mizdrak (2010: 179-180) „the success of a corporate social responsibility strategy depends on many factors, one of which is the system of accounting, which includes ready measurement methods, in particular with regard to balance sheet valuation, interpretation and recording of economic events, as well as reporting". Krasodomska (2010a: 338-339) points out that information created within the system of socially responsible accounting, similarly to the information generated in regular accounting, should be reliable, complete and delivered to the stakeholders/shareholders in time in order to use it in the decision-making processes. The information should be significant (inform about the most crucial aspects of the implemented social responsibility strategy), complete (take into account all the areas of company's operations) and comparable in time.

Also, it is frequently postulated that the contents of such reports should be integral with financial reports, accurately reflecting the real situation of the company. The trend is towards a high-quality, comprehensive business reporting. According to Roszkowska (2011: 145-146), the form and contents of social responsibility reports are to a large extent dependent on the general communication strategy of a company. If the company operates in a complete isolation, publishing the environmental, social and economic information is limited to simply presenting the data, without expecting any feedback. But if managers wish to establish lasting relations with the community, the exchange of information and opinions is vital in reporting. The published data collected in the course of bilateral communication are useful for both sides and affect future activities and directions of a company development.

Businesses are an integral part of the communities in which they operate. Companies' long-term success is based on continued good relations with a variety of parties – shareholders, non-governmental organizations, business partners, lenders, insurers, regulators, tax authorities, consumers, employees, investors, and local communities. Rectitude in abiding by the social norms is reflected, in particular, in respecting the rights of the most vulnerable stakeholders – those individuals and entities that have the weakest possibility of delivering their arguments and enforcing their rights (Marcinkowska, 2006: 410). Taking into account social, environmental and economic concerns, socially responsible companies aim to increase their value by creating a common value for different stakeholder group (Szadziewska, 2013: 258).

With CSR topic, also reporting issues are tightly connected. A postulate appears stating that the content of CSR reports should be substantively integral with financial reports, accurately reflecting reality. In Poland it was Samelak (2013: 179-181) who first attempted to establish a conceptual framework for integrated reporting by a socially responsible company – such integration may be based on the annual report concept, in which the operational report is the key part of the integrated report, or on the integrated report concept, in which a single document integrates all non-financial information (including the CSR report) with financial information by indicating relations and interrelations between said information types.

The integrated report appears to Dyląg and Puchalska (2014: 35-36) as a new report containing information on the economic, environmental and social aspects of the business – the integration of a wide range of information about the company in the form of a single, coherent and comparable format. They claim that the development of integrated reports should improve the quality of financial reporting and help to increase the confidence of public opinion and investors. Krasodomska (2014: 110) indicates two basic principles underlying the development of the concept of integrated reporting: accountability (the company's obligation to report to the stakeholders on the actions taken which results from the fact that the company receives consent to act from the public) and transparency (the way company disclose information to its external users – the information presented should reflect actual/true situation of the company). It is advisable for companies to start practicing integrated reporting and it is possible that it will emerge as a reporting standard in 2020 (Krasodomska, 2012b).

3. A quantitative analysis of CSR and integrated reporting scholarly publications

3.1 Research aim and method

The aim of the study was to identify publications concerning CSR and integrated reporting issues published over the years 2000-2015 to get an approximate picture of the popularity of the concepts as topics of research studies among Polish authors. In order to determine the degree to which CSR issues are discussed in Polish literature on the subject we have analyzed the resources included in two databases: BazEkon and EBSCO; we have also used the web search engine Google Scholar. It should be noted that the results of the performed analysis need to be interpreted with caution due to the application of a limited set of keywords.

BazEkon, a Polish database, was founded in 1993. It is being developed in a collaborative partnership of the libraries of Polish universities from Krakow,

Wroclaw, Poznan, Katowice, Szczecin and the Warsaw School of Economics. The database comprises the bibliographic descriptions of articles from scientific and economic periodicals, scientific publishing series of economic departments and faculties, as well as scientific institutions, including NGOs. The database allows publications to be searched with the use of keywords, publication year and publication language. The results can be sorted by two types of sources: journals and research papers.

EBSCOhost is a well-known research database, which offers a broad range of full-text and bibliographic data. In our study we have limited the EBSCO resources to two databases: Business Source Complete and Academic Search Complete. Business Source Complete is a comprehensive database of business-related sources and information and Academic Search Complete is a multidisciplinary academic database that includes peer-reviewed journals, as well as periodicals, reports and books. The search was limited to publications in scientific journals (peer-reviewed), including conference proceedings. Publications were checked one by one paying attention to whether they concerned CSR issues and were written by Polish authors.

Google Scholar is a freely accessible web search engine that indexes the full text or metadata of scholarly literature across an array of publishing formats and disciplines. Our Google Scholar search focused only on scientific publications (options „include patents” and „include citations” were not chosen).

The study was performed in three stages. The aim of the first one was to identify publications concerning the CSR notion in general. In the second stage, we concentrated on these, which refer to the CSR and corporate accounting or reporting. In the third stage of the research our aim was to identify publications related to the integrated reporting concept.

3.2 CSR as the topic of Polish scholarly publications

The aim of the first stage of the study was to identify the number of publications dedicated to CSR issues in general over the years 2000-2015.

BazEkon, EBSCO and Google Scholar resources were examined with the use of such keywords as „społeczna odpowiedzialność biznesu” (in English „corporate social responsibility”). Table 1 presents the results.

Table 1. The number of publications by Polish authors dedicated to the CSR issues indexed in BazEkon, EBSCO and provided by Google Scholar in 2000-2015

Year	BazEkon	EBSCO	Google Scholar
2000	0	0	0
2001	1	0	3
2002	8	0	3
2003	7	0	4
2004	7	0	7
2005	20	0	28
2006	30	0	38
2007	32	0	26
2008	81	0	67
2009	108	0	121
2010	140	0	101
2011	196	2	187
2012	130	4	214
2013	208	18	322
2014	231	15	266
2015	136	25	246
Total	**1335**	**64**	**1633**

According to the data presented in table 1, the number of publications dedicated to the CSR concept increased over the years 2000-2015. BazEkon and Google Scholar provided many more results (13335 and 1633 respectively) than EBSCO (64), which is not surprising given that few Polish scientific journals are included in EBSCO database, and it is still a big challenge for Polish researchers to get published in foreign journals indexed in it. A noticeable increase in the number of publications in BazEkon and Google Scholar as well as EBSCO occurred in 2005 and 2013, respectively.

According to the BazEkon, in the first half of the analysed period (2000-2007), on average 13 publications per year were issued, while in 2008-2015 – the number went up to about 154 per year. Important increases in the number of publications can be observed in the year 2008 in relation to 2007, in 2011 in relation to 2010 and in 2013 in relation to 2012. The largest decreases were identified in the years 2015 vs. 2014 and 2012 vs. 2011.

Table 2. Characteristics of the publications on the CSR issues included in the BazEkon in 2000-2015

Publication in:	No. of publications
Polish	1188
English	138
Research Paper	842
Scientific Journal	493

Only 10% of all Polish authors' CSR publications included in the BazEkon are written in English (table 2). Twice as many publications are published in universities' research papers as in scientific journals.

An analysis of the publications indexed in EBSCO database revealed 64 studies by Polish authors and the vast majority of them – 58, were published over the years 2013-2015. It should be noted that the significant increase in the number of publications in 2013 may have resulted not only from an increase in the academia interest in the CSR concept, but also from an increase in the number of Polish resources (such as research papers) indexed in EBSCO database.

The search performed with the use of the Google Scholar web search engine allowed the scope of publication sources to be extended. It should be noted that not all scholarly research papers and journals which are being published in Poland are included in BazEkon. However, a similarity can be observed in the number of publications included in BazEkon and that identified in Google Scholar within the research time frame. Like the BazEkon, Google Scholar also revealed an increase in the number of publications since 2005. As regards the first half of the analysed period (2000-2007), Google scholar provides information on an average of 13 publications per year (similar to BazEkon), while in 2008-2015 – the number is about 190 per year (more than BazEkon).

In the second research phase, we made an attempt to identify publications related to CSR and corporate accounting or reporting.

Table 3. The number of publications regarding CSR and accounting and CSR and reporting indexed in BazEkon in 2000-2015

Year	2000	2001	2002	2003	2004	2005	2006	2007	2008	2009	2010	2011	2012	2013	2014	2015
No. of publications	0	0	0	0	0	1	0	0	4	3	1	2	5	4	7	14

According to the research results, BazEkon included 41 studies dedicated to the issues of CSR and accounting (13) and CSR and reporting (28) which were published over the years 2005-2015. Since 2008, they appeared in the database every year. The highest number was published in 2015 (14). Only two publications were written in English, 19 were published in research papers and 22 in scientific journals.

Table 4. The number of publications regarding CSR and accounting and CSR and reporting indexed in EBSCO in 2000-2015

Year	**2000**	**2001**	**2002**	**2003**	**2004**	**2005**	**2006**	**2007**	**2008**	**2009**	**2010**	**2011**	**2012**	**2013**	**2014**	**2015**
No. of publications	0	0	0	0	0	0	0	0	0	0	0	1	0	8	6	7

Due to the importance of the EBSCO database on the international academic level, we searched the EBSCO database resources with the use of Polish and English keywords. This allowed us to identify 22 papers in total, published in 2011 and 2013-2015. The publications were carefully checked in order to avoid double counting.

The use of Polish keywords („społeczna odpowiedzialność biznesu and rachunkowość" and „społeczna odpowiedzialność biznesu and sprawozdawczość") yielded 9 results. These were CSR publications written by authors representing accounting discipline. They were mostly papers in the Polish language, published in the Research Papers of Wroclaw University of Economics.

13 more papers were identified using English keywords („corporate social responsibility and accounting and Poland or Polish" as well as („corporate social responsibility and reporting and Poland or Polish"). Four of them were published in 2013, four in 2014 and five in 2015. They were published in the Research Papers of the Wroclaw University of Economics (in Polish or in English), Copernican Journal of Finance & **Accounting, Accounting** & Management Information Systems, Journal of Environmental Planning & Management, Engineering Economics, Journal of Advanced Research in Law & Economics, or Problems of Management in the 21st Century (in English).

Table 5. The number of publications regarding CSR and reporting and CSR and accounting identified with the use of Google Scholar web search engine

Ye	2000	2001	2002	2003	2004	2005	2006	2007	2008	2009	2010	2011	2012	2013	2014	2015
No. of publications	0	0	0	0	2	4	7	12	22	14	21	32	35	83	59	63

The web search engine Google Scholar allowed us to identify the highest number of publications dedicated to the CSR issues and at the same time to accounting/reporting topics in comparison to BazEkon and EBSCO databases. The first publication appeared in 2004 and since then their number increased over the periods 2005-2008, 2010-2013 and 2014-2015. The most papers were published in 2013 (83).

3.3 Identification of papers referring to the integrated reporting concept

In the third study stage we focused on the publications concerning the integrated reporting problem.

Integrated reporting is a relatively new concept. The Integrated Reporting Council (originally as a Committee) was established in 2010 and the <IR> Framework was published in 2013. Table 4 presents the results of the analysis of publications referring to this concept and identified in the BazEkon , EBSCO databases and using Google Scholar. The search term was „sprawozdawczość zintegrowana" (in English integrated reporting).

The search performed with the term „sprawozdawczość zintegrowana" allowed us to identify 8 papers in the BazEkon database published over the years 2000-2016, mainly in scientific journals, such as Theoretical Journal of Accounting.

Table 6. The number of publications by Polish authors dedicated to the integrated reporting issue indexed in BazEkon, EBSCO and identified with the use of Google Scholar web search engine in 2011-2015

Year	BazEkon	EBSCO	Google Scholar
2011	0	0	0
2012	2	0	3
2013	1	3	12
2014	3	3	14
2015	2	2	12
Total	**8**	**8**	**41**

EBSCO database resources were searched with the use of the term „sprawozdawczość zintegrowana" as the keyword. 5 papers were identified. The search with the English phrase „integrated reporting" and „Poland or Polish" yielded 3 more results.

The use of the Google scholar web search engine allowed 41 publications to be identified, the first one appearing in 2012.

In conclusion, it can be said that Polish academia has taken more and more interest in CSR issues since 2001 but a significant increase in the number of publications on the topic has been observed only since 2005. The reason could be the process of CSR development and implementation in the corporate practice in Poland. According to Wachowiak (2013, p. 81), companies operating in Poland started to implement specific CSR projects in their operations in 2004-2005.

Only 3% of CSR publications included in BazEkon referred to accounting and reporting issues. In the case of Google Scholar, it was 22%. The highest percentage was observed in the results provided by the EBSCO database – 34%. Few papers by Polish authors are indexed in this database, but still quite many of those related to CSR refer at the same time to accounting and reporting. Integrated reporting is quite a new topic but it has been more and more popular in Polish scientific literature since 2012.

4. CSR disclosures as a research topic

4.1 Research aim and method

Studies on CSR disclosures are particularly popular among the Polish accounting academia. In Poland, such studies developed later than in Western Europe and in the USA. The first papers on CSR started to appear in Polish literature on the subject in the 1980s. Polish research in the field of CSR accounting must be assessed with the history of Poland in mind. Polish market started to develop after 1989 following the fall of the communist system. Between the end of the second world war and the 1980s, there was no place in Poland for private capital, non-profit organizations or corporate philanthropy. Therefore, society's expectations from enterprises were different than abroad. Polish citizens mistrust private capital and the level of social trust in general is very low among Polish people (Jastrzębska & Legutko-Kobus, 2014: 50). The survey conducted in 2008 by the research agency On Board PR and PBS DGA revealed that more than 70% of Poles were convinced that companies engaged in CSR for promotion of their products and to improve their image. That is why Polish companies were skeptical about the efficiency of disclosing the information on their CSR activity, especially philanthropy. However since the years 2010-2012 the CSR concept has started to be more and more popular in Poland both for business and for the media (Banaszkiewicz & Makowska, 2012)

Table 7 presents selected local and international journals, where Polish authors have published their papers on CSR in Polish or English. According to the data included in the table, 14 papers were published in Theoretical Journal of Accounting. The Journal has been published by the Research Council of the Accountants Association in Poland since 1977. It features articles written by Polish and foreign authors, in Polish and English.

Table 7. Selected journals which include Polish authors' publication on the CSR reporting

Journal	Language	No of Papers
	Local Journals	
Theoretical Journal of Accounting (published by the Accountants Association in Poland)	Polish English	13 1
Research Papers of the Wroclaw University of Economics	Polish	9
Studia Oeconomica Posnaniensia- Poznań University of Economics and Business	Polish	5
Research Papers of the Cracow University of Economics	Polish	4
***Acta Universitatis Lodziensis, Folia Oeconomica* -Research Papers of the Lodz University**	Polish	4
	International Journals	
Quality & Quantity	English	1
Social Responsibility Journal	English	1
Engineering Economics	English	2
Social Sciences	English	1

Internationally recognized journals which published papers by Polish authors include: Quality & Quantity, Social Responsibility Journal, Engineering Economics, and Social Sciences. Studies presented in the paper were also published in Research papers of Universities in Gdansk (2 papers), Szczecin (2) and Olsztyn (1), as well as in Studies and Papers of the Collegium of Management and Finance distributed by the Warsaw School of Economics (3). Apart from journals, authors referred to 11 books and 9 books' chapters by Polish academics dedicated to the CSR issues.

The aim of the study presented below is to evaluate the scope and development of Polish research in the field CSR reporting since the 1980s till present. In order to achieve the above mentioned objective we conducted a literature review. Our analysis concentrates on papers on the CSR disclosures and covers the time period from 1984 to 2015, giving us the possibility to assess the problem in a longitudinal perspective.

4.1 Research studies referring to the CSR disclosures presented in the Polish accounting literature

Studies on CSR disclosures in Poland are thought to have been pioneered by Jarugowa from the University of Lodz (table 7). In her first paper on CSR, she described the role of accounting for managers and society (Jarugowa, 1984). Her suggestions and research interests were based on the observations of business trends on western markets. She underlined the fact that information presented to society had to be useful for decision making. Accounting could be used to support the acceptance of business activity. Moreover, in order to fulfill the goal of accounting, according to Jarugowa (1984), financial data had to be supported by non-financial information. The scope of information had to take into consideration the following aspects: information importance, accuracy, aggregation and timeliness. Naglińska (1984), following the example of Jarugowa (1984), extended in her paper the traditional approach explaining that an enterprise was responsible to shareholders, to other stakeholders and society as a whole. She stated that accounting should measure the company's responsibility and allow the organization to disclose it. Therefore the paper was an introduction to the future discussion on the CSR measurement and future problems concerning business units (in the capitalism times). Moreover, the author thought that accounting had to reveal how the company's activities influenced the level of environmental pollution, usage of non-renewable resources, public security, health and education, civil rights and many other aspects of social life. Therefore, according to Jaglińska (1984), it was necessary to create a system of internal and external reporting in order to inform all stakeholders about all aspects and results of corporate activity. At the same time, it was obvious that the reports should be clear, easy to understand and rewarding for users. She divided the goals of social accounting into three groups (Jaglińska, 1984):

1. identification and measurement of the difference between social benefits and costs of social responsibility,
2. checking if the company's policy is consistent with the system of ethical norms, on the one hand, and social expectations on the other hand,
3. reporting on the corporate social responsibility results.

Table 8. Selected Polish authors' research studies concerning CSR disclosures and integrated reporting (1984-2016)

Main topic	Author	Main research method
Requirements for reporting on CSR activity	**Jarugowa (1984)** **Paglińska (1984)**	Literature analysis Literature analysis
Obstacles for developing social accounting	**Wołkowski (1984)**	Literature analysis
Evidence, importance and forms of the CSR in accounting	**Burzym (1990)** **Stępień (2001)**	Literature analysis Literature analysis
The role of accounting in the development of social responsibility of enterprises	**Marcinkowska (2004)** **Gabrusewicz (2005)**	Literature analysis Literature analysis
Measures of the efficiency of communication with stakeholders on the CSR activity	**Marcinkowska (2006)**	Literature analysis
Measurement of effects of CSR activity and providing the relevant information	**Stępień & Wydymus (2007)** **Krasodomska (2010a),** **Bielińska-Dusza & Pająk (2012)** **Szadziewska (2013)** **Kowalak (2014)** **Szczepankiewicz (2014)**	Literature analysis Literature analysis Literature analysis Case study Content analysis Literature analysis
The quality and content of CSR reports	**Gabrusewicz (2010),** **Krasodomska (2010b)** **Michalak (2010)** **Banaszkiewicz & Makowska (2012)** **Kuźbik (2012)** **Hąbek (2014)** **Macuda *et al.*, (2015a, 2015b)**	Literature analysis Literature analysis Content analysis Literature analysis Literature analysis Questionnaire survey Content analysis
Usefulness of integrated reports	**Marcinkowska (2012)** **Karmańska (2013)** **Szadziewska (2014)** **Wildowicz-Giegiel (2014)** **Zuchewicz (2014)** **Mazurowska (2014)** **Sikacz (2014)**	Literature analysis Literature analysis Literature analysis Literature analysis Literature analysis Literature analysis Content Analysis

	Macuda (2015)	Literature analysis
	Walińska (2015)	Literature analysis
Integrated reporting in the Polish companies practice	**Krasodomska (2012a, 2013b)**	Content Analysis
	Szczepankiewicz (2013a, 2013b, 2014)	Content Analysis
	Tatarska (2013)	Content Analysis
	Michalczuk & Mikulska (2014)	Content Analysis
CSR reporting in the light of legitimization theory	**Krasodomska (2013a, 2014)**	Literature analysis
	Waniak-Michalak & Michalak (2013)	Content analysis, cluster analysis
	Matuszak (2015)	Literature analysis
	Zyznarska-Dworczak (2015)	Literature analysis
Information on CSR in activity statements (management commentaries) or other reports	**Chojnacka (2014)**	Content analysis of activity statements
	Krasodomska (2015a)	Content analysis, disclosure index
Using the accounting system to inform, measure and control CSR activity	**Gabrusewicz (2014)**	Literature analysis
Factors influencing CSR reporting development	**Hąbek, Wolniak (2015)**	Questionnaire survey
	Waniak-Michalak & Michalak (2016)	Content analysis, regression analysis

Because social accounting also requires taking into consideration non-financial information, Paglińska (1984) considered regulations of this part of accounting and reporting in the form of GAAP or IAS to be impossible. However, as Jaglińska explained, fluctuation of social goals and their hierarchy made the introduction of social accounting into companies in Poland in the 1980s even more difficult. Jarugowa (1984) also tried to find the reason for the development of social accounting. She stated that the principal factor behind the growing importance of social accounting was the recognition of the role of man as the subject of labour activity and not only as a means to achieving goals. According to Jarugowa (1984), the companies' responsibility may be considered in isolation or in cooperation with many partners in the social context. In the case of the former, accounting serves as a measure of the achievement of goals while in the latter case the added value and the surplus in the form of the net production also have to be measured. In the same year, Wołkowski (1984) insisted that in the area of social accounting companies should report, most of all, on the expenditures and other provisions for the employees, environment and the whole society (mostly consumers). The author also evaluated the development of social accounting in countries other than Poland: Germany, Japan, France and the USA. He concluded that the main obstacle for this process was the resistance of business to the expectations of social organizations and groups.

Since the beginning of the 1990s, authors have focused their attention on the place of social accounting within the accounting system and the directions of its evolution in Poland. Burzym (1990) and Stępień (2001) tried to answer the following questions: what is the evidence, importance and forms of CSR in accounting and what is the influence of this notion on the accounting evolution in the area of environment and human capital. Marcinkowska (2004) and Gabrusewicz (2005) also emphasized the growing importance of the accountability concept in business operations and attempted to identify the role of accounting in the development of social responsibility of enterprises.

After the accession of Poland to the UE and along with the economic growth of the country, there occurred some changes in the attitudes of society and companies to CSR. Companies started to manage their CSR strategies and, at the same time, more and more publications on CSR reporting began to appear in the Polish academic literature.

Marcinkowska (2006) used the examples of selected corporations to present how business entities applied the CSR policies in order to satisfy stockholders' interests and how decisions should be made and controlled by shareholders. Marcinkowska started scientific discussion on the importance of corporate efficiency measures for stakeholders. According to her, a company is obliged to construct the measures of communication efficiency with stakeholders which will simultaneously measure the quality of the corporate governance system. The same issue was stressed by Stępień and Wydymus (2007) and Szadziewska (2013). They indicate that society must be able to control economic events whose effects impact upon individuals and the natural environment. However, organizations may also benefit from the control. Companies could use the accounting system to measure the effects of the CSR activity and provide the relevant information. Corporations should adjust the CSR strategy to their activity and goals and balance the benefits of this process for the company and society with the expenditures. Krasodomska (2010a) indicated the new challenges to the accounting information function posed by the implementation of the CSR concept in the business practice. Continuing the issue of the CSR measurement, Krasodomska (2010a) and Bielińska-Dusza and Pająk (2012) presented the examples of the CSR measures used by companies in different areas of social and environmental activity. Krasodomska (2010a) distinguished economic indicators (i.e. return on investment), ecological measures (i.e. CO2 emission), employees indicators (i.e. average salary of women/ average salary of men), measures of work security (i.e. number of accidents/ number of employees), indicators of social engagement (financial donations for philanthropic activity) and measures of cooperation with business partners (payables turnover in days). Marcinkowska (2012) suggested different tools to measure the non-financial achievements of a company, including the evaluation of stakeholders' expectations, such as balanced scorecard or accountability scorecard, intangible assets monitor and the performance prism. According to the author, the performance prism might be the most useful tool for stakeholders. It measures corporate achievements in five perspectives: stakeholders' interests, stakeholders' contribution, strategy, processes of the strategy implementation and resources used.

CSR reports content issues were relevant to the problems of CSR measurement and efficiency ratios. Kuźbik (2012) indicated that the CSR activity was very important for companies, but not all companies knew how to report on CSR. He concluded that the CSR report (prepared according to the GRI guidelines) could be useful only if it considered stakeholders' requirements. Research conducted by Macuda *et al.*, (2015a, 2015b) among Polish public companies listed on the WSE showed also that 30% of CSR reports in Poland are not prepared according to the GRI standards and only 18% of the companies had their CSR reports verified by an independent external auditor. Michalak (2010) checked the extent to which sustainability reporting standards were used in Poland. His research revealed that 67 out of 100 biggest companies underlined in their reports high importance of CSR but only 6 of them prepared CSR reports according to the GRI standards (they were companies from banking and oil industry). Gabrusewicz (2010) presented the view that financial statement and other reports on the CSR activity should contain the answers to the following questions:

1. what is the value of the company's activity within the CSR?
2. how does the CSR activity influence the corporation's results?
3. do the costs of CSR (i.e. environmental protection) exceed the benefits of these actions?

In 2014, Kowalak even suggested the measures for evaluating the CSR activity of companies' management of sewage and garbage.

Gabrusewicz (2010) defined social responsibility accounting taking into consideration the burden and benefits for society resulting from the activities of a particular entity presented in a qualitative or descriptive form. On the other hand, Krasodomska (2010b) stated that the content of social reports depended mainly on the enterprises' approach, because there were no universally accepted regulations in this regard. Measures of CSR used by companies often differed and thus were uncomparable. Moreover, the measures were also not subjected to verification by auditors. Companies might adopt one of the three models of CSR reporting:

1. presenting the information on the CSR activity as a supplement to the financial information,
2. determining the company's financial result adjusted for the effect of CSR, in full integration with financial accounting,

3. replacing financial accounting with a full model of costs and benefits of CSR to evaluate the performance of an enterprise from the point of view of all stakeholders.

According to Krasodomska (2010b), enterprises in Poland currently use the first model.

Since 2012, researchers in Poland have become interested in integrated reports (Marcinkowska, 2012; Krasodomska, 2012b; Wildowicz-Giegiel, 2014; Szadziewska, 2014; Chojnacka, 2014; Mazurowska, 2014; Sikacz, 2014; Macuda *et al.*, 2015b; Walińska, 2015). Most of the papers concerning integrated reports in Poland use a literature review or an analysis of legal acts as research methods. Authors conclude that integrated reports should be introduced in Poland in the near future.

Marcinkowska (2012) describes tools of accounting used for communicating information on CSR, such as: value added statement, expanded value added statement and CSR report. She underlines the usefulness of integrated reports. Szadziewska (2014) indicates that integrated reports should explain the relationships between strategic goals of the company and the economic and environmental aspects of its functioning. Szczepankiewicz (2014) even claims that the traditional financial statement does not present relevant information on the company's achievements and risks. However, an increase in the amount of information in integrated reports does not mean higher quality of the disclosure. Zuchewicz (2014) suggests that integrated reports should include mainly financial information while non-financial information should only be supplementary. The same problem has been raised by Walińska (2015). She even doubts if it is the right time to introduce integrated reports in Poland. Moreover, she fears that financial data will be replaced by non-financial information. A totally different opinion is held by Karmańska (2013) who states that accounting should not incorporate CSR issues and be used for reporting on CSR activity. According to her, financial information presented in this way might be manipulated. Therefore CSR reports should constitute separate documents. At present, integrated reports in Poland are chaotic and illogical. Chojnacka (2014) examined activity statements (management commentaries) of listed companies in Poland in order to determine if they contained any information on their CSR activities or at least where such information might be found. Her research revealed that some organizations presented information on CSR, but not all CSR activities were connected with their corporate strategy and the way CSR information was disclosed varied significantly.

As the number of Polish companies that prepare integrated reports increases, more and more researchers investigate their practices in this regard. A literature review (Krasodomska, 2015b) reveals the informative content of the following companies' integrated reports to have been analyzed in Polish literature: LOTOS, GAZ

SYSTEM and Scanmed Multimedis (Krasodomska, 2012a, 2013b), LOTOS, GAZ-SYSTEM, Scanmed Multimedis, TAURON Polska Energia and Grupa RWE SA (Szczepankiewicz, 2013a, 2013b, 2014), LOTOS (Tatarska, 2013), Zakłady Azotowe SA (Michalczuk & Mikulska, 2014). In general, the authors share the opinion that companies present information in integrated reports in a diverse manner, which makes any comparison difficult. They also follow the Integrated Reporting Framework guidelines more or less strictly.

In recent years, researchers in Poland and across the world have started to examine the determinants of CSR disclosure and motives of CSR reporting. Krasodomska (2013a, 2014) has tried to explain the phenomena of CSR through the legitimization theory. Waniak-Michalak and Michalak (2013) have discovered the level of CSR disclosure in companies in Poland to be dependent on the characteristics of management boards (age and experience of the chairperson). At the same time, they conclude that few companies disclose information about the impact of CSR activities on customer value creation. Zyznarska-Dworczak (2015) suggests that the legitimization might be internal and external and that accounting could help to present a company as socially responsible both to external stakeholders and its employees and shareholders.

Another article by the same authors (Waniak-Michalak & Michalak 2013) reveals that the motives of corporations in Poland for developing CSR activities are similar to those of the organizations in the USA. However, Polish companies seem to be motivated more strongly by the fact that their competitors realize CSR strategy than by the fact that their stakeholders expect them to do so. Yet another article by these authors (Waniak-Michalak & Michalak 2016) shows corporations to be more willing to disclose information on CSR activity in the social area if they belong to the group of the biggest donors, i.e. if the donation is significant. Hąbek and Wolniak (2015) have discovered that managers and researchers have totally different opinions on the determinants of CSR reporting. However, the main conclusion is that the government needs to engage in the development of CSR reporting.

In 2014, Gabrusewicz described the role of the accounting system in delivering necessary information for the management of the CSR strategy. He stated that the CSR manager should collect important data from the company's ledger and journal. Krasodomska (2015a) has analyzed CSR disclosures in management commentaries of selected banks. She concludes that the quality of CSR disclosures in bank management commentaries in Poland has increased over time although the banks do not prepare integrated reports.

In conclusion, it can be said that Poland is a country where CSR is at an early stage of development (Hąbek, 2014). Most of research papers concern the content of CSR reports and, since 2014, of integrated reporting. However, articles in Polish are rather theoretical and do not present the results of empirical research , as opposed to articles of Polish scientists published in languages other than Polish. Research interests of Polish authors in the area of CSR reporting concentrate on factors influencing CSR reporting and the quality of these reports. This can be accounted for by the fact that the sample of CSR reports is still small in Poland (37 reports in 2014). However, assuming that the CSR concept becomes more widespread in Poland in the near future, the research in this field is likely to gather momentum.

5. Conclusion

The profit-maximizing rule proposed by the traditional theory of economics as one and only aim of business operations does not explain the behavior of many types of companies which we observe nowadays. Although this approach still has many supporters, business executives more and more often recognize the importance of non-economic purposes, declare them as part of the companies' mission and assume responsibility for their implementation.

This corporate behavior is in line with the CSR concept. In Poland, it has been developing for about 15 years. Initially, it consisted in raising money for charities and in sponsorships, and was viewed primarily as a marketing activity. Nowadays, Polish companies have become aware of the advantages of implementing CSR in their long-term strategies, as for example, an opportunity to stand out in the market, to achieve tangible benefits or to avoid some types of risks.

In 2010, the concept of integrated reporting emerged mainly owing to the GRI and the development of sustainability reporting over the years. The idea of CSR has drawn attention to the importance of non-financial information for a comprehensive assessment of business activities. However, there are some important differences between the CSR and integrated reporting. CSR reporting targets a wider stakeholder audience than does integrated reporting and it focuses on impacts on the environment, society and the economy rather than on the value creation over time.

The above mentioned changes in the way companies operate and report on their performance are reflected in accounting research. In Poland, as in other countries across the world, academia representatives conduct studies referring to the inclusion of the CSR concept in the accounting framework, mainly concentrating on voluntary corporate disclosures and integrated reporting practices.

The discussion presented in this paper is based on the analysis of the BazEkon and EBSCO databases, Google web search engine, as well as a thorough examination of 67 papers, 39 of which concerned CSR reporting and 9 focused on integrated reporting.

According to the study results, the first accounting publications dedicated to the CSR concept appeared in Poland in 2005 (as identified in BazEkon), 2011 (according to EBSCO), and 2004 (as indicated by Google Scholar). Integrated reporting, as a moderately new concept, was the topic of the first scholarly publications in 2012 (BazEkon, Google Scholar) and 2013 (EBSCO). The total number of publications increased over time to reach: 14 (Bazekon), 7 (EBSCO) and 63 (Google Scholar) works on CSR issues and 8,8 and 41 papers on integrated reporting, respectively, in 2015. Few papers included in the databases were written in English and none of them was published in the top accounting journals (with the highest impact factors).

Our research revealed that CSR is widely presented in Polish literature. Most papers referred to the use of GRI standards and benefits of the CSR for the companies. Only in recent years in Poland more empirical studies in the field of CSR reporting were conducted and discussion about integrated reporting started. Some authors were skeptical about usefulness of integrated reports and were against the increase of non-financial information in the reports. The others stated that integrated reports should replace traditional reports which did not present relevant information on the company's achievements and risks. Only a few researchers applied statistical tools or conducted interviews or surveys. The interests of Polish researchers in the area of CSR reporting focus on factors influencing CSR reporting and the quality of CSR reports.

Small number of research articles on CSR disclosures in Poland may result from the fact that the communist regime in Poland fell just 20 years ago and that CSR is a new concept for Polish companies. However, we can conclude that along with an increase in the number of CSR reports in Poland, the research in this field can also be extended. In the light of the above, it seems that the possibilities of future research on CSR literature in Poland are extensive. It could focus on the more thorough quantitative and qualitative analyses of the studies conducted by the Polish academia, particularly with a view to finding out whether they are published in internationally acknowledged journals, prepared in collaboration with foreign scholars, or performed with the use of more sophisticated methods. Authors believe that further development of Polish literature on CSR issues could be beneficial not only for the accounting science itself, but also for Polish students of accounting, accountants, regulatory authorities and companies.

References

Banaszkiewicz, A. & Makowska, E. (2012) "Społeczna odpowiedzialność biznesu w kontekście wybranych aspektów kulturowych XXI stulecia" [Corporate Social Responsibility Accounting in the Context of the Selected Cultural Aspects of the Twenty-first Century], *Copernican Journal of Finance & Accounting*, vol 1, no. 1: 9-21

Bartkowiak, G. (2011) "Społeczna odpowiedzialność biznesu w aspekcie teoretycznym i empirycznym" [Corporate social responsibility in theoretical and empirical aspects], Difin, Warszawa

Bernatt, M., Bogdanienko, J. & Skoczny, T. (2011) "Społeczna odpowiedzialność biznezu. Krytyczna analiza" [Corporate Social Responsibility. Critical analysis], Wydawnictwo Naukowe Wydziału Zarządzania Uniwersytetu Warszawskiego, Warszawa

Bielińska-Dusza, E. & Pająk, W. (2012) "Metodyczna koncepcja badania społecznej odpowiedzialności przedsiębiorstwa w kształtowaniu strategii zrównoważonego rozwoju" [Methodological Concept of Corporate Social Responsibility Research in the Development of Strategies for Sustainable Development], *Acta Universitatis Lodziensis, Folia Oeconomica,* no. 265: 154-170

Broniewska, G. (2012) "Wytyczne i standardy społecznej odpowiedzialności biznesu" [Guidelines and standards of corporate social responsibility], *Acta Universitatis Lodziensis, Folia Oeconomica*, no. 265: 7-16

Brzozowski, T. T. (2010) "Rola i zasadność społecznej odpowiedzialności biznesu w warunkach integracji europejskiej" [The Significance and Legitimacy of Corporate Social Responsibility in the Conditions of the European Integration Process], *Przedsiębiorczość – Edukacja*, no. 6: 113-125

Burzym, E. (1990) "Rachunkowość jako podstawa rachunku z tytułu społeczno-ekonomicznej odpowiedzialności przedsiębiorstw" [Accounting as the base of reporting corporate social responsibility], *Zeszyty Naukowe AE w Krakowie*, no. 329: 1-11

Burzym, E. (1993) "Społeczny i ekologiczny aspekt współczesnej ewolucji rachunkowości" [Social and ecological aspect of modern evolution of accounting], *Zeszyty Naukowe AE w Krakowie*, no. 401: 5-20

Burzym, E. (2008) "Społeczna funkcja rachunkowości" [The social function of accounting], *Zeszyty Teoretyczne Rachunkowości*, vol. 45, no. 101: 71-86

Chojnacka, E. (2014) "Raportowanie danych w obszarach środowiskowym i społecznym w publicznych spółkach sektora energetycznego" [Reporting environment and social data in public companies in energy sector], *Prace Naukowe Uniwersytetu Ekonomicznego we Wrocławiu*, no. 329: 45-53

Dołęgowski, T. (2005) "Od etyki gospodarczej i etyki biznesu do Corporate Social Responasability i koncepcji rozwoju zrównoważonego [From economic ethics and business ethics to Corporate Social Responsibility and sustainable development concept], in: eds. Brdulak, H. & Gołębiowski, T., *Zrównoważony rozwój przedsiębiorstwa a relacje z interesariuszami [Sustainable development of the company and stakeholder relations]*, Oficyna Wydawnicza SGH, Warszawa

Dyląg, R., Puchalska, E. (2014) "Raportowanie zagadnień środowiskowych i społecznych" [Reporting on social and environmental issues], *Zeszyty Teoretyczne Rachunkowości*, vol. 75, no. 131: 23-45

Gabrusewicz, T. (2005) "Próba objaśnienia roli rachunkowości w społecznej odpowiedzialności korporacji" [Social responsibility of the corporation (the role of accounting)], *Zeszyty Teoretyczne Rachunkowości,* vol. 29, no. 85: 34-48

Gabrusewicz, T. (2010) "Rachunkowość społecznej odpowiedzialności w kształtowaniu zasad nadzoru korporacyjnego" [Corporate Social Responsibility accounting for creating the rules of corporate governance], C.H. Beck, Warszawa

Gabrusewicz, T. (2014) "Zdolność systemu rachunkowości w zakresie zaspokojenia potrzeb informacyjnych w realizacji koncepcji zrównoważonego rozwoju" [The ability of the accounting systemto satisfy information needs in the concept of sustainable development], *Studia i prace Kolegium Zarządzania i Finansów*, no.130: 109-117

Galimska, A. (2015) "Sprawozdawczość społecznej odpowiedzialności przedsiębiorstw wydobywających gaz łupkowy w Polsce i Stanach Zjednoczonych" [Corporate Social Responsability reporting among shale gas producers in Poland and the USA], *Studia Oeconomica Posnaniensia*, vol. 3, no. 1: 18-35

Gasparski, W. (2007) "Wykłady z etyki biznesu. Nowa edycja uzupełniona" [Lectures on business ethics. New edition supplemented], Wydawnictwo WSPIZ im. Leona Koźmińskiego, Warszawa

Gołaszewska-Kaczan, U. (2009) "Zaangażowanie społeczne przedsiębiorstwa" [The social involvement of an enterprise], Wydawnictwo Uniwersytetu w Białymstoku, Białystok

Hąbek, P. (2014) "Evaluation of sustainability reporting practices in Poland", *Quality & Quantity*, vol. 48, no. 3: 1739-1752

Hąbek, P. & Wolniak, R. (2015) "Factors influencing the development of CSR Reporting Practices: Experts' versus preparers' points of view", *Engineering Economics*, vol. 26, no. 5: 560-570

Hopkins, M. (2015) "Foreword", in: S. O. Idowu, R. Schmidpeter, M. S. Fifka (Eds.) *Corporate Social Responsibility in Europe. United in Sustainable Diversity*, Springer, Switzerland.

Haglińska, Z. (1984) "Rachunkowość odpowiedzialności społecznej przedsiębiorstw kapitalistycznych" [Accouting of corporate social responsibility of capital enterprises], *Zeszyty Teoretyczne Rachunkowości,* no. 7: 15-21

Jarugowa, A. (1984) "Rachunkowość społeczna na tle tendencji rozwoju rachunkowości" [Social accounting in the light of accounting development], *Zeszyty Teoretyczne Rachunkowości,* no. 7: 5-14

Jastrzębska, E. & Legutko-Kobus, P. (2014) "Rola i działania biznesu na rzecz budowania kapitału społecznego w Polsce" [Role and business activity for social capital creating], *Mazowsze Studia Regionalne*, no. 15: 49-75

Karmańska, A., (2013) "Nauka rachunkowości, proces poznawczy, paradygmaty i prawda" [The science of accounting, cognitive process, paradigms and truth in accounting – a handful of findings and reflections], *Zeszyty Teoretyczne Rachunkowości*, vol. 71, no. 127:125-146

Kowalak, R. (2014) "Kluczowe mierniki dokonań w zakładach gospodarowania odpadami" [Key performance indicators for the waste disposal plants], *Prace Naukowe Uniwersytetu Ekonomicznego we Wrocławiu*, no. 329: 180-190

Krasodomska, J. (2010a) "Perspektywy rozwoju informacyjnej funkcji rachunkowości w kontekście społecznej odpowiedzialności przedsiębiorstw" [Development Prospects for the Accounting Informative Function and the Issue of Corporate Social Responsibility], *Studia i Prace Uniwersytetu Ekonomicznego w Krakowie,* no. 14: 334-341

Krasodomska, J. (2010b) "Rachunkowość a idea społecznej odpowiedzialności przedsiębiorstw w dobie kryzysu ekonomicznego" [Accounting and the social responsibility concept in times of economic crisis], in: ed. Micherda, B., *Rachunkowość wobec kryzysu gospodarczego [Accounting in the face of the economic crisis]*, Difin, Warszawa

Krasodomska J. (2012a) "Ewolucja sprawozdawczości finansowej w kierunku sprawozdawczości zintegrowanej na przykładzie spółekNovo Nordisk i LOTOS" [The evolution of financial reporting in the direction of integrated reporting on the example of companies Novo Nordisk and LOTOS], in: ed. Micherda, B., *Kierunki ewolucji sprawozdawczości i rewizji finansowej [Directions of reporting and auditing evolution]*, Difin, Warszawa

Krasodomska, J. (2012b) "Zintegrowana sprawozdawczość spółek w 2020 roku" [Integrated Reporting of Companies in 2020], *Zeszyty Teoretyczne Rachunkowości*, vol. 66, no. 122: 101-110

Krasodomska, J. (2013a) "Sprawozdawczość przedsiębiorstw w świetle teorii legitymizacji" [Corporate Reporting in the light of the Theory of Legitimization], *Studia i prace Kolegium Zarządzania i Finansów,* no. 130: 39-51

Krasodomska, J. (2013b) "Sprawozdawczość zintegrowana – aspekty teoretyczne i praktyczne" [Integrated Reporting - theoretical and practical aspects], in: ed. Remlein, M., *Rachunkowość odpowiedzialności społecznej – teoria i praktyka [Socially responsible accounting – theory and practice],* ZPW „M-DRUK", Poznań: 65-87

Krasodomska, J. (2014) "Integrated reporting and the directions of its development", *Olsztyn Economic Journal*, vol. 9 no. 2: 109-118

Krasodomska, J (2015a) „CSR disclosures in the banking industry. Empirical evidence from Poland", *Social Responsibility Journal*, vol. 11, no.3: 406-423

Krasodomska, J. (2015b) "Sprawozdawczość zintegrowana jako nowy obszar badań naukowych w rachunkowości" [Integrated reporting as a new area of research in accounting], *Zeszyty Teoretyczne Rachunkowości*, vol. 82 no. 138: 77-92

Kuźbik, P. (2012) "Kreowanie przestrzeni odpowiedzialności w świetle praktyki organizacyjnej" [Creating an area of responsibility in organizational practice], *Acta Universitatis Lodziensis, Folia Oeconomica*, no. 265: 85-93

Macuda, M. (2013) "Społeczna odpowiedzialność biznesu na przykładzie szpitala" [Corporate social responsibility on the example of the hospital], in: ed. Remlein, M., *Rachunkowość odpowiedzialności społecznej – teoria i praktyka [Socially responsible accounting – theory and practice]*, ZPW „M-DRUK", Poznań: 88-96

Macuda, M. (2015) "Rachunkowość odpowiedzialności społecznej – raportowanie zagadnień środowiskowych" [Social responsibility accounting – environmental reporting], *Studia Oeconomica Posnaniensia*, vol. 3, no. 1: 97-111

Macuda, M., Matuszak, Ł. & Różańska, E. (2015a) "Ujawnienia o CSR na przykładzie spółek notowanych na GPW w Warszawie" [Disclosures of CSR on the example of companies listed on the Warsaw Stock Exchange], in: ed. Remlein, M., *Teoria, praktyka, polityka rachunkowości [Theory, practice and policy of accounting]*, ZPW „M-DRUK", Poznań: 145-157

Macuda, M., Matuszak, Ł. & Różańska, E. (2015b) "The concept of CSR in accounting theory and practice in Poland: an empirical study", *Zeszyty Teoretyczne Rachunkowości*, vol. 84, no.140: 115-137

Marcinkowska, M. (2004) "Społeczna odpowiedzialność przedsiębiorstw – wpływ na zawartość raportów rocznych" [Corporate social responsibility – inluence on the content of year reports], *Acta Universitatis Lodziensis, Folia Oeconomica,* no. 181: 265-274

Marcinkowska, M. (2006) "Władztwo korporacyjne w kontekście społecznej odpowiedzialności przedsiębiorstw" [Corporate Governance in the context of corporate social responsibility], [in:] ed. Rudolf, S., *Tendencje zmian w nadzorze korporacyjnym [Tendency of changes in corporate govenrance]*, Wydawnictwo Uniwersytetu Łódzkiego, Łódź: 409-428

Marcinkowska, M. (2012) "Rachunkowość społeczna – czyli o pomiarze wyników przedsiębiorstw w kontekście oczekiwań interesariuszy" [Social accounting – or how to measure companies' performance in the context of stakeholders' expectations], *Prace Naukowe Uniwersytetu Ekonomicznego we Wrocławiu,* no. 271: 501-525

Matuszak, Ł. (2013) "Wycena sprawozdania finansowego w realizacji koncepcji społecznej odpowiedzialności przedsiębiorstwa" [Valuation of financial statements in the implementation of the CSR concept], in: ed. Remlein, M., *Rachunkowość odpowiedzialności społecznej – teoria i praktyka [Socially responsible accounting – theory and practice]*, ZPW „M-DRUK", Poznań: 97-109

Matuszak, Ł. (2015) "Raportowanie o społecznej odpowiedzialności przedsiębiorstw (CSR) za pomocą narzędzia legitymizacji przedsiębiorstw" [CSR reporting as a tool of corporate legitimacy], *Studia Oeconomica Posnaniensia*, vol. 3, no. 1: 113-134

Mazurowska, M. (2014) "Dylematy rachunkowości społecznej odpowiedzialności" [Dillemas of social responsibility accounting], *Studia Oeconomica Posnaniensia*, vol. 2, no. 8: 38-52

Michalak, J. (2010) "Standardy sprawozdawczości zrównoważonego rozwoju i stopień ich zastosowania w Polsce. Perspektywy rozwoju na podstawie wyników badań empirycznych" [Sustainability Reporting Standards: the Level of Application in Poland and around the World and the Prospects for Progress in the Light of Empirical Questions], *Studia i prace Uniwersytetu Ekonomicznego w Krakowie*, no. 2: 26-38.

Michalczuk G. & Mikulska T. (2014) "Sprawozdanie zintegrowane jako produkt finalny rachunkowości społecznej" [Integrated reporting as a final product of social accounting], *Zeszyty Naukowe Uniwersytetu Szczecińskiego*, vol. 827, no. 69: 197-207

Mizdrak, I. & Pogodzińska-Mizdrak, E. (2013) "Społeczna odpowiedzialność w działalności banków na przykładzie Banca Popolare Etica" [Social Responsibility in Bank Activities Exemplified by Banca Popolare Etica], *Studia i Prace Kolegium Zarządzania i Finansów*, vol. 130: 53-77.

Nakonieczna, J. (2008) "Społeczna odpowiedzialność przedsiębiorstw międzynarodowych" [Corporate Social Responsibility of international companies], Difin, Warszawa

Paszkiewicz, A. & Szadziewska, A. (2011) "Przejawy społecznej odpowiedzialności w działalności przedsiębiorstw" [Aspects of Social Responsibility in Business Activity], in: eds. Gierusz, J. & Martyniuk, T., *Kluczowe problemy teorii i praktyki rachunkowości [Key problems of the theory and practice of accounting], Prace i Materiały Wydziału Zarządzania Uniwersytetu Gdańskiego*, vol. 1, no. 1: 77-90

Pogodzińska-Mizdrak, E. (2010) "Koncepcje społecznie odpowiedzialnego gospodarowania i inwestowania szansa rozwoju rachunkowości" [Corporate Social Responsibility, Environmental Social Governance and Social Responsibility Investment as a chance for accounting], *Zeszyty Teoretyczne Rachunkowości*, vol. 56, no. 12: 175-184

Remlein, M. (2015) "Doświadczenia polskich grup kapitałowych w zakresie zintegrowanej sprawozdawczości" [The experience of polish corporate groups in integrated reporting], *Studia Oeconomica Posnaniensia*, vol. 3, no. 1: 149-166

Różańska, E. (2014) "Finansowa ocena projektów badawczo-rozwojowych w przedsiębiorstwie społecznie odpowiedzialnym" [Financial assessment of research and development projects in a socially responsible company], *Prace Naukowe Uniwersytetu Ekonomicznego we Wrocławiu*, no. 344: 434-445

Roszkowska, P. (2011) "Rewolucja w raportowaniu biznesowym. Interesariusze, konkurencyjność, społeczna odpowiedzialność" [The revolution in business reporting. Stakeholders, competitiveness, corporate social responsibility], Difin, Warszawa

Samelak, J. (2013) "Zintegrowane sprawozdanie przedsiębiorstwa społecznie odpowiedzialnego" [Integrated report of a socially responsible company], Wydawnictwo Uniwersytetu Ekonomicznego w Poznaniu, Poznań

Sikacz, H. (2014) "Raportowanie o ryzyku płynności w kontekście społecznej odpowiedzialności przedsiębiorstwa w wybranych grupach kapitałowych" [Reporting of Liquidity Risk in the Context of Corporate Social Responsibility in Selected Capital Groups], *Zeszyty Naukowe Uniwersytetu Szczecińskiego*, no. 65: 719-729

Stępień, M. (2001) "Idea społecznej odpowiedzialności przedsiębiorstw i jej wpływ na ewolucję rachunkowości" [Social responsibility accounting concept and its influence on the accounting evolution], *Zeszyty Teoretyczne Rachunkowości*, vol. 4, no.60: 177-195

Stępień, M. (2003) "Rachunkowość a ochrona środowiska w opinii biegłych rewidentów (wyniki badań ankietowych)" [Accounting and environmental protection in the opinion of the auditors (survey results)], in: ed. Sojak, S., *Historia, współczesność i perspektywy rachunkowości w Polsce [History, contemporaneity and perspectives of accounting in Poland]*, Wydawnictwo Uniwersytetu Mikołaja Kopernika, Toruń: 69-82

Stępień, M. & Wydymus Z. (2007) "Rola rachunkowości w kształtowaniu społecznej odpowiedzialności jednostki gospodarczej" [The Role of Accounting in Creating Corporate Social Responsibility], *Zeszyty Naukowe Uniwersytetu Ekonomicznego w Krakowie*, no. 750: 79-99

Szadziewska, A. (2013) "Rola rachunkowości w pomiarze efektywności działań CSR" [The Role of Accounting in Measuring the Effectiveness of CSR Activities], *Prace i Materiały Wydziału Zarządzania Uniwersytetu Gdańskiego*, no. 4: 257-277

Szadziewska, A. (2014) "Prezentowanie informacji na temat społecznej odpowiedzialności w sprawozdawczości zewnętrznej przedsiębiorstw" [Presenting Social Responsibility Information in Corporate External Reports], *Prace Naukowe Uniwersytetu Ekonomicznego we Wrocławiu*, no. 329: 261-270

Szczepankiewicz, E. (2013a) "Ryzyka ujawniane w zintegrowanym sprawozdaniu przedsiębiorstwa społecznie odpowiedzialnego" [The Risks Disclosed in the Integrated Statements of a Socially Responsible Company], *Ekonomika i Organizacja Przedsiębiorstwa*, no. 5: 71-82

Szczepankiewicz, E. (2013b) "Informacje tworzące wartość rynkową w raportowaniu biznesowym" [Information creating the market value of the reporting business], *Kwartalnik Nauk o Przedsiębiorstwie*, no. 3: 33-42

Szczepankiewicz, E. (2014) "Zintegrowane sprawozdanie przedsiębiorstwa jako narzędzie komunikacji z interesariuszami" [Integrated report on socially responsible companies as a tool of communication with users], *Prace Naukowe Uniwersytetu Ekonomicznego we Wrocławiu*, no. 329: 271-281

Tatarska, M. (2013) "Sprawozdawczość zintegrowana na przykładzie Grupy Lotos SA" [Integrated Reporting on the Example of the Lotos Group Joint Stock Company], *Prace Naukowe Uniwersytetu Ekonomicznego we Wrocławiu*, no. 314: 187-199

Wachowiak, P. (2013) *Wrażliwość społeczna przedsiębiorstwa. Analiza i pomiar* [Corporate social sensitivity. Analysis and measurement], Szkoła Główna Handlowa w Warszawie – Oficyna Wydawnicza, Warszawa.

Walińska, E. (2015) "Zintegrowany raport – początek końca sprawozdania finansowego?" [Integrated report – beginning of the end of financial statements?], *Zeszyty Teoretyczne Rachunkowości*, vol. 82, no. 138: 151-165

Waniak-Michalak, H. & Michalak, J. (2013) "Customer value creation through corporate disclosure on society-oriented activities, do CEO's characteristics influence the scope of disclosure?", *Social Sciences*, Vol. 81, no. 3: 43-54

Waniak-Michalak, H. & Michalak, J. (2016) "Corporate and NGOs' voluntary disclosure on collaboration. Evidence from Poland", *Inzinerine Ekonomika-Engineering Economics*, vol. 27, no.1: 98–108

Wildowicz-Giegiel, A. (2014) "Wyzwania przed sprawozdawczością finansową związane z raportowaniem o kapitale intelektualnym i społecznej odpowiedzialności" [Challenges of financial reporting associatedwith reporting the intellectual capitaland the social responsibility of enterprise], *Prace Naukowe Uniwersytetu Ekonomicznego we Wrocławiu*, no. 329: 300-307

Wołkowski, J. (1984) "Z praktyki rachunkowości społecznej w niektórych krajach kapitalistycznych" [From practice of social accounting in some market oriented countries], *Zeszyty Teoretyczne Rachunkowości*, no. 7: 47-55

Wyrzykowski, M. (1986) "Pojęcie interesu społecznego w prawie administracyjnym" [The concept of public interest in administrative law], Wydawnictwo Uniwersytetu Warszawskiego, Warszawa

Zbiegień-Maciąg, L. (1996) *Etyka w zarządzaniu* [Ethics in management], Centrum Informacji Menedżera, Warszawa

Zuchewicz, J. (2014) "Sprawozdawczość jednostki społecznie odpowiedzialnej za swoje dokonania" [CSR in reporting entity's performance], *Prace Naukowe Uniwersytetu Ekonomicznego we Wrocławiu*, no. 329: 326-333

Zyznarska-Dworczak, B. (2015) "Zrównoważona rachunkowość zarządcza w świetle teorii legitymizacji" [Sustainable Management Accounting in the Light of Legitimacy Theory], *Zeszyty Teoretyczne Rachunkowości*, vol. 82, no.138: 181-189

Żemigała, M. (2007) "Społeczna odpowiedzialność przedsiębiorstwa" [Corporate Social Responsibility], Oficyna a Wolters Kluwer business, Kraków

Appendix A

Selected publications by Polish authors representing the accounting discipline referring to the CSR and integrated reporting issues

Author(s)	Key issues investigated	Research method and theory	Language	Source (international or local; accounting or general; book or book chapter or journal)	Key findings
Banaszkiewicz & Makowska (2012)	CSR	literature analysis	Polish	Local/accounting Journal	▪ accounting should encounter selected aspects of culture, such as activities to protect the environment and society
Bielińska-Dusza & Pająk (2012)	CSR, sustainability development	literature analysis	Polish	Local/general Journal	▪ companies must develop and measure achievements of the CSR activity
Broniewska (2012)	CSR standards	literature analysis	Polish	Local/general Journal	▪ guidelines of SA 8000, AA 1000 and ISO26000 standards could be useful to the leaders of the organizations – these standards facilitate the implementation of social and environmental problems as well as the stakeholders` service
Brzozowski (2010)	CSR	literature analysis	Polish	Local/general Journal	▪ the main problem concerns the possibilities of working out an agreement in order to recognize the common values shared by key member states of the EU – good place for an achievement of consensus in this matter is the business arena, it seems probable that business will be the most neutral field to achieve harmony in social issues during the European integration process

Author(s)	Key issues investigated	Research method and theory	Language	Source (international or local; accounting or general; book or book chapter or journal)	Key findings
Burzym (1990)	CSR, accounting	literature analysis	Polish	Local/general Journal	▪ accounting should play greater role in presenting information on CSR
Burzym (1993)	environmental and social issues	literature analysis	Polish	Local/general Journal	▪ accounting evaluates and nowadays should present social and ecological aspects of business activity ▪ accounting should provide information to stakeholders in order to enable monitoring and evaluation of the company's activities from the point of view of compliance of its objectives with the social objectives and its contribution to social welfare
Burzym (2008)	social function of accounting	literature analysis	Polish	Local/accounting Journal	▪ accounting defined as „a universal, flexible, entity oriented system of information and ▪ control, determined by the balancing method, which is inseparably linked with it by the cognitive method, making possible a numerical representation of the generation, flow and distribution of value and resulting settlements between entities” ▪ importance of social responsibility of enterprises and the resulting need to measure business efficiency understood as socio-economic efficiency

Author(s)	Key issues investigated	Research method and theory	Language	Source (international or local; accounting or general; book or book chapter or journal)	Key findings
Chojnacka (2014)	reporting of environmental and social issues, activity statements	content analysis of activity statements	Polish	Local/accounting Journal	▪ according to law regulations environment and social data can be presented in the Report of the Management Board on operations ▪ analysis of this report in chosen Polish public companies in energy sector confirms that the reporting level of given issues is different among companies – some companies prepared the separate part concerning social responsibility but presented activities were not always connected with a company's strategy; given companies did not inform about additional CSR reports ▪ due to the varied report structure it limits the utility of this reports as the source of nonfinancial information ▪ CSR activities are not always connected with a company's strategy and companies did not always inform about additional CSR reports

Author(s)	Key issues investigated	Research method and theory	Language	Source (international or local; accounting or general; book or book chapter or journal)	Key findings
Dyląg & Puchalska (2014)	reporting of environmental and social issues	literature analysis content analysis	Polish	Local/accounting Journal	▪ significance and effectiveness of the integration of companies' business strategy with the strategy of sustainable development is increasingly being emphasized ▪ corporate reporting is changing constantly following the trend characterized by a broader approach to business activity, involving not only the economic perspective but also the perspective of the environment and society – reporting on corporate social responsibility is one of the concepts supporting the implementation of the sustainable development strategy
Gabrusewicz (2005)	CSR, accounting	literature analysis	Polish	Local/accounting Journal	▪ the concept of accountability in the operations of business entities is important as well as in CSR activity
Gabrusewicz (2010)	socially responsible accounting	literature analysis	Polish	Local/accounting Book	▪ CSR increases the reputation and trust of the company ▪ accounting plays great role in increasing transparency of the organization and enables to use benefits of CSR by the corporation
Gabrusewicz (2014)	sustainability development, accounting	literature analysis	Polish	Local/general Journal	▪ with the increasing interest in the concept of sustainable development economists have noted that they do not have the appropriate methods for measuring its extent or effectiveness

Author(s)	Key issues investigated	Research method and theory	Language	Source (international or local; accounting or general; book or book chapter or journal)	Key findings
Galimska (2015)	CSR reporting	literature analysis	Polish	Local/ accounting Journal	▪ CSR reporting concerns companies engaged in the exploration and extraction of shale gas ▪ globalization and constantly increasing expectations of stakeholders force companies to produce reports which cover the results of economic activity more extensively than the previously offered accounting reports ▪ CSR reporting by Polish shale gas producers is often inadequate and lacks comparability by reason of adhering to different guidelines
Hąbek (2014)	sustainability reporting practices	questionnaire survey	English	International/general Journal	▪ sustainability reporting is not widespread in Poland but increasing demand in this field from stakeholders is not noticed
Hąbek & Wolniak (2015)	CSR reporting practices	questionnaire survey	English	International/general Journal	▪ CSR reports' preparers' and external 'experts' have a different view on reasons to issue a CSR report
Jaglińska (1984)	socially responsible accounting	literature analysis	Polish	Local/accounting Journal	▪ nowadays responsibility is extended to other stakeholders than only to shareholders, and to society ▪ accounting must reveal how the activities of the company influence the level of environment's pollution, usage of not-renewable resources, public security, health and education, civil rights and many other social aspects of life

Author(s)	Key issues investigated	Research method and theory	Language	Source (international or local; accounting or general; book or book chapter or journal)	Key findings
					▪ it is necessary to create the system of internal and external reporting in order to inform all stakeholders on all aspects and results of the corporate's activity ▪ social accounting requires taking into account non-financial information ▪ accounting and reporting regulations in the form of GAAP or IRS may be impossible ▪ reports should be clear, easy to understand and rewarding for users
Jarugowa (1984)	social accounting	literature analysis	Polish	Local/accounting Journal	▪ accounting may be used as the source supporting the acceptance of the business activity ▪ information presented to society must be useful for decision making ▪ financial information should be supported by non-financial information ▪ information aspects should be the following: importance, accuracy, aggregation and timeless ▪ principal reason for developing the social accounting was the recognition of the man as the subject of work, not only as the mean for goals' achievement ▪ responsibility of companies may be considered in the isolation or in the cooperation of many partners in social context

Author(s)	Key issues investigated	Research method and theory	Language	Source (international or local; accounting or general; book or book chapter or journal)	Key findings
Jastrzębska & Legutko-Kobus (2014)	social capital, CSR	literature analysis, content analysis	Polish	Local/general Journal	▪ level of civil trust in Poland is low and therefore small development of CSR
Karmańska (2013)	integrated reports	literature analysis	Polish	Local/accounting Journal	▪ knowledge-based economy triggers the circumstances and factors that the academic accounting community should carefully identify, investigate and evaluate in terms of value contributed to the development of accounting practice and theory
Kowalak (2014)	CSR	literature analysis	Polish	Local/accounting Journal	▪ waste disposal plants do not use measurement system and do not evaluate their activity
Krasodomska (2010a)	CSR, informative function of accounting	literature analysis	Polish	Local/general Journal	▪ social accounting and social reporting are important research splits within the accounting discipline ▪ it is necessary to measure corporate CSR achievements in social and environmental areas with the use of indicators which refer to e.g.: economic performance, ecological issues, employees, work security, social problems and cooperation with business partners

Author(s)	Key issues investigated	Research method and theory	Language	Source (international or local; accounting or general; book or book chapter or journal)	Key findings
Krasodomska (2010b)	CSR, accounting	literature analysis	Polish	Local/accounting Book chapter	▪ companies needs to satisfy the needs of various stakeholders ▪ CSR should be discussed in several areas: economical, sociological, ecological, ethical ▪ CSR standards needs to be implemented by companies ▪ connection between CSR and accounting has to be stressed
Krasodomska (2012a)	CSR, integrated reporting	literature analysis, case study	Polish	Local/accounting Book chapter	▪ integrated reporting concept is an important and needed notion ▪ comparative analysis of Novo Nordisk and LOTOS integrated reports allows for the positive assessment of both companies disclosure practices
Krasodomska (2012b)	integrated reporting	literature analysis	Polish	Local/accounting Journal	▪ it is possible for the integrated reporting to became a reporting standard in 2020 among others due to the promotion actions taken, by IIRC, GRI, AICPA and the European Union
Krasodomska (2013a)	reporting, legitimization theory	literature analysis	Polish	Local/general Journal	▪ legitimacy theory has a particularly wide application in regard to voluntary environmental and social disclosures made by companies, as exemplified by the selected empirical studies presented in the paper

Author(s)	Key issues investigated	Research method and theory	Language	Source (international or local; accounting or general; book or book chapter or journal)	Key findings
Krasodomska (2013b)	integrated reporting, legitimization theory, stakeholder theory	literature analysis, case study	Polish	Local/accounting Book chapter	▪ an analysis of CorporateRegister.com data, and the integrated reports drawn up by three companies operating in Poland: LOTOS, GAS SYSTEM and Scanmed Multimedis allows to state that this concept gains in popularity, and the reliability of the information presented in integrated reports is particularly important
Krasodomska (2014)	integrated reporting, legitimization theory	literature analysis	English	Local/general Journal	▪ integrated reporting is an issue is also worth addressing within contemporary accounting research, paper identifies Polish authors dealing with this problems in their studies published in the years 2011-2013
Krasodomska (2015a)	CSR disclosures in banks	content analysis, disclosure index, legitimacy theory	English	International/general Journal	▪ identification of information on CSR included in the management commentaries of selected banks operating in Poland, and evaluation the disclosures with regard to their quality, diversity and the ways they change over time allows to state that banks tend to include CSR disclosures in the management commentary ▪ banks present CSR information in diverse manner, focusing mainly on community involvement

Author(s)	Key issues investigated	Research method and theory	Language	Source (international or local; accounting or general; book or book chapter or journal)	Key findings
					▪ the quality of CSR disclosures in 2011 was higher as compared with 2005
Krasodomska (2015b)	integrated reporting	literature analysis	Polish	Local/accounting Journal	▪ identification of the main research gaps in integrating reporting as a result of an analysis of: papers indexed in EBSCO and Emerald databases, problems indicated by the IIRC in cooperation with ACCA and IAAER, studies accepted for presentation at the EAA Congress in Glasgow in April 2015, and Polish authors' publications ▪ as the main desirable research topics were identified problems related to: the business model, the value concept, the six capitals, the quality and materiality of integrated reports, satisfaction of users with integrated reports as sources of information, as well as the role of accountants and external auditors in the development and verification of integrated reporting
Kuźbik (2012)	CSR	literature analysis	Polish	Local/general Journal	▪ it is necessary to inform people about fulfilling their expectations about the organization's activities for the common good and future generations
Macuda (2013)	CSR, hospital	literature analysis	Polish	Local/accounting Book chapter	▪ CSR concept is spread also in hospitals

Author(s)	Key issues investigated	Research method and theory	Language	Source (international or local; accounting or general; book or book chapter or journal)	Key findings
Macuda (2015)	socially responsible accounting, CSR reporting, environmental issues	literature analysis	Polish	Local/ accounting Journal	▪ stakeholders expect greater transparency of information concerning the impact of the company activity on environmental, social and economic issues ▪ lack of consistency and uniform practices in reporting on corporate social responsibility impedes comparability between companies ▪ integrated reporting is the future of corporate reporting – should provide a coherent, consistent, transparent and comparable financial and non-financial information
Macuda *et al.* (2015b)	CSR, accounting	literature analysis, content analysis	English	Local/ accounting Journal	▪ among Polish public companies listed on the WSE (also listed in the WIG-Poland index) only 6% operate in a socially responsible manner according to the RESPECT criteria, and less than 4.6% of all companies listed in the WIG-Poland and 70% of RESPECT index companies prepare separate CSR reports ▪ out of all the companies that prepare separate CSR reports, 93% prepare ESG reports, but to a different scope ▪ out of all the companies preparing separate CSR reports, 70% followed the GRI Guidelines

Author(s)	Key issues investigated	Research method and theory	Language	Source (international or local; accounting or general; book or book chapter or journal)	Key findings
					▪ percentage share of companies whose CSR reports were verified by an independent external auditor is not very high - 18% ▪ among the companies preparing separate CSR reports (listed in the RESPECT Index) only one prepared an integrated annual report (for the year 2012)
Marcinkowska (2004)	CSR, annual reports	literature analysis	Polish	Local/general Journal	▪ corporations must disclose on financial, environmental and social aspects
Marcinkowska (2006)	CSR	literature analysis	Polish	Local/general Book chapter	▪ company must construct the measures of the efficiency of communication with stakeholders which will be, in the same moment, measures of the quality of the corporate governance system
Marcinkowska (2012)	social accounting	literature analysis	Polish	Local/general Journal	▪ the most useful for stakeholders tool is the performance prism, which measures the achievements in five perspectives: stakeholders interests, stakeholders contribution, strategy, processes of implementation the strategy and resources
Matuszak (2015)	CSR reporting, integrated reporting	literature analysis	Polish	Local/ accounting Journal	▪ CSR disclosing to the public information in the form of financial reports, CSR reports or integrated reports can be used by companies to pursue strategies to obtain, maintain and recover legitimacy

Author(s)	Key issues investigated	Research method and theory	Language	Source (international or local; accounting or general; book or book chapter or journal)	Key findings
					▪ disclosure of non-financial information (same as disclosure of financial information) should be verified by external auditors to confirm their credibility – otherwise, the information will be part of the marketing strategy of a company that does not motivate to conduct socially responsible business (this requires a higher degree of formalization and regulation) ▪ CSR disclosures should not be only a consequence of the danger of losing legitimacy, but must arise from the conviction of the management team about the responsibility for the company activities
Mazurowska (2014)	integrated reports	literature analysis	Polish	Local/ accounting Journal	▪ system of accounting should provide information on the methods and results regarding the implementation of the CSR concept in business entities
Michalak (2010)	CSR reports	content analysis	Polish	Local/accounting Journal	▪ CSR is important, however small number of CSR reports is prepared according to GRI standards
Michalczuk & Mikulska (2014)	integrated reporting, CSR reporting,	literature analysis content analysis	Polish	Local/general Journal	▪ preparing the standard for integrated reporting is undoubtedly a crucial step towards information reporting in the context of the growing needs of company

Author(s)	Key issues investigated	Research method and theory	Language	Source (international or local; accounting or general; book or book chapter or journal)	Key findings
	social accounting				stakeholders – (1) it would enable to include all the spheres of business activity of a company in one document which would primarily emphasize the importance of the connection between corporate strategy, financial performance and the social, economic and environmental context of its activities; and (2) it would allow the creation of a global platform for enterprise reporting accomplishments within the concept of social responsibility and sustainable development
Mizdrak *et al.* (2013)	CSR in banks	literature analysis	Polish	Local/general Journal	▪ ethical banks give a positive example of the implementation of the idea of good CSR practices in the business activity ▪ moral (ethical) predicates are as important and justified as empirical cognition in economic sciences
Paszkiewicz & Szadziewska (2011)	CSR	literature analysis	Polish	Local/general Journal	▪ CSR concept combines the elements of economic sciences, social sciences and philosophy

Author(s)	Key issues investigated	Research method and theory	Language	Source (international or local; accounting or general; book or book chapter or journal)	Key findings
Pogodzińska-Mizdrak (2010)	CSR, accounting	literature analysis	Polish	Local/accounting Journal	▪ success of a corporate social responsibility strategy depends on many factors, one of which is the system of accounting, which includes ready measurement methods, in particular with regard to balance sheet valuation, interpretation and recording of economic events, as well as reporting ▪ social responsibility accounting should integrate, on a voluntary basis, social and environmental concerns in business operations and in interaction with stakeholders of a company in long-term perspective
Roszkowska (2011)	CSR, reporting	content analysis	Polish	Local/general Book	▪ form and contents of social responsibility reports depend on the general communication strategy of a company – if the company operates in a complete isolation, publishing the environmental, social and economic information is limited to simply presenting the data (without any feedback); but if managers wish to establish lasting relations with the community, the exchange of information and opinions is vital in reporting (data collected in the course of bilateral communication)

Author(s)	Key issues investigated	Research method and theory	Language	Source (international or local; accounting or general; book or book chapter or journal)	Key findings
Różańska (2015)	CSR reporting standards	literature analysis	Polish	Local/ accounting Journal	▪ GRI Guidelines with other general corporate social responsibility initiatives developed at the international level should be combined
Sikacz (2014)	CSR, reporting	content analysis	Polish	Local/general Journal	▪ there is a need to include in CSR reporting liquidity risk – the information contained in these reports is limited to provide basic, quantitative reporting data
Stępień (2001)	CSR, accounting	literature analysis	Polish	Local/accounting Journal	▪ there is a significant influence of corporate social responsibility on the accounting evolution in the area of environment capital and human capital
Stępień (2003)	environmental issues	literature analysis	Polish	Local/accounting Book chapter	▪ environmental awareness among societies increases ▪ implementation of corporate social responsibility idea is a manifestation of the development of accounting theory and practice arising from economic and social changes
Stępień & Wydymus (2007)	CSR, accounting	literature analysis	Polish	Local/general Journal	▪ society must have possibility to control economic events whose effects impact upon individuals and the natural environment ▪ companies may use the accounting system in order to measure the effects of CSR activity and provide the relevant information

Author(s)	Key issues investigated	Research method and theory	Language	Source (international or local; accounting or general; book or book chapter or journal)	Key findings
Szadziewska (2013)	CSR, accounting	literature analysis	Polish	Local/general Journal	▪ accounting should enable to gain information on environmental and social activity of companies
Szadziewska (2014)	CSR, reporting	literature analysis	Polish	Local/ accounting Journal	▪ CSR reporting allows companies to build transparent and trust-based relationships with their stakeholders
Szczepankiewicz (2013a)	integrated reporting	content analysis	Polish	Local/general Journal	▪ integrated reporting is the next step of reporting evolution
Szczepankiewicz (2013b)	integrated reporting	content analysis	Polish	Local/general Journal	▪ integrated reports should focus on the company's strategy ▪ the new approach to corporate disclosures should not lead to the information overload ▪ analyzed companies (LOTOS, GAZ-System, Skanmed Mulitimedis) present information in the integrated reports in a very diversified manner, what makes it difficult to compare
Szczepankiewicz (2014)	integrated reporting	literature analysis	Polish	Local/ accounting Journal	▪ in order to start integrated reporting following rules should be introduced: significance of information, complexity of information and fulfilling stakeholders' needs
Tatarska (2013)	integrated reporting	content analysis	Polish	Local/ accounting Journal	▪ the main advantages of integrated reporting include the possibility to obtain the holistic picture of company's achievements, and to make more effective economic decisions

Author(s)	Key issues investigated	Research method and theory	Language	Source (international or local; accounting or general; book or book chapter or journal)	Key findings
					▪ costs and labour-intensiveness are the main problems related to integrated reporting
Walińska (2015)	integrated report	literature analysis	Polish	Local/accounting Journal	▪ in integrated reports the financial information should be presented in the highest extend and non-financial information should be only a supplement
Waniak-Michalak & Michalak (2013)		content analysis, cluster analysis	English	International/general Journal	▪ level of CSR disclosure depends on the characteristics of management boards (age and experience of a chairman person)
Waniak-Michalak & Michalak (2016)	CSR reporting	content analysis, regression analysis	English	International/general Journal	▪ key factors determining the amount of information on philanthropic partnerships displayed by corporations and charities on their websites and in CSR reports are on the side of corporation: NGO being a corporate foundation and belonging to the group of biggest donors
Wildowicz-Giegiel (2014)	CSR, reporting	literature analysis	Polish	Local/ accounting Journal	▪ in spite of the growth of an interest in integrated reports of enterprises, the creation of universal principles of reporting which would ensure the credibility and the comparability of delivered information is not successful
Wołkowski (1984)	social accounting	literature analysis	Polish	Local/ accounting Journal	▪ companies report most of all on the expenditures and other provisions for

Author(s)	Key issues investigated	Research method and theory	Language	Source (international or local; accounting or general; book or book chapter or journal)	Key findings
					employees, environment and the whole society (mostly consumers) ▪ main obstacle for developing social accounting is the resistance of business to the expectations of social organizations and groups
▪ Zuchewicz (2014)	▪ social reporting	▪ literature analysis	▪ Polish	▪ Local/ accounting ▪ Journal	▪ traditional reporting, presented by entities is too complicated and over extensive and it does not meet information needs of more and more CSR aware organization shareholders, who make numerous decisions of local and international nature exerting impact on the surrounding reality ▪ possibility of developing an integrated financial statement extended by non-financial aspects referring to CSR for ecological, ethical and social specific operations
▪ Zyznarska-Dworczak (2015)	▪ CSR and other reports	▪ content analysis	▪ Polish	▪ Local/accounting ▪ Journal	▪ a proposals for treating internal social responsibility accounting (sustainable management accounting) as a tool for sustainable business legitimation

Permissions

All chapters in this book were first published in JAMIS, by Bucharest University of Economic Studies; hereby published with permission under the Creative Commons Attribution License or equivalent. Every chapter published in this book has been scrutinized by our experts. Their significance has been extensively debated. The topics covered herein carry significant findings which will fuel the growth of the discipline. They may even be implemented as practical applications or may be referred to as a beginning point for another development.

The contributors of this book come from diverse backgrounds, making this book a truly international effort. This book will bring forth new frontiers with its revolutionizing research information and detailed analysis of the nascent developments around the world.

We would like to thank all the contributing authors for lending their expertise to make the book truly unique. They have played a crucial role in the development of this book. Without their invaluable contributions this book wouldn't have been possible. They have made vital efforts to compile up to date information on the varied aspects of this subject to make this book a valuable addition to the collection of many professionals and students.

This book was conceptualized with the vision of imparting up-to-date information and advanced data in this field. To ensure the same, a matchless editorial board was set up. Every individual on the board went through rigorous rounds of assessment to prove their worth. After which they invested a large part of their time researching and compiling the most relevant data for our readers.

The editorial board has been involved in producing this book since its inception. They have spent rigorous hours researching and exploring the diverse topics which have resulted in the successful publishing of this book. They have passed on their knowledge of decades through this book. To expedite this challenging task, the publisher supported the team at every step. A small team of assistant editors was also appointed to further simplify the editing procedure and attain best results for the readers.

Apart from the editorial board, the designing team has also invested a significant amount of their time in understanding the subject and creating the most relevant covers. They scrutinized every image to scout for the most suitable representation of the subject and create an appropriate cover for the book.

The publishing team has been an ardent support to the editorial, designing and production team. Their endless efforts to recruit the best for this project, has resulted in the accomplishment of this book. They are a veteran in the field of academics and their pool of knowledge is as vast as their experience in printing. Their expertise and guidance has proved useful at every step. Their uncompromising quality standards have made this book an exceptional effort. Their encouragement from time to time has been an inspiration for everyone.

The publisher and the editorial board hope that this book will prove to be a valuable piece of knowledge for researchers, students, practitioners and scholars across the globe.

List of Contributors

Odysseas Pavlatos
Athens University of Economics and Business, Greece

Jadranka Mrsik and Ninko Kostovski
University American College, Skopje, Macedonia

Dragoş Mangiuc
Bucharest University of Economic Studies, Romania

Justyna Fijałkowska
University of Social Sciences

Beata Zyznarska-Dworczak and Przemysław Garsztka
Poznan University of Economics and Business

Eleftherios Aggelopoulos
University of Patras, Greece

Maria-Silvia Săndulescu and Cătălin-Nicolae Albu
The Bucharest University of Economic Studies, Romania

Mateja Jerman
University of Primorska, Slovenia

Halina Waniak-Michalak
Lodz University, Poland

Małgorzata Macuda
Poznań University of Economics and Business, Poland

Joanna Krasodomska
Cracow University of Economics, Poland

Index

N

O

P

Q

R

S

T

CPSIA information can be obtained
at www.ICGtesting.com
Printed in the USA
LVHW060905030122
707669LV00002B/354

9 781647 260712